Harmonise Your Heart

Dear Emma,
wishing you a
harmonised heart
everyday.
    Love + blessings,
    Denise
      ♡
    x   x
      x

Denise Davis

Disclaimer: The ideas in *Harmonise Your Heart: The Badass Way* represent those of the author as of the date of publication. The book is for informational and educational purposes only to aid and support emotional wellbeing and personal development.

The information in this book is not a substitute for professional medical advice. If you are suffering from any physical or psychiatric condition, please seek the help of the appropriate qualified health professional. Any use of information in this book is at the reader's discretion and risk.

The author and publisher cannot be held responsible for any loss, claim, or damage arising out of use, or misuse of the suggestions made, or the failure to take medical advice.

While the author has made every effort to provide accurate information at the time of publication, the author and publisher do not assume and hereby disclaim any liability to any party for loss, damage, or disruption caused by error or omissions. Whether such errors or omissions result from negligence, accident or other cause.

Every effort has been made to represent this product and its potential for personal and professional development there is no guarantee that using any or all of the suggestions and processes will work for you in the way they have for the author. Any links to websites are for information purposes only and are not warranted for content, performance, accuracy or any other implied or explicit purpose.

In the event you use any of the information as a constitutional right, the author assumes no responsibility for your actions.

ISBN Number: 978-1-8383274-0-8

Publisher: Heart Alchemist Publishing

Orders: signed copies of *Harmonise Your Heart: The Badass Way* with a personalised dedication and bulk discount are available. You can contact the author at www.denisedavis.co.uk

Paperback and e-book via www.amazon.co.uk and www.amazon.com

ENDORSEMENTS

Anne Jirsch, bestselling author and international FLP Trainer

People are feeling lost in these uncertain times, many people have told me they feel "disorientated" or "out of sync". Denise's book will gently bring you back to balance. It is filled with techniques and ideas to realign you. Whatever stage you are at right now, there will be something here to help you move forward in life with ease.

Denise Kennedy

Harmonise Your Heart is a profound exploration of self-love, respect for oneself, and love for life to harmonise your heart. It offers insights and knowledge, with scientific backing, to assist you. The author has offered a beautiful gift of real spiritual value and practical expertise to support you fully on your journey. Thank you, Denise, for letting me read your book; it inspired and motivated me to write the content for my new website.

Davina Mackail, Hay House Author of *Feng Shui Made Easy* and *The Dream Whisperer*

From the experience of her own healing journey, Denise has compiled a "bible" of remedies for healing our hearts. This is a book to keep on your shelf – a reference manual you can immerse yourself in for major healing or dip into whenever you need a self-love boost.

Pamela Cullinane

Thank you, Denise, for the privilege of reading your book. Your book was both emotionally moving and inspiring in many ways. What you wrote felt so true and emotive, I could relate to many issues you have experienced. Your journey is full of truth and light, even in the darkest of times – well done.

Blue Marsden MA author of *Soul Plan: Reconnect With Your True Life Purpose*

A candid description of an emotional rollercoaster that opened the door to a path of self-healing. As is so often the case with those who have emerged from life's myriad of obstacles with the gift of deeper awareness, Denise has much to share. What she offers is not only her own compelling story of self-discovery but also a rich and practical compendium of some of the most modern and effective holistic practices designed to help us all "harmonise our hearts".

Barbie Brinkman

Denise shows a great depth of knowledge in the area she has chosen to write about. This is exampled by case histories and personal experience. This is a book filled with love and hope for the reader. It gives one a thirst for greater knowledge in the subjects that are covered. Denise's personality shines through, I felt she enjoyed writing the book – her writing flows and is organised. Denise is a fabulous, relaxing and friendly writer. Thank you for asking me to read this, Denise. It was so informative and interesting. I feel privileged. Thoroughly recommended.

Simon Hodges

Denise has written an open and emotional story of her beautiful, colourful life – an inspired, authentic reflection of her journey on her lovely little bus. Throughout the book, Denise has offered the reader many opportunities to reflect upon their own life through the different stories, the searching questions she has asked and the insightful guidance – both intuitive and factual – she has freely given. The book is beautifully littered with "precious gifts" of wisdom and learning for anyone willing to move forward with courage to revivify their inspired authentic self. I have known Denise for some years now and it has been a privilege and a pleasure to have been invited as a guest on her lovely little bus. I wish her well, as always, and wish her the continued success and happiness that she deserves.

Sian Goodspeed, "Flying Start Tuition"

Harmonise Your Heart takes the reader on a fascinating journey of self-discovery. Through telling her life story, with all its ups and downs, Denise shares much of the wisdom she has gained along the way – both on a personal level and also through her many years of experience as a teacher, coach, healer, wife and mother. This is a must-read for anyone striving to be the best possible version of his or herself.

PR

I have thoroughly enjoyed this book and found it well-written. As it's a personal journey, the way the author has shown how she dealt with the journey and shared experiences made me feel very connected, as my journey was very similar. The book is "simple" in its approach to healing on emotional and spiritual levels. I think anyone will find it an asset on their bookshelf and a very helpful insight into how to heal our hearts.

Alison White

A very personal journey told with searing honesty, coupled with a plethora of techniques to help you overcome your own challenges in life. Select what resonates with you to help you grow.

Maxine Middleton-Budd

Harmonise Your Heart is a guide for healing the heart through a blend of holistic therapies and self-reflection to create balance, peace and inner harmony. Through the sharing of the author's own open and honest personal journey, it explores the unfolding of life through the ups and downs. It shows how we can come to a place of more peace, when we learn to live from a place of authenticity and from the heart.

At the end of each chapter, there is an invitation for the reader to explore and work through questions, combined with lots of great tools to use in day to day life, taken from a range of holistic therapies to create balance and peace in the heart. This truly is a handbook with all the tools to heal, soothe, tune and calm the heart, where the reader can grow through thought-provoking self-reflection and a wonderful experiential sharing of life.

Libby Bellhouse

Jump aboard the tour bus for a fascinating and information-packed journey through the landscape of self-discovery. Stop off to explore the research and thinking behind each topic before trying out the various and varied exercises. There will be plenty of 'Ah Ha!' and 'Oh Yes!' moments along the way. I found that the questions posed every now and then during the telling of the author's life story, were particularly thought-provoking.

Foreword

Many people are dissatisfied with life and don't know how to get started on a healing journey. For some, they despair and feel they have left it too late to walk away from what they know and make alternative choices. Others are distressed and lack the personal motivation to move on from heartache and take action toward their dreams; but it does not have to be that way. *Harmonise Your Heart: The Badass Way* will show you how to readdress the balance, liberate your life and create a blessed future. Lucky you!

I am excited that you found this book, or it found you. Whatever stage in your life you find yourself at, *now* is the perfect time to change, take back control, step up, walk your talk and thrive! You no longer have to go it alone or stagger blindly into your future. With the concepts shared in *Harmonise Your Heart* and Denise's words of wisdom, you are equipped with powerful tools and techniques to help you live a joy-filled life based on your unique needs and values.

Denise's compelling story of overcoming personal setbacks, mixed with her experience as a professional coach, will leave you feeling understood, further helping you to overcome fear and uncertainty and will move you forward in life with clarity and confidence. I recommend you read this book in its entirety, to reduce stress, overcome emotional overwhelm and to help you recognise where you gave away your power. The signposts shared will help you learn how to take back control of your life, supporting you to gain an understanding of how your negative thinking habits and limiting beliefs hold you back from achieving your heart's desires.

If you are contemplating divorce, coming out the other side of the hellhole of a relationship breakup, experiencing empty nest syndrome or pondering a new career, you are not alone. Denise Davis, Heart Alchemist, author, and speaker will support you to find true happiness and offer you a roadmap to discover a greater connection with yourself.

With a badass attitude, the author shares her personal story and professional journey, which will help you to liberate your life and find the courage and confidence within to overcome significant life challenges and setbacks using your intuition and manifestation techniques. *Harmonise Your Heart* offers you a choice of strategies to enhance your self-awareness and raise your vibration to gain heart coherence. Using the principles shared, you will discover how to overcome self-sabotage and fear – moving beyond your current situation. The heart-based exercises support you to move confidently forward in the direction of your dreams with a sense of self-accountability, responsibility and unfailing self-belief.

Denise's humorous, raw and straight-talking guide is guaranteed to support you in regaining a sense of personal power and will leave you with your confidence soaring to new heights, and a desire to live your life on purpose! Whether you are contemplating a career move, considering leaving a relationship or dusting yourself down from the aftermath of the rollercoaster we call

♡

life, *Harmonise Your Heart* seriously helps overcome setbacks, guiding you to create a life you love – not by chance but by design.

Take control of your future NOW and start as you mean to go on – The Badass Way!

Wendy Fry – Transformational speaker, emotional health consultant and writing coach. Bestselling Author of *Write from Your Heart*, *Mothers and Daughters* and *Find YOU Find LOVE*.

Contents

Part One

Introduction

Life is very much like a bus journey. It has constant stops, changes in route, and sometimes mishaps. When you were born, you boarded your bus and met your parents. At some point your parents will step off your bus, leaving you to continue your journey alone. Along the way, other people will board, some of them significant – siblings, friends, children, and possibly the love of your life. Upon departure, some will leave a permanent vacuum. Others may go unnoticed, simply here for a reason or a season, but not for the entire ride. This journey of life will be full of joy, sorrow, dreams, expectations, magic and miracles, hellos, see you soon's and last farewells. I believe the relationships built in this life are far more important than financial rewards and accolades. Having positive relationships allows you to make the best of yourself, and therefore the most important people in your life will have an enormous impact on your success. Think about it: do you want your journey to be chaotic, with people hanging out of the windows, clinging on to the bumper, sitting on the roof, or even trying to drive your bus? Or will you choose a smoother ride? Imagine a ride where you are in control of who is on your bus, where you are firmly in the driver's seat, with nothing untoward impacting your driving. If this sounds beneficial, then you need to be aware and proactive – ensuring you take back control of your steering wheel.

You never know at which stop your journey will end. So, it's important to live as impeccably as possible. Be authentic, act with integrity, love and compassion, to be the best person possible. Radiate your love out into the world, to those you care for, strangers, to all sentient beings and the world at large. Then, when the time comes for you to step down and leave your seat empty, those left behind will have happy memories to sustain them through the pain of your loss. You will rest more peacefully knowing that you did the best you could with the knowledge and resources you had.

I wrote this book to share my story of the practical things, therapeutic processes and tools that have helped me on my journey of self-discovery. When my marriage broke up over sixteen years ago, I had a choice to make. I could sink to the darkest depths of despair, or I could swim with the current of life. I had seen others go through trauma, using drink, drugs or shopping as a coping mechanism and I even knew people who had opted out of life altogether. I didn't want this for myself. I was devastated, my heart was in despair and my mind in constant turmoil. I felt so lost, desperately alone with no idea of where and how to start over. But there was only one choice for me – I had to keep swimming, to live another day. Today, I feel truly liberated and free, with more self-awareness, self-love and happiness. I have found inner peace, trust and faith in the Universe. I've had fun travelling, exploring new cultures and taken up new hobbies. Now, I want to inspire you to do the same.

I firmly believe that we choose our family before incarnating on Earth, which in turn helps us to experience lessons for our soul's evolvement. The family you choose will have a huge bearing on your growth – but both the positives and negatives contain lessons to be learned. For instance, if the family you choose means you will suffer abuse, then this can help you to learn compassion from awful conditions, how to persevere in the face of adversity and how to show kindness that perhaps wasn't demonstrated to you. In spirit, before coming into form, you understand that everything you experience helps your soul learn and grow. However, on a human level it is extremely difficult to understand why horrible things happen to you and even more disconcerting to acknowledge that you chose for them to happen.

By reading this book, you will become more proactive and less reactive to life. You'll learn how to feel in control of your emotions and how to get in touch with the inner you – moving away from feelings of devastation and towards feelings of liberation and freedom. Essentially, you'll learn how to choose and create a life you love. To do this, you have to change your mindset and behaviours. As Einstein once said, 'Insanity is doing the same thing repeatedly and expecting different results.' This book will help you to take action, transforming your outlook and putting you firmly in control of your own life bus.

Of course, it's not all heart-led! There is a genuine science to making positive changes, which I explore later in the book. It is possible to reset your mind and body to equilibrium – to live a life with more resilience, control, understanding, focus, fun and fabulousness. When reading this book, it's important for you to understand that everything is energy, that life is about vibrations and that we are all connected to one another. How you feel and behave affects the world. I believe that we are slowly coming to the realisation that we are one human race, regardless of our differences. Many more people are working towards collaboration with a win-win for all (service to others and self) instead of the outmoded competition model focusing on service to self only. This is a good thing for overall togetherness and unity.

The Structure of This Book
This book is full of suggestions on how you can become an improved version of yourself. At the end of each part, I have given you an invitation to fulfil and questions to explore – helping you to achieve more insight and awareness of where you are right now. Asking purposeful questions enables you to tap into your own resourcefulness. In turn, this elevates your confidence, as you begin to recognise the potential within you and to shift your perspective towards a positive and proactive approach. It's always fabulous to watch my clients blossom from a bud to a fully-fledged flower in all their glory and I take such pride in assisting them to develop. I wish the same for you too!

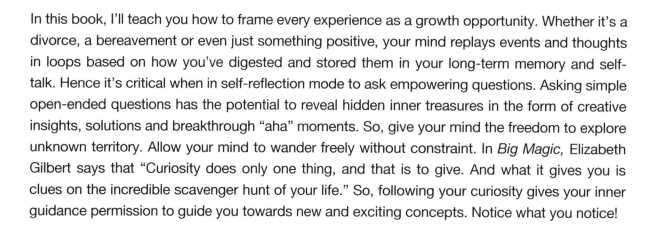

In this book, I'll teach you how to frame every experience as a growth opportunity. Whether it's a divorce, a bereavement or even just something positive, your mind replays events and thoughts in loops based on how you've digested and stored them in your long-term memory and self-talk. Hence it's critical when in self-reflection mode to ask empowering questions. Asking simple open-ended questions has the potential to reveal hidden inner treasures in the form of creative insights, solutions and breakthrough "aha" moments. So, give your mind the freedom to explore unknown territory. Allow your mind to wander freely without constraint. In *Big Magic,* Elizabeth Gilbert says that "Curiosity does only one thing, and that is to give. And what it gives you is clues on the incredible scavenger hunt of your life." So, following your curiosity gives your inner guidance permission to guide you towards new and exciting concepts. Notice what you notice!

Greater Connection to Yourself

Throughout this book, I will make constant reference to the value of harmonising your heart. This reconnects you to your inner guidance system, bringing you back to the essence of you! I have written about your heart on a physical and energetic level and I will demonstrate why it is important for it to be in balance. I have shared what harmony means for me and how self-care, self-respect and self-esteem, plus honouring your body and heart's wisdom, are all components of self-love. Most importantly, there are suggestions on what you can do to bring your heart more into harmony.

I am very grateful to you, dear reader, for giving me the chance to assist you, just as I have guided so many others. I feel blessed that you've picked up this book and that you will benefit from the lessons within just the same as I have. This book is a culmination of my journey, of wisdom learned from years of trials, tribulations, healing and teaching.

Before we begin with the essential lessons, I would like to tell you about me. I want to share my story, so that others can take heart and inspiration from what I have experienced along my own bus route and how I took back my steering wheel. It is rather lengthy, so if you don't wish to read this then that's totally fine too! If so, just hop over to part two of this book and start reading from there. You can then return to my story, if you choose to, later on. Just know that I am here for you, as a caring fellow human being; we are on this journey of life together.

My Story

My Impoverished Childhood

I was conceived at an inconvenient time, as my dad was due to be conscripted into the RAF. Despite my parents being married, I was unplanned, and I believe I was unwanted. To add to this, once my dad discovered the pregnancy, he set about buying items like train sets – as he wanted a boy. When I was born, we were so poor that I had to sleep in a drawer, as there wasn't any money for a crib. We lived in a slum, with mould growing on the walls (it was so bad that even animals wouldn't be allowed to stay in such conditions nowadays). It was a harsh entrance to the world indeed.

As a child, I was very sensitive, shy and timid. I always felt that I didn't quite "fit" in, and that many of the other kids didn't seem to be like me. My favourite book was *Pookie* by Ivy L Wallace. This was the story of a little rabbit, who had tiny, ineffectual wings. Feeling unlike all the other rabbits, he went out into the world to seek love and acceptance. Another story that resonated with me was *The Ugly Duckling* by Hans Christian Andersen. You can see a pattern emerging here already – I dreamed of a life where I was cherished for who and what I was, not one where I was marginalised for my differences. I also loved *The Magic Far Away Tree* and *The Famous Five* series, both by Enid Blyton, which enabled me to live in an alternative world, albeit temporarily.

- Take a moment and think of what pattern(s) have shown up in your life. How do they present themselves? What issues do they cause?

- Now, consider if these patterns are working for you. You will find suggestions to make changes further in the book.

Entry to School

My first day at school was terrifying! The teacher had an awful temper and was enraged when I misunderstood where to write my name on my exercise book. She had no thought or consideration for the fact that I was only five, and that her reaction could have a lasting effect on my learning. I recall her face being contorted with rage, and the veins on her arms bulging with apoplectic fury! This just consolidated my belief that I was a "waste of space" and not good enough. My babysitter had already instilled this feeling in me, because she loved my baby sister, but was very harsh and hurtful to me. Once she even hung me out of the window in our two-storey flat! I was so scared that the fear has erased my memory of why she did this. I believe this may have been the beginning of my fear of heights, which I gratefully let go of during my NLP training. All of this was in addition to having a violent and angry dad, of whom I was absolutely petrified (I would often wet myself with fear when he was in one of his terrible moods). So, it was a rough start, to say the least. With maturity and an understanding of my dad's background, the journey he went through, and what contributed to his frustrations with life, I now have compassion for his journey as well as my own. Neither of my parents had a family role model growing up, and perhaps this contributed to the way I was raised. My mum was raised in an orphanage

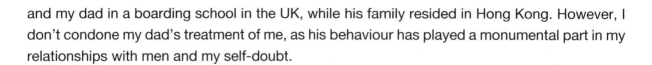

and my dad in a boarding school in the UK, while his family resided in Hong Kong. However, I don't condone my dad's treatment of me, as his behaviour has played a monumental part in my relationships with men and my self-doubt.

Having finally settled in my school in London, we then moved to Hemel Hempstead when I was six. Given how long it had taken me to get to grips with my previous school, it was unsurprisingly challenging to start afresh somewhere different. To compound my feelings of not belonging, I had to wear NHS glasses with a patch over my left eye, and second-hand clothes, which were bought from a girl in my school (she made a great show of telling everyone that the clothes had been hers). Plus, I had a large mole on my right thigh, which people called "the devil's mark". All of this resulted in me being teased and bullied, not just by pupils but also by teachers too, who seemed to adore my more outgoing sisters but dislike the quiet, shy me. As a teacher myself, I have learned from my own negative experiences, taking enormous care to praise the children in my classes, and not to put them down. I find that there is always at least one aspect of a task that you can use for praise. This positive feedback has built my students' self-esteem and motivation to continue learning, and their parents have given me great feedback too.

After a while, I made a very close friend at school, named Faye. She looked like a little blonde angel, and seemed content spending time with me. Unfortunately, after a year she moved away, which only left me feeling sadder and more bereft. In addition, the house we'd moved to was yet again dreadful. It had no bathroom or hot water, with only an outdoor toilet. One night when I needed to use the loo, I suffered a massive jolt of electricity, because the light switch was hanging loose – I was terrified, it shook me to my core! But I was too afraid to mention my distress to my parents, so I went back to bed alone, sad and hurt. After all, I was the eldest, and was always expected to be brave and strong for my three siblings, who I often had responsibility for. Another contributor to my fear of falling was because my dad had removed the wall to a bedroom that I shared with my two sisters, as he had renovation plans. The absence of the wall meant we were able to see the room below us. If we got too close, we could fall down into the room underneath us, which was a possibility if you misjudged it in the dark.

Our neighbours across the road had a son around my age, and so I often went to their house for a bath and the occasional sleepover. Once, when I was nine, my friend's dad touched my developing breasts when he was putting me to bed (I was a very early developer, with my period starting at the same time). Following this, I still went to see my friend but I stopped regularly going to his house for sleepovers, although I didn't tell my parents why.

It seemed I continually had to face and deal with my challenges all on my own, as my parents were wrapped up in their own pain and life issues. I felt as if telling them of my experiences would add further burdens to their already challenging lives, and so I kept my own counsel. From an early age, the world seemed an extremely unkind and hurtful place to live for my kind and sensitive soul.

Spirit Visitations

Further daunting events occurred in my new home in Hemel Hempstead, especially when I was in the hypnagogic state just before sleep. I would often see faces close up to me, without understanding what they were or what they wanted. Naturally, this petrified me! My coping mechanism was to recite the Lord's Prayer repeatedly until the faces went away. I did not understand at the time that my visions were spirit, coming to reassure me I was not alone and that they were with me. This happened every night for quite a long time, alongside reoccurring scary dreams of being chased but escaping at the last minute. When discussing our youth with my youngest sister, she confirmed that she too had experienced similar things. What I hadn't realised until developing my spirituality was that my heightened sensitivities are because I have strong clairsentient capabilities, as well as being fairly clairaudient, claircognizant, clairvoyant and able to channel the higher realms as well as the deceased. I explored these gifts further for many years as an adult, and I now help others to unlock their gifts too. As I'll explain later in this book, I believe everyone is intuitive (psychic) and has healing powers – it's just that some of you have stronger gifts and maybe are more aware than others.

Failure

In the final year of junior school, I failed the 11+ by a tiny margin, as did another girl in my class. There was only one place available, so instead of allowing one of us the opportunity to expand and fly by going to grammar school, they decided it would be best to send us both to a comprehensive school. This failure coloured my life hugely, leaving me with enormous doubt about my capabilities. Once I left school at sixteen without qualifications, I studied all manner of things through choice and have continued learning until this day. I overcame my fear of learning, and now I love studying, especially when it is a subject I am interested in – I feel it is important to learn and grow until we leave this mortal coil. Many friends had suggested my continued studying was to prove to my dad that I wasn't stupid, as he was extremely disappointed in my 11+ failure. I still continued after he died, so this didn't resonate with me. However, when studying various elements such as Human Design and Soul Plan readings, personality assessments and more, I discovered that continuous learning is part of my make-up and destiny.

Family Suicide Attempts

Growing up, I had to look after my three younger siblings, as both my parents worked full-time. They separated when I was eleven, but maintenance from my dad wasn't always forthcoming, and this meant that my mum had to work almost constantly to keep us afloat. Initially, we lived with our grandparents (on my dad's side, as Mum had no parents to offer support), but this too had real challenges. In the latter years of my grandparents' marriage, which was volatile at times, my granddad attempted suicide. I absolutely adored my granddad – who was great fun – so I found this deeply distressing. He eventually left my nan the day after their ruby wedding anniversary, for his childhood sweetheart. This broke my poor nan's heart, leaving her alone to take care of their adult son, who had severe epilepsy.

Whilst all this was going on, a science teacher at my high school took a shine to me. He kept me in detention frequently and took me out on "dates" after school. Initially I felt obliged to do his bidding, as he had authority over me, plus I was flattered – all the other girls in school fancied him. Later I discovered he was twenty-six to my thirteen, and married, with a baby on the way! Despite his having dominion over me as my teacher, I eventually found the courage to end our "romantic" enforced relationship (there was no physical consummation). My teacher became overcome with guilt from all the subterfuge and lies, so to offload his burden he confessed to his wife. He told me that her response was that she would cite me in their divorce, which to a young child was a frightening proposition. I had no comprehension of what this meant, just that they would hear the case in court and would perceive me as guilty. I blamed myself for the situation, feeling that I'd done something dreadfully wrong and that "the affair" was my fault! It wasn't until many years later in my fifties that I had an epiphany. I realised that I was a very young, vulnerable child with no father figure in my life, and that this teacher had taken advantage of my people pleasing tendencies. He had been fulfilling his own wants and needs, but ignored mine. Upon realising this, I finally forgave myself, and was proud that I had been courageous enough to break his manipulation and control.

Unfortunately, that wasn't the end of it. My teacher exacted revenge because of my curtailing our activities together. He relentlessly pursued my mum, eventually charming and winning her over, which culminated in them sleeping together. This news he imparted to me with glee. My mum was entirely oblivious to what had gone on between us, as I never shared my problems, believing that she had enough to contend with as a single mum working full time with four children. It must be said that, at this time, divorce was almost unheard of. My parents were the only ones I knew who got divorced – it was almost like being a pariah, as if something was terribly wrong if you were unable to live together as a family. On reflection, I've noticed that I always protected other people's feelings (especially those I loved) hence not sharing my worries.

- Take a moment and think if there have been any times when you have put other people's feelings before your own, making you less important. Can you imagine how your life would be different if you had made yourself a priority sooner?

- Return to a specific incident and imagine the circumstances in a more positive light. Notice the difference in the way you feel, sense and think.

Sex and Distrust

Having left my grandparents' home, we were divided even further as a family. My two younger sisters were placed in a children's home, and my mum, baby brother and I lived with my aunt and uncle. During this time my mum tried to commit suicide, after a broken love affair. I now felt even more responsible for the wellbeing of my siblings, and felt a need to closely monitor my mum. In 1970 we finally had a council house to ourselves, but it didn't last long, as my mum met and married my stepdad – who moved in during the same year.

As my mum's "right-hand man" I felt abandoned; I was no longer her confidante. In addition to this, my dad was spending more time with his newly acquired ready-made family and new baby. I found this extremely difficult, as my mum and I had always been so close, sharing responsibility, whereas now I had a bully of a man dictating all the rules (so now two scary, bullying and controlling men in my life, albeit with my dad taking a much lesser role). My stepdad, when giving orders to me and my siblings, behaved like a sergeant major in the army commanding his troops. This was in complete contrast to my mum's parenting style, which was less rigid and more compassionate. A habit my stepdad developed shortly after moving in with us, was that he would come back early from the pub because he thought my boyfriend (who later became my fiancé) and I were having sex (it was a great deterrent so we waited until I was of a legal age). Eventually my stepdad asked me to have sex with him, because he wanted to be my first lover, to show me the ropes. But again I summoned my inner strength and declined his offer. I never told anyone about this!

After a few years it became obvious that my stepdad was an alcoholic and struggling to cope; he eventually tried to kill himself and was admitted to a nearby psychiatric unit. So, three people in close proximity to me (that I was living with at the time), tried to escape their pain and leave the planet. With hindsight it explains to me why, when as an adult and extremely low, feeling very sad without a strong purpose, I would ask the Universe to 'Beam me up Scotty' – to return "home" to where I believed everything was brighter and formless as described in Sunday school. Life on earth felt bleak; I didn't know what to do or where I fitted in.

My fiancé ended our relationship almost a year later, before my seventeenth birthday, as he felt we had become more like a brother and sister. This was a gift, to be honest, as he had been jealous and controlling. After that, instead of following a family pattern of despair and wishing to leave earth, I enjoyed my liberation. With my newly found freedom I had fun and dated a few men briefly, before becoming smitten with someone who I also allowed to disrespect me. Of course, it didn't start out that way. In the beginning he was very keen and attentive but once he had me "hooked" he changed. The relationship eventually ended because he wanted to change our status from exclusive to open (meaning he could see other people) which was untenable for me.

In my early years, I was very much in the habit of always trusting people, assuming they had ethics and values like me. Oh how young and naive I was! Things and people are not always as they seem, some people put a positive spin on everything to ensure they get what they want. My trust of everyone led me to being raped twice. The first guy took advantage when we were at his place watching a film together. The other guy, on a different occasion, knowingly took advantage of my being inebriated. Again I told no one, as these two boys were part of our social group, and one was immensely popular and loved by everyone. I also had a huge fear of authority, meaning I was very frightened about the police getting involved. In my mind, I felt as if people would only blame me, telling me that I was silly to trust the boys, and that I shouldn't have been drinking in the second incident. Throughout the whole of my life, my sexual relationships have been few and far between, as I prefer to have sex within a loving, committed relationship. Still, I believe it is better to be trusting of people and a bit of a softie, than to be a hard-nosed cynic who is distrusting of everyone and everything. I realise there are lessons from every situation and that I grow wiser and stronger from them.

As you'll have guessed, I didn't grow up blessed with wonderful role models to guide me. Instead, I just "felt" my way through life. Yes, I experienced some situations that were certainly not fabulous, and not all happenings made it into this book, but they all made impressions on me, creating who I am today. As you will discover later in the book, for those emotions and beliefs that didn't contribute to my having a happy life, I had coaching and healing to help me move forward in a better way. In part seven, I'll demonstrate how you create your world with your thoughts and beliefs. My story is a testament to the fact that, despite horrible situations and events, you can still feel good, just as long as you make the necessary changes.

- What kind of role model are you to those at home, at work and socially?

- Do you know where your values and ethics come from? Have you questioned whether you fully agree with them?

Meeting My Future Husband

The first time I met James, I was out at a nightclub in Hemel Hempstead. I was seventeen years old. I was actually out with his cousin (whom I worked with) and she'd asked James for a lift home, as they lived near each other. He said no, but offered me a lift instead! At the time it's fair to say that I was a bit anti-men, having come out of a couple of relationships where I had been treated badly. So, I told him in no uncertain terms, 'No thanks, I'm perfectly capable of taking myself home.'

Despite my frosty response, later in the night James asked me to dance. I said yes and from that point onwards he didn't leave my side. When he asked if he could take me out, I declined, telling him that I wanted to be single; I was enjoying my newfound freedom to do what I pleased, as and when I wanted. I told him that we'd see each other out and about anyway and this turned out to be true, as over a brief period of time he seemed to be at every single gathering I attended. In the end I capitulated and agreed to go on a date with him. He seemed a decent guy with a fabulous smile, sparkly eyes and brilliant sense of humour, always making me laugh. Apparently, after a couple of weeks he had told his friend he was going to marry me, although it was months later when he told me about his early thoughts and feelings. Scarily and sponta-neously, I told James I loved him first and then waited an agonising two days for his response! It's fair to say that his eventual proposal wasn't quite how he had planned it or how I'd expected it. We were on a weekend away with his football friends (he managed two football teams) and all a little bit worse for wear, as we'd drunk a fair bit and were thoroughly enjoying ourselves. Having asked to marry me near the end of the evening when he was inebriated (he fell off his bar stool straight after asking me), I suggested he asked me again in the morning when sober – as I wasn't completely sure he meant it; I wondered if he may regret his spontaneity when he woke up. It turned out he didn't and I accepted his (sober) proposal the very next day.

As it was only around six weeks into our relationship; I suggested it would be best to wait until he had gone on his two-week holiday to Lloret de Mar, and after I went on my vendage (grape picking) in Beaujolais (both of which were booked before meeting each other). The vendage was supposed to be for three months, but ended up being only six weeks. Unlike most people, I embrace change, as it staves off complacency and boredom. If I really want to do something then I will do it, despite my fear. So, I gave up my permanent job at a publishing house in Hemel Hempstead and headed for France. Many people thought I was crazy to take off on a whim, but I didn't pay attention to this. After six months we were officially engaged and it was time to discuss wedding dates. Eventually, we settled on St Mary's Church in Hemel Hempstead, to be married in July 1976. I was so happy and so in love.

With hindsight, there were early warning signs that not everything was rosy regarding our relationship. I totally ignored these signs, putting them down to my jealous emotions, which were perceived to be a problem by both of us. I simply hadn't considered that James's insensitive behaviour was only exacerbating my feelings. One incident that particularly stands out was when we were on a group holiday with his friends down in Cornwall, where he allowed a girl called Penny to sit on his lap – leaving me standing there like "Billy no mates" with hurt feelings. I didn't understand why he hadn't asked her to stop. I was made to feel that my emotions weren't normal and unreasonable. This occurrence was a bone of contention and we argued horribly about it. The holiday wasn't as fabulous as I had anticipated and I was violently sick with a bug for a few days. In my naivety, we hadn't taken any extra precautions. I didn't know that being ill meant my contraceptive pill wasn't effective – and this led to me becoming pregnant.

Another occasion that I found difficult to understand, was James's response to his close friend making a pass at me. His friend said to me that James was sleeping around and that I should sleep with him to get my own back. When I told James about this, he listened to me, but then dismissed it and still invited his friend to our wedding. His feeble excuse was that he had attended his friend's wedding, so he had to invite him in return. This was a powerful indicator that he was putting his friend's feelings before mine and maybe even his own! At the time I thought it was really off and still do! From my perspective, it meant that he was more of a conformist and concerned with what others thought of him than I'd initially suspected, as most of the time he seemed a maverick like me.

Looking back, our relationship was very lopsided until I matured and grew. James is almost four years older than me, so often I would bow to his knowledge or suggestions in the belief that he knew better than I did. He had unwittingly stifled me with his controlling suggestions, which apparently were for my own good, even on simple things like tennis lessons. I asked for a racket from my future mother-in-law for my 18th birthday, which I duly received. However, James told me I wouldn't be able to play well, as my wrists were too tiny and weak. I totally bought into his opinion and so never played! I trusted that, as a tennis player, he had more experience and insight. Instead I played badminton, because he said it would suit me better. Funnily enough, my youngest daughter is petite like I was and now successfully plays tennis against others at her local club, often winning matches. Based on what I learned from my marriage, I instilled in our children the importance of trying things out, to see whether they liked them or if they were suitable, before dismissing them out of hand.

Going back to the story, my mum was the one who realised I had missed periods, noticing that I was getting larger – even though it was early days. However, after examining me, my GP said I wasn't expecting a baby – but he didn't take a test. Instead, he gave me pills to bring about my period. Eventually as I kept "blossoming", I requested a test, which proved positive. My mum was fabulous and said that whatever I decided she would help me and that I didn't have to go ahead with the wedding if I didn't want to. By now I was already in love with this tiny baby inside me and I knew I would keep him whatever the consequences of our relationship. As a result of the pregnancy (and still being in love), we brought the marriage forward by a year and only had six weeks to organise it, instead of twelve months!

Our Marriage

After our wedding in July 1975, there was a further warning sign I hadn't initially noticed. It became apparent that James had no intention of changing his life in any way and that I would have to continue to adapt. I would have to compromise what I wanted, for his benefit. This meant that on Saturdays and Sundays he still played football matches and trained two nights a week. This trend of him putting his own needs first continued throughout our marriage. When I initially encountered this, I perceived it as selfish and inflexible, with no consideration for how I felt or what my needs were. As I know now, this was his way of "putting his oxygen mask on first" meaning he was better equipped to support the family having done this. At the time I felt a bit neglected, because we'd moved to a place where I didn't know anyone. I didn't drive either, so it was very difficult for me to visit friends or family in our hometown. With this in mind, I was exceedingly lonely at first, especially since the estate was new and we were one of the first couples to move in – the whole site was still in construction. Our son, born near Christmas that same year, was a frustrated and bright little thing who cried loads, hardly sleeping day or night. James became quite adept at cooking, due to the amount of time I spent looking after our baby, who needed constant consoling. Even though I was extremely sleep deprived and lonely, James still went to his football meetings, with life appearing to carry on as normal for him. In the latter years when he became too old for football, it became golf all day Saturday with two evenings playing squash. To reiterate, this was him taking care of his needs, which I now know is important. At the time, however, I didn't understand this – so I felt hurt.

After the birth of our daughter in 1977, I started working as a waitress for a few evenings a week. This was an escape for me. For the first time in years, I wasn't just a mummy or a dutiful corporate wife. I had a small window of time where I could just be me, albeit rushing around as the restaurant was always busy. The highlight was when I'd arrive home after midnight with one cold meal wrapped in aluminium foil, which we both would share, as it was such a treat.

Our Children

Upon the arrival of our children, I really came into my own. I realised that as their primary carer I was their main advocate, the inspiration that they needed to become beautiful little people, caring and loving. This gave me strength and confidence. I no longer needed to drink for "Dutch courage" when socialising. I wanted to be an excellent role model for our children. Unfortunately, as a human and a mum still learning, I initially used fear to try and control our kids, as this is how my dad raised me. But, once I became aware of what I was doing, I questioned whether I really wanted to be that kind of person. I changed my patterns and habits (which it should be said were a part of societal norm at the time) and as a result my adult children have never taken on the old family pattern of smacking their kids, which is certainly more in line with society today.

Gradually, as our marriage continued, I lost "me" and lacked confidence, consumed with family and work life. My weight increased. I struggled to reduce it, even with going to gym classes four times a week and eating a healthy and limited amount of food. I felt fat and ugly – akin to my childhood feelings when I had to wear a patch over one eye. Even though James knew my vulnerabilities, particularly my jealousy of other women (especially ones he was overly friendly with) he continued to do as he wished, regardless of fanning the flames of my pain and hurt. When James neglected me, sat or danced more with other women or suchlike, I didn't feel special, nurtured or cherished. It felt as if the only way his life had changed after marriage was that he was now financially responsible for me and our children. He still continued with his sports and spending time with his friends, whereas my body had undergone significant changes. Likewise, my career was placed on hold; once again I was doing menial jobs to help support the family income. On top of this I was a corporate wife, accompanying James to business events, making polite small talk with the correct social graces.

Looking back, I suspect that my insecurity stemmed in part from male figures in my family having affairs and friends' husbands who had numerous affairs. While some of the men stayed in the marriages, high emotions were always present thereafter, whilst others left, creating abandonment and betrayal issues. My nan (who I later discovered was clairvoyant and a healer) was portrayed by my granddad as highly-strung and neurotic, in her belief that he was having affairs, unjustly so because eventually it came out that everything she had "seen and felt" was true. This becomes relevant later in my story, as a similar thing occurred to me. With hindsight, I wish I'd been aware of this – had I known the truth of the matter, that my nan and I were highly similar, then we could have had a better relationship. As it was, I always felt closer to my granddad.

Once our children were all going to school, I trained to become a primary school teacher. This was a nurturing role, occupying a lot of my time. I studied for my qualifications (even my degree) by doing night classes, as I was teaching during the day and transporting our children to after-school activities on weekdays evenings and the weekends. So, my studying was carried out once the children were all in bed. I had no time to think about life and its turn of events or how things didn't always happen as expected. I just continued on the hamster wheel, spinning back and forth in a frazzled and reactive manner.

My First Business

When interest rates were low, we bought a slightly bigger house to accommodate our growing family. However, immediately following this there were massive rate increases in quick succession, which hit us hard! We were in the red every month, placing an enormous strain on James as he was the main breadwinner. He shielded me from many of his worries, as men did in those days, believing it was his responsibility to shoulder the financial burdens alone. The constant pressure led him to have a mental breakdown, but prescription drugs helped him to get through; eventually he learned to manage without them and became far more resilient. It's fair to say that life was fairly bleak for a while. Financially, we struggled even to buy food. Luckily, we found a shop in the next town where you could pay using a credit card (remember these were simpler times).

Then, a friend who was already working in the Middle East offered James a job overseas. I thought this was a brilliant plan. I had always been ready to explore and travel and realised it would help us to get back on our feet financially. So, in 1979, we moved to Qatar (where we eventually lived for five years). James flew out six weeks before me to sort out accommodation and other practicalities. I followed, with our two very young children in tow. This was my first time flying; I was alone with two tiny children for the seven-and-a-half-hour flight. Upon arrival at Doha airport, it was strange to see what looked like twelve-year-old children brandishing enormous guns. I was grateful to be reunited with James, as we had been apart for six weeks and had really missed each other (it was the first time we'd separated since our marriage).

Gosh, Doha was so different to anything I could have imagined. During my first fortnight, a British bank manager was shot dead. Our daughter became distraught with night visions that we couldn't see or help her with. We were undecided and conflicted about whether to stay or go home. However, neither of us are quitters, so we stayed. Somehow, as a family, we slowly adapted to our new life. I didn't fully settle until I was able to drive and get myself about, instead of being reliant on others taking me out to coffee mornings to make macramé pot-holders or such like. Being imprisoned behind a six-foot wall, unable to get out independently and missing

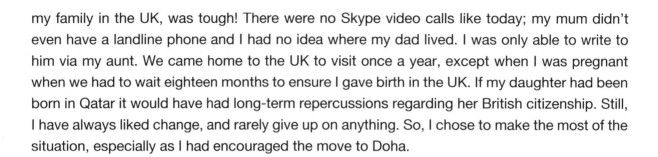

my family in the UK, was tough! There were no Skype video calls like today; my mum didn't even have a landline phone and I had no idea where my dad lived. I was only able to write to him via my aunt. We came home to the UK to visit once a year, except when I was pregnant when we had to wait eighteen months to ensure I gave birth in the UK. If my daughter had been born in Qatar it would have had long-term repercussions regarding her British citizenship. Still, I have always liked change, and rarely give up on anything. So, I chose to make the most of the situation, especially as I had encouraged the move to Doha.

For a short time I worked in an office. Then, I contracted pleurisy. I continued to work, as I didn't realise how unwell I was, until it got so bad that I needed medical help. The pain had gone from my lungs all the way down my right leg, affecting my ability to walk. This gave me time to think about what I wanted to do whilst overseas. When a new boss arrived, who was a bully, this reinforced my feelings that office work wasn't for me. I left the company and got a job working at a nursery school for a while, which I really loved, as it fulfilled my dream of teaching. This culminated in my decision to run my own private nursery school, to help our family economy and to give me more autonomy. Originally, everyone thought I was crazy, as there were other nurseries readily available, coupled with the fact that I was almost seven months pregnant with our third child and shortly due to go home to the UK to give birth. However, James knew I was fully committed to the idea, and was great with practical support, so helped me prepare the rooms for my small nursery. He also fully supported us financially, so that I didn't have to focus on anything apart from my work and our family. My small school was highly successful, with numerous parents placing their unborn babies on my waiting list. I absolutely loved the children and it really seemed like I had found my life purpose. I have to mention that James was an excellent dad, spending time playing with our children and helping with their homework (as I did). Unlike some of my friends' husbands, he also did some chores around the home too.

Bereavement

As a family we had finally settled into our new way of life, with fulfilling work and a fabulous social life. Baby number three, another daughter, was born at the beginning of 1982. We had been living in Doha three years at this time. Then, out of the blue, my mum died. She was just forty-nine years old. James answered the phone and when he tried to tell me the devastating news I just screamed at him not to say anything. Somehow, before being told, I had sensed it. I just didn't want it to be true. Obviously, I was absolutely distraught and beside myself with shock and grief! I had only just seen my mum a few months earlier, when we had our baby christened back in the UK. At the time, she looked the best she had in years – slimmer, happier and healthier. I was only twenty-six, with three very young children. Our baby daughter was just eight months old, so my hormones were still raging all over the place. That was the worst time of my life (up to that point). It felt like someone had physically ripped my heart out of my body; my physical and emotional pain was unbearable and indescribable!

During this time, James was absolutely brilliant. As a husband and dad he was a real rock for us. He even took my brother and sister to see my mum's body at the funeral parlour and helped us with all the admin and paperwork. He is very practical, with an astute mathematical and logical mind, which makes us a great team – as I emotionally support our children and he takes care of the practical stuff.

Seeking solace, I went back to the church I used to attend before I lived in Doha. There, I was told that my mum was in Hell, as she didn't attend church on a weekly basis. This felt incredibly unjust, as my mum had read the Bible, believed in God and always treated others as she wished to be treated, readily helping family and friends in their times of need. I thought to myself, *isn't that what the Church espouses?* Inconsolable, my youngest sister and I consulted a medium, who gave us information about conversations we'd had the previous day, plus other information only we could know, which proved to us that there was an afterlife. I found it highly reassuring to be told that my mum wasn't in Hell and that she was okay in her alternative place. Following this, however, things took another turn in my marriage. James was very uncomfortable with spirituality, as it scared him. He asked me to refrain from taking part in any such activities. I duly obeyed him, because I wanted him to be happy and it was easier to keep the peace that way. Interestingly, I failed to take into account my own needs. Hindsight is a wonderful thing. I'd allowed myself to be subjugated again, without even realising it.

Back to Qatar

Having emptied my mum's house and had the funeral in the UK, we returned to Doha. I found this exceedingly difficult, as I had left my middle sister (aged twenty-three) still in long-term residence in hospital with her new baby, plus my youngest sister who was only twenty-one, who had recently been left by her husband (for her best friend) with two very young children. My brother was only seventeen, so we brought him to live with us.

Although James had been brilliant in the immediate aftermath of my mum's death, once we moved back to Doha and settled back into "normal life" he really struggled to support me emotionally. In truth, he was at a complete loss and just didn't know what to do when I was emotional and distressed. He distanced himself, not knowing what to say or how to comfort me. This enhanced my sadness and compounded my pain. Just two weeks after my mum's passing he told me I should stop crying! This wasn't an easy time for any of us, adapting to the new dynamics of an extra person living with us, as well as the grief from my mum's loss. It was

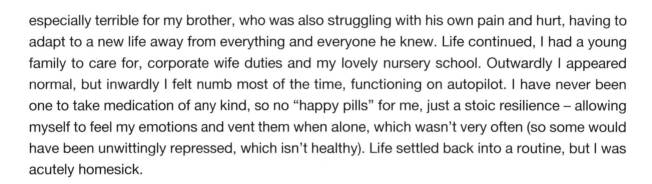

especially terrible for my brother, who was also struggling with his own pain and hurt, having to adapt to a new life away from everything and everyone he knew. Life continued, I had a young family to care for, corporate wife duties and my lovely nursery school. Outwardly I appeared normal, but inwardly I felt numb most of the time, functioning on autopilot. I have never been one to take medication of any kind, so no "happy pills" for me, just a stoic resilience – allowing myself to feel my emotions and vent them when alone, which wasn't very often (so some would have been unwittingly repressed, which isn't healthy). Life settled back into a routine, but I was acutely homesick.

Soon after we arrived back in Doha, I began to receive nightly spirit visitations. This left me terrified, as I was unsure initially of what was happening to me, who or what it was, what it meant or what I was supposed to do. Having blocked myself from such visits since I was six, this came as an immense surprise. Not only did I have night-time visitations when relaxing to go to sleep, but I also had terrible difficulty doing my meditations in the day, because being in this relaxed state was an ideal condition for spirit contact. I clung to my husband each night, sometimes hysterical, especially when I felt touches on my body. In the end I "knew" it was my mum coming to visit. It still freaked me out a bit, even though I believed she was probably coming to comfort me. Strangely, once I fully embraced spirituality many years later after my divorce, I welcomed contact – learning to appreciate that this was really just a friendly way of saying, 'Hello, we're here with you for support.'

In 1983, after spending just one year in Doha, my brother left. He went to live with friends back in the UK. Unbeknownst to James, I contacted a psychic in the UK and sent a lock of my hair for her to do psychometry, to give me a reading. I wanted advice about returning to the UK myself. I was still feeling guilty that I had left my younger siblings to fend on their own. I also had concerns that we would get used to the "ex-pat lifestyle", which we wouldn't be able to sustain once returning to the UK. Another issue was that our kids were cute little blondies, which attracted a lot of unwanted attention. Eventually, I had to confess to James that I had contacted a psychic, because the advice was for him to seek a work position before returning to the UK, otherwise it would be an unmitigated disaster. He implemented this, which turned out extremely well. Hurray, we were off! Thanks Doha for all the pleasurable times and learning.

Goodbye Qatar, Hello England
We eventually returned to the UK in May 1984, another big adjustment period for us as a family. We'd rented out our house whilst living in Doha, so we returned to the same house, considering the "known" to be an easy and safer option than moving elsewhere, which we had explored. In 1986, a year after our fourth and final child was born, we moved to a bigger home around

the corner. I worked at a private school as a teacher whilst studying for my degree to obtain qualified teacher status (I had a Nursery Nurse qualification from Montessori). Then, just before completion of my dissertation for my degree, my middle sister died on the operating theatre table due to a heart attack, which had been induced because of a long-term health problem, caused by a negligent operation. She was thirty-five years old. Yet again, I never got the chance to say, 'Goodbye, I love you, thank you for being part of my life – may your spirit soar high.' At the same time, my youngest sister had a new love (eventually becoming her third husband) and became completely insular in her new relationship, which interestingly followed a parental pattern. Usually I would have sought her company so we could console each other, but this wasn't an option now, as she only had eyes and ears for her new beau. Fascinatingly my brother is quite insular in his marriages too, although much more so with his first wife. With this in mind, I felt utterly bereft, as James yet again had zoned out and was unable to comfort me.

My marriage was undergoing a rocky patch and on top of this there was the added challenge that my deceased sister had elected me to be her son's guardian. This was understandable, because at the time this was discussed James and I were the stable couple of the family. Plus, when my nephew was younger he often came and stayed with us temporarily when my sister was admitted to hospital. This all changed though once my nephew became old enough to go to school. His mum chose her friend, who lived a couple of doors from his house with boys of a similar age, to become his official foster parent. As a foster parent she was awarded financial support for looking after him, which wasn't forthcoming for family. This arrangement was approved by the Social Services because it facilitated continuity for my nephew, allowing him to attend his local school when his mum was in hospital, instead of coming to stay with us, which would have entailed him having to attend a different school temporarily. While I was of course happy to care for him, James's work situation made this incredibly challenging. As a senior quantity surveyor he was responsible for millions of pounds of business and if he got just one figure wrong then the company could make a huge loss. He said that he just couldn't take on this guardianship and added financial burden, plus the practicalities of another child who was the same age as our youngest daughter. Bear in mind he had already taken on temporary responsibility for my brother previously.

As I said, we were going through a rough patch – James threatened to leave if we took my nephew in. This was something he felt he was unable to cope with at the time, as his primary responsibility was for his own and our family's care. Thus, my nephew remained with his foster family. Although this wasn't new for him, as he had spent long periods living with his foster family whenever his mum was hospitalised, it left him feeling that our family abandoned him (in the end social services felt, as before, that for continuity he should continue to live with his foster family).

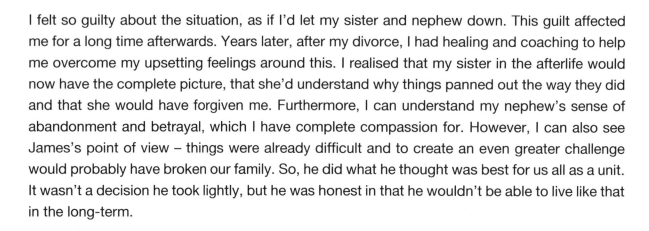

I felt so guilty about the situation, as if I'd let my sister and nephew down. This guilt affected me for a long time afterwards. Years later, after my divorce, I had healing and coaching to help me overcome my upsetting feelings around this. I realised that my sister in the afterlife would now have the complete picture, that she'd understand why things panned out the way they did and that she would have forgiven me. Furthermore, I can understand my nephew's sense of abandonment and betrayal, which I have complete compassion for. However, I can also see James's point of view – things were already difficult and to create an even greater challenge would probably have broken our family. So, he did what he thought was best for us all as a unit. It wasn't a decision he took lightly, but he was honest in that he wouldn't be able to live like that in the long-term.

After my sister's death, I spent five years going back and forth to London to fight for compensation on behalf of my nephew. Due to a faulty operation, where the colon had been cut but not sealed up, waste had gone directly into her stomach. This meant that for much of her life, my sister relied on being fed by a machine for twelve hours every day. She'd had a dreadful quality of life, all because of an incomprehensible medical mishap. This negligence and the medical problems that followed were directly responsible for her death. All of this meant that the emotional wounds I'd suffered from losing my sister couldn't heal properly until the court case was over. I got a little compensation for my nephew, which he used as a deposit for a cheap house much further north, but it was certainly miniscule compared to what she would have got had she lived.

My Jealousy Rears Its Ugly Head...

Prior to my sister's unexpected passing, James had bought tickets for us to attend Ascot races with friends. He and our friends decided that we would still attend, even though it was only two weeks after my sister's death. Perhaps they thought it would take my mind off the hurt and pain, which perhaps was well-meaning but also very naïve, or maybe selfishly they still just wanted us all to go. I was very fragile emotionally and it all ended in disaster! At the end of the event, when the band began playing, James went off with an unknown female who came and asked him to dance. I felt abandoned by him in my time of grief and I stormed off with no intention of waiting around for him to return. When my friends returned to our hired limo, they dropped me off at the hotel before going home themselves. This utterly ruined our supposed "romantic night away", which was an extremely rare opportunity for us to bond – as it was challenging with four kids, the costs of babysitters and accommodation charges.

Once James returned to our hotel, we had an honest and frank discussion, which culminated in us both saying we still loved one another and would make more of an effort to keep our marriage intact. It transpired that we had both been considering separation, but hadn't talked it through with each other. On my part it was because I was emotionally and physically exhausted, so I hadn't felt up to starting such a difficult conversion, which I usually did whenever I felt we needed to sort things out. Although my instigation of such conversations had worked well for many years, eventually we'd become complacent and started to make less effort. On my part, it felt like James just wanted more time with friends for extra golfing holidays and less time with me. To add to this, his overseas golfing trips entailed the men spending nights at brothels, with the justification that it afforded them to drink until the early hours. Some of the men used this as an excuse to partake in the services of the girls, but I like to think that James didn't – and I always believed him when he said that he hadn't. After all, he had free sex on tap at home whenever he wished (our sex life was brilliant and frequent until he fell out of love with me years later). That being said, he still hadn't curbed his excessive flirting with other women in front of me and said he had no intention of changing. He informed me that if I didn't like it, then we should stay in.

Now, I realise that I allowed myself to be disrespected due to my love for James and fear of his leaving me. This was a pattern created in my early teens, of giving the steering wheel of my bus to others by being a people-pleaser. I realise now that it is better to be alone than to be treated badly. Being single means my expectations are never mismanaged by a significant other. I only wish I had known then about therapy/coaching, so I could have released my issues around trust in committed relationships. Both of us would then have been more conscious and aware of our behaviours and reactions, helping us to choose differently.

Ask yourself this, dear reader:

- Are you allowing yourself to be taken for granted, to be mistreated or disrespected?

- If the answer is yes, then by whom? How can you take steps to change this, and start treating yourself with love and respect?

Yet Another Death

Just under a year after my sister's death, my dad passed. There was a lot of pain around this. Due to close family listening to my dad's ramblings when he was on morphine – about a dispute over a cross-stitch that he'd gifted my deceased sister (which he wanted back), I wasn't allowed to travel in the family car to the service or invited back to his flat for the wake. I found this hard, as we had become much closer since his illness, and felt completely alienated by family who had wanted to exclude us. To add to this, no family or friends came to speak to me and my sister (who supported me) either before or after the service. Now I truly felt like an orphan!

I realised that – having taken responsibility for my siblings my entire life – I now needed to release some of this, to concentrate on my own family. My siblings were all adults and therefore self-accountable for their choices and decisions. I hadn't realised that always having me around to rely on may have hampered them, disempowering them and preventing them from learning through their own challenges and outcomes. I felt such a relief when I realised this; it was as if someone had lifted a boulder from my shoulders.

- What can you let go of today that will help you feel relieved?

- Are you allowing others to learn from their challenges, or are you giving them too much assistance?

Workplace Bullying

Following this, I wanted a change of scenery and new challenges. I left the private school education system, moving to state sector. Unfortunately this got off to a rough start, as the headmistress in my first school constantly bullied me. It was a tough school to work in and had a huge turnover of teachers. The previous year all staff had left, which I only found out having accepted the position. To add to this, I was given a group of children termed "the challenging class". Even though I worked extra hard to please the headmistress, this was to no avail. In fact, my attempts only appeared to aggravate her further – resulting in her jesting about my efforts during staff meetings. At this point, even my own children were questioning why I would stay at the school, as I regularly came home from work in tears. But, as I've said, I don't quit. I wanted to honour my class, showing the children who had been labelled "difficult" that not all adults give up and run away when things get tough.

After the year was up, I left that school and worked as a supply teacher. The parents were so appreciative and very sad that I was leaving, but completely understood why, as they had seen the head's mistreatment of me. Again though, I was putting other people's needs before my own. My working as a supply teacher suited us better as a family, as I only did it two or three times a week, meaning I had more time for the family. Our lives were already frenetic and on top of working I was running the kids to activities after school and on weekends. When I reflect on what I said earlier, about acting as a role model for my children, I realise that in some areas I was brilliant, whilst in others I sadly fell short. If only I knew then what I know now! I have apologised to my adult children for my shortcomings when they were younger, saying that I did the best I could at the time with the knowledge I had, but realise that my best at times just wasn't good enough. I am so grateful that as a family we have frank and open discussions together, even disagreeing on things at times, but still retaining our loving relationships.

- Do you express your needs to those close to you? Whose needs do you put before your own?

- Do you do this willingly or grudgingly?

Beginning of the End

I had experienced extreme menopausal symptoms for a couple of years. By the time I hit forty-three years of age, I thought it was time to finally consult with a doctor. The doctor said I could take HRT, as it was natural and would give me relief. I had previously used black cohosh and other natural products, which failed to bring any relief for the extreme itching under my arms or on my calves. Nor did they reduce my occasional angry outbursts (which were incredibly alien to me as I had a fear of becoming my dad) or the tremendous hot flushes – day and night – that created excessive sweating resulting in an extremely red face. I can remember being told by a male friend to tone down my makeup when I wasn't even wearing any! Fortunately, HRT relieved all these symptoms and I began to feel more like myself again. However, things were about to turn negative at home again.

Once James was promoted to director at the company he worked for, where he was respected and placed on a pedestal, I felt he expected a similar reception at home. In his mind, he was king, and we shouldn't question it. James changed from a loving, caring father and husband, to someone who had little interest in our family, leaving it to me to tell him what was happening in our children's lives. Work took up more of his time, with meetings in the evenings, so he took extra downtime with his friends to counteract this. Prior to this we had done Ballroom and Latin American dancing together and played mixed doubles badminton. Now, these stopped and were never replaced with anything else. I believe that doing things together and separately was the foundation of our marriage, as well as good communication and a sense of fun. With the end of these, I saw that there was now a fatal flaw in our partnership. We had always said that once our children became adults, we would use this as a chance to try new things, making more time for "us" and have fun. But now, James wanted the exact opposite. I was obviously very sad at this state of affairs, as I had looked forward to spending more time together, even if it had been mainly at home.

- Do you have a vision of what you want your future to look like? If not, then how will you know what steps you need to take?

- Do you want to be healthier, fitter, change your job, be socially active, try new hobbies and travel more? What would your ideal life look like? What will you see, feel, hear and sense?

One thing that left me feeling incredibly uncomfortable during these latter years was James's newly found naturist tendencies. When our children were growing up, we often walked around the house naked, but were appropriately very modest around other people. He would always tell me and our daughters off when we were near windows for wearing just our undies, despite living in a tiny close and overlooking fields. So, it was a complete 180 when he decided that he wanted to go to nudist beaches when on holiday, to get his kit off for an all-over tan. He had always been a bit of a sun fanatic, but this was taking it to a more extreme level! Personally, I had always felt body dysmorphic and uncomfortable with my looks and that was even the case when I was slim and weighed much less. Having given birth to four children and now a size sixteen, I definitely didn't have a dream figure anymore. This made me feel even more body conscious. I detested it when gorgeous nymph-like and youthful beauties surrounded James when we were on the beach or at the pool, as he spent a long time looking at them or so I believed. I felt that I was found wanting! I would have loved to feel as free and easy as he did and understood the appeal, but I just felt extremely self-conscious and disliked being around naked people even though I was clothed. It was a bit different when we were totally secluded, but even then I couldn't relax in case anyone came across us and so only did it a couple of times. This meant that I no longer enjoyed our holidays, as James always wanted to go somewhere he could disrobe. Part of this was that he loved an all-over tan, but I'm sure it was the feeling of freedom too. I swam out and took my swimming costume off a couple of times when no-one was nearby – and it felt great – but I really struggled to put it on again when treading water in the deep sea, so I didn't repeat that. Again, with us not doing joint activities and this new uprising, it showed we were becoming more misaligned in what we wanted from our marriage.

During the process of writing this book, I had a lengthy discussion with a friend about whether I should include James's naturist behaviour. My concern about writing this was down to how our children and James would feel if they read the book, as I know from past discussions that they believe we shouldn't air our "dirty linen" in public. However, everything I've written is my truth and played a large part in my unhappiness. This is about how I felt, not a criticism of James, who was a good example of being body confident and having courage of his convictions. My intention in including this is to help others understand more about me – not to upset my family. I have since discussed the content with James and our family, so they are aware. James was magnanimous and wished me well with the book.

When having this discussion with my friend, I realised that I felt a real sense of anger. To this day, I'm unsure of why that was, as I very rarely feel angry. Maybe it was because I feel that James was insensitive to my feelings and didn't care enough to nurture me. Or, maybe the anger was directed at myself, for being complicit and going along with the circumstances despite the upset it caused me. In truth, I think it's probably a combination of the two. James was a product of his generation, in that he had been raised to believe his word (as a man and head of the household) was law and that because he was the main breadwinner who earned much more than I did, he had the right to dictate major decisions. Maybe if he had been more sensitive and caring, he would have taken onboard the fact that I was extremely uncomfortable with his wanting to disrobe, especially when we were away together (maybe he could have carried these out when on his "lads" golfing trips instead). This is in contrast with my sons, who are equally a product of their generation – a generation which recognises marriage as being as about equality, regardless of gender, age or earnings.

A few months after our eldest daughter got married and moved up to Cheshire, I noticed that James was becoming distant and beginning to pull away from me energetically. I knew he was close to our daughter, so considered it may have been him missing her, but somehow I understood it wasn't that. I felt the changes within him before he recognised them himself. I just "knew" my past visions and dreams were being realised, that he no longer loved me. I had dreamt of him being with other women on many occasions. In one dream I saw my wedding ring rolling down the hill away from me, like a giant hoop, signifying the end of my marriage. James had taken to different behaviours now, such as doing push-ups in the bathroom when he thought no-one was watching (these could have been explained as improved self-care) and there were other subtle changes too. When I eventually plucked up the courage to ask him, sharing my thoughts and feelings, he said I was paranoid and needed to see a psychiatrist! Apparently everything was absolutely fine. This reflected what my nan had contended with. James wasn't being honest with himself or with me; it later emerged that he had become close to someone else at work. In the earlier years of our marriage this was something I had suggested could happen. Did I bring this about by expressing my thoughts and feelings? Was it an idea that I had planted as a seed in his mind to later fulfil? Or, was it something entirely different – who knows? The bottom line though was this: James had fallen out of love with me. Even if he continued to believe otherwise, I felt and knew it in my heart.

Looking back, I now realise that James's disinterest led to me feeling depressed. We only had our youngest daughter living at home now, but even she was rarely ever there (hardly surprising given the atmosphere), so I was feeling empty nest syndrome as well. I was unsure about what to do with my life and it felt as if everything was tumbling down around me. As a highly sensitive person (HSP) I feel other's feelings, both on a personal and collective level, so I checked in to see if the emotions were mine – which this time they were. Many months later, James finally confirmed what I already knew and felt – he no longer loved me. He asked if I wanted to stay together, with the understanding that we would live separate lives in the same house. For me, this wasn't an option. At forty-eight almost forty-nine, I deserved to have a life filled with love. (I often describe this as having a new Mercedes car and then being asked to swap it for a rusty old banger.) To top this off, James said not to tell his mother what was happening, as she was already highly distressed from my father-in-law having a stroke. With our extra busy lives, plus fitting in visits to the hospital, I had no time to sort out my prescription for HRT. This lead to my depression becoming more noticeable, but still not being fully acknowledged or recognised by us. Again, there was no understanding about what I was going through from James. I was just expected to carry on as I always had – being strong and capable.

Unfortunately, James's father never recovered from his stroke and died. At the time, we already had a holiday booked. I didn't want to go, not just because of my father-in-law's death, but because we were no longer a loving couple. However, James insisted, so that everything would appear to be normal to his family. Needless to say it was the worst holiday ever – when sharing a bed I was having to almost fall out of it to ensure we had no contact (sadly I was desperate to snuggle up as we had always done). I declined James's offer for us to remain in a platonic relationship, with him staying in the house, so he suggested he would leave and go to live with his mother. I told him that this wasn't a sensible idea, proposing that now his mother was living alone she might end up relying on his being around and feel bereft again when he left. In the end, I said he should stay until he could organise his own accommodation. This would also afford him time to take stock and review his life. At the time I hadn't envisaged it taking very long.

When James first said that he no longer loved me, I didn't just give up. First, I suggested we sought help before his making a final decision to leave. So off we went. To say this marriage counselling session was disappointing, would be an understatement! The woman facilitating the discussion seemed to be incredibly biased towards James. Her suggestion was that he booked in half-an-hour a week to spend time with me! James didn't want to do that, he said the counselling was a waste of a time and refused to attend any more sessions. I agreed, as it hadn't been very beneficial. Needless to say, this wasn't a success. A relationship certainly won't work if only one person wants to be in it and spending just thirty minutes per week is no way to rectify that.

During this period, I was crying on a daily basis. James was giving me very mixed signals – one day he was talking to me and being extra friendly and then on other days he was completely blanking me. A good example of this was when we went to London to watch "The Lion King", where he took me to the Oxo Tower for a cocktail beforehand. We wandered around London holding hands (instigated by him). The next day he barely spoke to me – it was as if I were completely invisible. Oh so much crying, with my expectations being constantly dashed! During this period I had a few sessions with a coach for weight loss. I was so impressed with my outcome of letting go of some of my unhealthy emotions and reducing some of my excess weight (which was apparently why James had fallen out of love with me) that I began to hope he would change his mind. In hindsight, it was very silly of me to think this.

For a period of time, I continued to attend James's business meetings, acting as a corporate wife. However, eventually I told him that I could no longer play happy families. That being said, I respected his wish for me not to tell his mother until after he left. This meant I still had to maintain this façade when taking her out on our fortnightly trips alone and on our regular family visits, to keep up appearances. This repression of my thoughts and feelings created even more devastation in my heart, mind and body. After nine months of James telling me that he would be leaving and then failing to, I eventually told him that this couldn't continue – the way I was living daily was untenable and akin to purgatory. His response was that his place would be ready in two weeks. But I'd had enough; I just needed to be alone and come to terms with everything. So, I made him leave that very weekend. I wasn't prepared to put up with the feeling of being in limbo anymore.

- Where can you take your power back?

- How can you manage your expectations, so they are not always dashed?

Of course, that wasn't the end of it. Upon leaving, James dangled a carrot. He said, 'Let's give it six months. We can meet up monthly and see how things are.' Essentially, I felt he was implying that if anything changed, he may come back. It took me many months before I even told anyone (apart from our children) that he'd left; I didn't even tell my siblings or close friends. I just needed to lick my wounds and come to terms with it. This had a big impact on my work and everything else too, as I was quiet and no longer an open book. With him being their dad, our kids naturally felt sorry for James and asked me to have him over for our usual Christmas Day (at this point we didn't know about his affair). I said yes to this, because I wanted everyone to be as happy as possible. Again, I gave the steering wheel of my bus to others. My thoughts and emotions were all over the place and were intensified each Wednesday when James would ring me to chat and on Saturdays when he came to visit me. I was unsure about his mixed messages, so in order to keep my sanity, I requested that he stop. I also said that it would benefit his new loveship, as he would not have to divide his attention.

To this day, James maintains that he left me because he didn't love me and not because he met someone else. When speaking to my stepmother (my dad's second wife) months later, she told me she had known since the summer that James was having an affair, because when they were on the beach at Studland as a family they had seen him. Upon walking nearer to him, they realised it wasn't me whom he was with. So, they changed direction. Interestingly, they never told me about this until after I said he'd left. During one of our monthly meetings, I did bring this up, asking James if it was true. This was when he first confessed to seeing someone from his work, which he had done whilst still married to me. Again, he reiterated that he hadn't left her for me, it was just that he only loved me platonically now. Upon admitting this, he became quite emotional and upset, so I held his hand and said, 'Everyone deserves to be happy, so you needn't feel guilty.' To this day I stand by this – I have repeated to James and family that 'Everyone deserves to be happy and true to themselves.'

This conversation reaffirmed to me that my intuition had been correct all along. I was not mentally ill, as he had suggested, just very intuitive to the emotions of others. I had realised, even before James did, that he had fallen out of love with me. My only regret was that he hadn't waited until he left me before seeing someone else. It would have been kinder and we could even have all been friends. Initially I did suggest to our children that James and his new partner joined us at family get-togethers, but their emotions were (understandably) very raw. They said that they couldn't deal with the idea of spending time with this new woman and me at the same time, plus they didn't want anything to do with their father anymore, let alone her. Over time, this has changed. I believe that my acceptance of everything and my encouragement has really helped our children to develop a good, renewed relationship with James and his partner. When I was invited by BBC Three Counties Radio to give my expert opinion on divorce and whether to stay together for the children's sake, I drew upon both my professional and personal experience. One of the suggestions I made to counteract complacency and act as a reminder of the sacred-ness of the union, was an annual renewal of the marriage license, which could be dissolved or renewed. I also mentioned that I had suggested to my husband that we live next door to each other, to inject some "mystery" and choice when spending time alone or together. This would help us to look forward to our "dates". James has since told me that if we had carried this out, our marriage would have survived. So, although these ideas may appear radical to some, for us it would have worked well. I used the example of my parents' divorce, explaining that the home was more peaceful and less fearful without the arguments, to show that from this perspective I don't believe in staying together for the children's sake.

- What can you do today to let others you care about know how much they mean to you?

- Do you listen to your intuition and follow its guidance?

- What boundaries can you set, so you get treated well? In what (healthy) ways can you let off steam when feeling angry or frustrated?

All Alone!

So, here I was, all alone and in despair after many years of marriage. I was now single, for the first time since the age of seventeen! I felt lost and afraid, with a whole host of other negative emotions and conflicting thoughts all whirling around in my head and body. I experienced extreme grief, from the loss of the future that I'd expected. I had no visions of what my life would look like now; the plan had been for me to retrain in floristry, with James taking some time out from his weekend golf so we could go away for occasional weekends together. Life would be easier financially, as there was only one year left of our son's time at university, freeing up more money for us to enjoy the fruits of our hard labour, to explore and have fun.

Now, I felt thoroughly overwhelmed and paralysed by the many changes I needed to make on a practical and emotional level! Having been in a relationship since I was seventeen, how on earth was I going to adjust to life as a singleton? I didn't even know where to start – times had changed drastically since then.

My New Beginning – Busyness

After James left me, I changed career, becoming a self-employed coach and healer. This was largely inspired by the sessions I had with my coach for weight loss. In conjunction with this, I was also learning floristry and doing supply teaching. I'd realised that my safety and security was greatly impacted by not having a partner, and this was especially magnified since I no longer had a guaranteed regular income from teaching. For transparency, the court awarded me some financial support (maintenance) from my husband – not enough to live on but it did provide me with a safety net. This maintenance has been a blessing at the times when I have been very ill and unable to work at all; I have thanked James for his continued support. Time to focus on creating abundance through work and other means. One silver lining of our split was that my weight was much easier to reduce now, since I no longer had snacks around the house (James had insisted on having these). In any case, life had to go on. It was sink or swim, and I am a great swimmer.

I put on a brave face for a while, ensuring that my life was very busy, as I wanted to avoid being all on my own. But, in this sense, I was developing unhealthy habits – clubbing and drinking to fill the void, as well as booking numerous activities, all so I could avoid brooding on my plight. However, eventually all my busyness took its toll. My feelings didn't have the chance for full expression, so eventually came out in a bout of full-blown depression. I cried buckets and couldn't even go to college. This was so unlike me. I'd never missed class when studying, as I'm someone who puts her all into every task, wanting to do my absolute best. Even though I was a complete mess I still managed to carry out our homework assignment. I remember taking it into college, crying all the way. Funnily enough, one tutor told me to say a sentence which I hadn't come across before: 'Every day and in every way I am getting stronger and stronger.' Later on I came across more of these expressions. I fervently hated feeling so hopeless, just wanting to live underneath my duvet, so I went to my doctor. She confirmed my suspicions that I was depressed. Because I didn't want prescription drugs, she suggested that I see a counsellor privately, as an NHS counsellor would take months to get seen.

Unfortunately, the counselling didn't work out too well, as the counsellor in question ended up telling me about her arduous life (it was tragic, as she was a paraplegic because of someone else's carelessness, amongst other disasters). Yet again, my empathic nature meant that, like others, she felt the need to tell me her story. To add to this, she also told me that I looked terrible, that I needed a more uplifting bra and to put some makeup on, with the added insult that I should try and audition for the TV show "Ten Years Younger". Unbelievable! Had I been less strong, these criticisms could well have tipped me over the edge. After a few sessions I found it difficult to tell the counsellor that I no longer needed her services, as I felt sorry for her and didn't want to hurt her feelings. Eventually I rang her and said that all was well or something to the effect that I no longer needed her. Later I made other arrangements to ensure I dealt with my emotional challenges.

In terms of new relationships, I did dabble a little, but not with any real success. During the six-month probationary period after James left (before we knew about his affair) I unexpectedly ended up dating a toy boy, which boosted my ego tremendously. My daughter told me off for this. She thought I should wait to see if James would change his mind and come back (once James had confessed to his affair, my daughter apologised for telling me not to date). It's fair to say that this new relationship was a rollercoaster of a ride; my emotions were high when he would call or text, then drop very low when he didn't contact me or meet up. Eventually, however, I took back control and finished things, as it didn't really serve my needs. I wanted to be in an equal, interdependent, committed partnership that had longevity. Our relationship had been based on a lie, as I did not know his correct age until much later. I discovered he was twenty years younger than me, the same age as my eldest son! Boy, did I do lots of journaling to release my angst. As well as writing down the tarot and other oracle card spreads I had done for myself, I also documented my aspirations and dreams, future visions and "knowings" I had regarding my children's future offspring and more.

After that, I didn't date for almost a year, to give myself space to recover from my hurts. However, on a night out, I was attracted to a guy who also had twinkly eyes and a lovely smile. I ended up dating him, another younger man this time but just by three years. He gave me emotional support, which was wonderful, but after a while I found out he was in debt and living on disability benefits. Once more I ended up being the financial supporter in the relationship (it was the same in the previous relationship towards the end), now with the added role of alpha male, which really wasn't my ideal loveship. We dated for five years on and off and stayed friends for eleven years in total. Again, not the wisest of choices, but we both helped each other and became more self-aware.

A Catalyst for Change

Hindsight has continually shown me that I am different; that I inadvertently act as a catalyst to help others change. This can be very challenging, especially when it is unexpected by me or them (obviously its different if they seek my services as a coach). My experiences tell me that others don't always welcome knowledge, especially when they haven't sought it, maybe because it often requires them to change.

A good example of this was when I was out with friends in a pub – a guy was chatting me up and asked to meet up for coffee. Unusually for me, I gave him my business card, because it had my number on it (I rarely give out my mobile number to men socially). Following this, I watched him for a while. He spent a considerable time in close proximity with a young female. This made me wary, as I only date exclusively and didn't want to waste my time or tread on someone else's toes. When in the toilets later, I noticed the young lady was also in there and I made an off the cuff remark. She told me that the guy in question was her boyfriend. When repeatedly asked why I had made that remark, I explained that her boyfriend had asked me out, reassuring her that I had no interest in pursuing it, since I'd assumed he was single when he approached me. Trying to be as kind as possible, I gently advised her that maybe she needed to consider what she wanted from a relationship.

Evidently, this got back to the guy in question, as when I left the venue he shouted some absolutely vile names at me. I just refused to give eye contact or respond. I wasn't taking any blame or criticism for this situation. I felt sad for the girl; she was upset, but at least now she knew his true character. On my part, I felt good that I hadn't been duped and left with my head held high. Hurray for my instincts and courage of my convictions!

Since then, I've spent lots of time discovering and enjoying time for myself. I did date a few other guys, but nothing came of it. My singledom has lasted nine years, because I've made the choice to only date a man when I experience a genuine connection of mind, body and soul. As yet I've not met one that I am physically attracted to, yet alone the rest of the package. I am open to giving and receiving love and look forward to meeting my beloved. I have made the

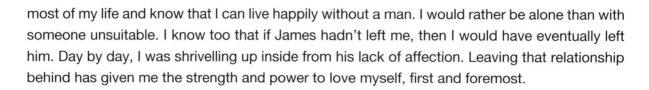

most of my life and know that I can live happily without a man. I would rather be alone than with someone unsuitable. I know too that if James hadn't left me, then I would have eventually left him. Day by day, I was shrivelling up inside from his lack of affection. Leaving that relationship behind has given me the strength and power to love myself, first and foremost.

In this way, my divorce has also benefitted me professionally. People now come to me because they're dissatisfied with their life and want to redress this. I call myself "The Heart Alchemist". Just as an alchemist changes matter from one state to another, I assist people with moving on, transforming despair to self-care, heartbreak to happiness, feeling distressed to feeling blessed, devastation to liberation. Within this book, I mention many of the processes that I use to help people, all of which helped me. This includes Time Line Therapy, NLP, Clinical Hypnotherapy, EFT, Inner Child Processes, Energetic NLP and Accelerated Learning, plus much more.

Growth

A while after James left, I wrote in one of my blog posts that I was grateful for the growth he'd given me; I knew that on a soul level we had agreed our situation before incarnating on earth. This meant we were part of the same soul group with a very close connection. His leaving afforded me the space to grow and find self-love. It took me longer to realise that if this was true for him, then it was also true for his partner. She must also be part of my soul group. So I have thanked them both in the ether for their gift of growth and liberation to me.

As I was learning more and more about myself during my countless coaching and healing trainings, I could discern what was good for my energy and what wasn't. In the end, most of my socialising palled because I was bored with the shallow lifestyle I was leading. Inane chitchat and gossip wasn't what I was about. I thirsted for more knowledge of what makes the world and people tick, so I spent less time socialising in that way. Knowing I still needed help for my extreme sadness and depression, I returned to the coach I saw previously for my weight issues. I had just one session for my depression – a mix of neuro linguistic programming and hypnotherapy. Amazingly, the outcome was brilliant. Using this alongside other trainings and tools meant that I became stronger, calmer, more confident and in control. During this time I also trained in other healing and coaching techniques, which led to more self-awareness, increased intuition, self-love and self-accountability. At the same time, I took spiritual develop-ment classes. Then, finally, I took full control of my bus and filed for divorce.

From Feeling Stressed to Feeling Blessed

Over the past sixteen or so years, I have fully embraced all things spiritual and self-developmental. The time since my divorce has been one of my greatest growth periods. I love learning, provided the topic interests me. I have spent my entire adult life fulfilling this desire for new knowledge. Fortunately, when I became a coach and healer, I finally learned to love my "gifts"; they help me empathise, watch my clients grow and fulfil their potential. Having taken back control and accountability for whatever happens in my life, I ensure I manage my thoughts, emotions and energy (in part seven, science explains that we co-create our reality with our beliefs and thoughts). As I'm human, I still have some down times, but they never last long – I always bounce back. Over the years I have become more self-aware and let go of my "poor me" and people-pleasing aspects, strengthened my boundaries and most importantly learnt to love and accept myself as I am – "warts and all!" I finally feel comfortable in my own skin.

I know now that my coaching and healing was very much a part of my personal journey and not just for business, as I had naively thought all those years ago. Throughout this time I've had coaching/healing when necessary to ensure that I'm in the best mental, emotional, physical and energetic space, which is important to me personally and professionally. I acknowledge that we are all a work in progress, perfectly imperfect human beings, all doing the best we can with the resources available to us.

I am pleased to say that James, his partner and I merrily mingle together at family gatherings and have discussions about our children. Time and therapy have been fantastic healers for me. I hold no recrimination and as I said earlier I've encouraged our children to have contact with their dad. Their relationship is now on a great footing – he contacts them regularly and they get together too. My belief that everyone deserves to live a contented life meant that I agreed with his decision to leave and put himself first, so he could have that fulfilment. I am glad that he is still in accord with the choice he made. Even now I still visit my ex mother-in-law and we exchange birthday and Christmas gifts. James and I still send cards to each other too.

Spirit Connections

The beginning of my understanding and awareness of my "gifts" really began when I attended my first "Mind Body Soul Fair" just a couple of weeks after James left. I chose a workshop where I expected to learn how to become a psychic, but in truth I didn't really know what to expect. I definitely wasn't expecting to be thrown in at the deep end, with instructions to partner up with strangers to give readings through various mediums such as crystals, ribbons, cards and more. For my first experience discovering crystals, I chose black onyx. This was highly appropriate, as I learnt that it is a protection gem which absorbs and transforms negative energy, helping to develop emotional and physical strength and stamina when experiencing grief, stress and confusion. My unknown partner and I were to hold our crystals, put our energy into them and then pass it back to our partner to give each other a psychometry reading. I was unsure of how to do this, but words came out that were apparently appropriate. After this I was paired with the teacher to give her a reading from the red ribbon she had chosen. Again, I had no idea how to do this, but somehow words spilled out from my mouth – I told her she had been a premature baby and carried on from there. I took a pause in my reading to tell her how wonderful her teaching was. She then asked if I knew I was clairsentient, which I didn't. The teacher said that I had instantly responded to her unseen anxieties about whether her teaching was good enough.

One of my colleagues at school told me about a spiritualist church near me. I missed going to church, but regular church left me feeling that something was missing. Upon attending this spiritualist church, I was fascinated and so grateful to have met people similar to me. It was only after a service here, when I went for healing myself, that I discovered I was a healer. The lady who was to give me a healing said that I had healed her headache. She invited me to become a healer through the church. In the end I decided upon Reiki Healing, because it was a much quicker way to obtain the qualifications and insurance to offer healing to clients. How strange that we have to jump through formal hoops to prove our natural gifts. I believe that everyone is a healer and psychic, but we all have varying strength of awareness and capabilities. All of this explains why I love watching "witchy woo" programmes like Bewitched, Charmed and Merlin. I sometimes feel a longing to be part of these worlds, where magic is an accepted and everyday occurrence. I love hearing about people who have telekinetic abilities and other such skills. Our lives do have magic in and we have so much more control that we realise. As I'll explain in part seven, it is our own thoughts and beliefs that create our current reality.

Indigo

When embarking on a year long spiritual and psychic development course in London, the teacher Tracey said she only accepted "indigos" to work with. This was the first time I had been called this and again it explained in part who and what I am. Some traits that indigos have, which I embody, are:

- Being a maverick who doesn't always conform to the norm;

- Heightened sensitivity;

- Intuition;

- Curiosity;

- Love;

- Creativity;

- A sense of justice;

- Intelligence (although I didn't believe this until I passed my degree, when I realised I was a quick learner with a good memory).

I have always been driven to make positive changes in the world. As a child I made up stories to amuse all the younger kids who lived nearby. They would clamour to sit down on the green outside my grandparent's house (where we lived at the time) whilst I story-told (always including a moral to the story). Later on, as a primary school teacher and now as a coach, healer, author and speaker, my aim is still the same – to bring about positive change. The empathy that I once felt was a curse, I now accept as a gift. Looking back, I noticed that I was and still am a sounding board for others telling me their life stories and soliciting my wisdom. Even when I was eleven years old, a neighbour would tell me her woes and want advice, as did my mum when she was considering a divorce.

In the middle of my spiritual development journey, I had a strange encounter at the Sound Healing Conference in London Colney. After chatting and saying goodnight to friends, I went to bed. Suddenly, my uncharged iPod came on of its own accord – it wasn't plugged in and I hadn't touched it since arrival. Recognising what this meant, I thanked spirit for contact, turned it off and went to sleep. Later, I was awoken by a bright, flashing light. I got up and looked out of the window to see if it was fireworks or lightning. Nothing! Something prompted me to look up, where I observed the ceiling light switching itself on and off repeatedly. For a brief moment I was afraid, but then concluded that spirit was just saying hi again. I said, 'Thanks for visiting, but I am going back to sleep now, so keep the light off please.' The remainder of the night was uneventful and peaceful.

Another example was when returning home from a training. The table lamp in my blue spare room was on. It is always switched off, as I live alone and nobody uses the room when I am away. However, I noticed that oftentimes this would be on when I got home, with seemingly no explanation. My son-in-law had noticed it too, as this happened once when my granddaughter slept in that room. When attending Reconnective Healing training, I learned that other people had experienced similar instances and that they'd put it down to our energy fields changing and upgrading.

Soul Calling

A few months before I turned sixty, I followed my soul's desire to live by the sea down in Bournemouth. Ever since I returned from Qatar I'd wanted to relocate to Bournemouth, so I was finally fulfilling my wish of thirty-five years. In addition to this, I had been coming down for forty years to visit my dad, plus every October for fifteen years for what I termed my "witchy woo" holiday – which was a group of like-minded people enjoying talks, meditations and workshops together. My children were concerned that I would be lonely, as I didn't know anyone, but this wasn't a worry for me as I knew I would be proactive in this regard. It was a massive wrench leaving our wonderful children and grandchildren in Hertfordshire/Bedfordshire. The timing was also terribly inconvenient and felt wrong on so many levels, because my eldest daughter was going through a divorce and moving close by to be near family. I'd said I would be there to give her emotional support. On top of this, my eldest son and his wife were having their first baby, and her parents lived a distance away. As a result of this, my relationship with my daughter became strained. I was still there for some support, occasionally driving up to look after the children on Tuesday evenings when she was without childcare facilities, and having them stay during the summer holidays for a short while (for a couple of years), but this wasn't the same as being close by and readily available each week for her childcare needs as I had promised. It was the hardest thing I have ever done, putting my own needs and desires first. I knew I needed to be near the sea, with like-minded people, to be free from stressful situations for my physical and emotional health. I completely understood my daughter experiencing feelings of betrayal and abandonment due to being let down by the two important adults in her life. But, I realised that if I didn't live my life for me at sixty, then when would I? After all, no-one knows how long we have left on the planet. Luckily, things are good between my daughter and I today. I am so grateful that we overcame this painful time, and that my daughter, although hurt, maintained our relationship. Meanwhile, I sought out a coach to heal my guilt at letting her down when she needed me most.

My move to Dorset, being drawn to the beauty and healing properties of the sea and forest was brilliant. I found my "tribe"– my precious people, friends with whom I can be authentically myself, who care and understand my spiritual aspects. I've had to start again professionally, building a successful one-to-one coaching practice down here, although I still work with clients in Hertfordshire and Bedfordshire when I visit family and stay over. I also work internationally via Skype/Zoom. Time, space and therapy has helped me recover from the grief of my youngest son emigrating to Australia in September 2010, which I felt as another tremendous loss. Wow, ten years has gone by in a flash! I am blessed to have three wonderful Australian grandchildren and a super daughter-in-law. By accepting my shadow side and shortcomings physically and energetically, plus fulfilling my own needs, I've learnt to love, honour, respect and support myself. I am finally at peace.

Errors of Judgement

One of the first books I read at the beginning of this journey of self-discovery was Louis Hay's *You Can Heal Your Life*. There are many affirmations in this book, with one of the most important being, 'I am whole and complete and all is well in my world'. Affirmations are a form of communication with your unconscious mind, which is always listening to and believing your thoughts and feelings. I use them daily, even more during testing times, to get me through my challenges. You can say them out loud, in your mind or write them in the present tense as if they have already occurred. It's a fabulous way to get in touch with the feeling that they have already happened. It's your command to the Universe, as well as helping your mind and body to create your affirmation in reality.

Unfortunately, there have been periods since my move to Dorset where I have made calamitous errors. I've had to use my affirmations and many other tools to help me cope with my newly found situations and unwanted feelings. I ended up losing my nest egg that I had downsized my home for, after investing a lot of money on a property-training programme. I used the funds I planned to help subsidise my pension, which I knew would be small due to us placing more into my ex-husband's private pension and the government unexpectedly increasing my retirement date by six years.

My investment came about because of synchronicities (events loosely connected to each other), which made me think that property was supposed to be part of my journey. I should have "tuned in" and not just blindly followed the "signs". It all started when I was at a workshop in London, where someone told me that I should work in property instead of coaching. I didn't take any notice at the time, as the idea didn't resonate with me. Then, a short while later, a friend asked me to go with her to London to attend a property day. Remembering what I'd been told at the workshop and looking forward to a day out, I went along to see what it was all about. The event was fascinating and I found it inspiring that one woman had created a property empire, turning over millions of pounds every year. I really liked the thought of providing affordable housing for those at the beginning of their home ownership journey. I spoke to a few other women at the conference, all of whom had followed the initial woman's guidance the previous year, when she had showed others how to implement her model of success. They'd made a profit and were apparently doing well. Of course, we weren't told about the ones who hadn't "made it", which I discovered much later!

I left the conference without signing up, but had filled in a feedback form requesting further information. The business owner personally rang me and made all sorts of wonderful promises, which I believed to be a verbal contract and so signed up for the course. But in the end these assurances and promises meant absolutely nothing! Along with me there were many business owners who joined the course too. They encouraged us to pursue property full time to ensure our success, resulting in a few people (including one top London headmistress) giving up their jobs. So, I put aside my coaching business in Dorset and concentrated on my foray into the property business.

The disappointments arrived thick and fast. First, it became apparent that we wouldn't be receiving coaching from the aforementioned female business owner. Instead, it would be a male trainer (representing her company). I wasn't the only person unhappy with this and made my feelings known both in person and in writing. To add to this, I felt that I somehow didn't fit into the group of my fellow property enthusiasts, as it was large and cliquey.

I worked hard making phone calls and weekly visits to a multitude of estate agents, doing letter drops to empty houses, scouting for possible suitable properties, attending networking events, watching videos, reading books and journals to learn more. I would often travel to and from properties with a surveyor to see if they were suitable to convert. I really felt that this time I had inspected the business thoroughly, to ensure it wasn't a scam, but later I discovered that even my research wasn't sufficient. Numerous problems began to appear early on. To start with, we were told to work fairly close to home for ease of regular inspection when project-managing the buildings. Then, when this wasn't fruitful for any of us down south (as house prices are exorbitant), we were told to try further afield, even as far north as Doncaster where the course owner worked. This led to some of us encroaching on each other's areas, turning up at the same buildings at the same time to view. For six months I was using the strategy suggested to me, finding extensive properties that could be split into two flats. But, when the figures didn't work to make a profit, I was told to change strategy and buy up commercial buildings and convert them to flats. Again, because of high prices locally and others already having rapport with the agents (having been in the business for years) this too was unsuccessful. My surveyor and I travelled to Poole, Bournemouth, Salisbury, Southampton and many other areas, but somehow the layout was always wrong or the numbers wouldn't stack up for conversion and profit. I did a private bid on a property in Basingstoke, where I thought I stood a fabulous chance, as they called me afterwards. However, they wanted my investors and me to buy the building without planning permission. Although the profits would have been vast, the risk was far too high. Understandably my investors wouldn't go along with it.

Once the course was over (it was extended to fifteen months because hardly anyone on the course had made a property deal), less than half the class had experienced any success at all! It seemed that many of us had just thrown our time and money away. No wonder she was a multi-millionaire – with thirty people paying £25,000 each for four weekend group trainings, some videos and calls. On top of this I had seven hours' travel expenses and three nights' accommodation costs for each in person event!

Another disastrous experience was when someone I knew recommended a guy who was using and selling bio-resonance machines. I had two sessions to help get rid of parasites in my body and I was so impressed that I enquired about purchasing it. Again, I was given a verbal contract with assurances that I'd be trained on both software types up to the top level. I didn't have the full amount and so I paid by instalments on my credit card. After a brief time, the seller had family difficulties and was taking on more clients, so couldn't fulfil his verbal contract for the training. I paid thousands of pounds for the machine, which was now not working correctly, nor did he give me the full training as promised. I tried to pursue it through official channels, but they couldn't do anything as it was difficult to prove. I had initially bought the machine because my daughter and I were experiencing health issues. I thought it would be helpful for us and something extra that I could add to my coaching and healing practice.

After these scams I felt terribly low and sad at myself for getting sucked in by supposed-ly spiritual people like me (both times those involved professed to be spiritual, but weren't really like me at all), they had no transparency, ethics or integrity. Still, just like I always do, I bounced back. I chose to acknowledge the money as a write off, to stop my continuously looping thoughts and feelings, which were stressing me out. My health was more important than money. Having made this decision I felt lighter, even though there wasn't anything left in my pot! Thankfully coaching, healing and self-exploration has enabled me to see why things happened and for what reason, although in the property instance I've yet to fully understand why. It transpires that I do occasionally need to have the same lesson twice – but as humans this is sometimes the case.

Moving On and Exploring

I adore exploring. Now in my mid-sixties, I am young at heart and still willing to try new things. Since my divorce I have been lucky to have had truly wonderful experiences and gone to fabulous places in the world, most of the time on my own. What a contrast to when I wouldn't even walk into a pub alone to meet friends or drive to Keele to see our daughter at universi-ty. When our youngest son was twenty-one and I was fifty, James gifted him with a wonderful birthday present – a free fall tandem skydive for two. I was the only one who would accompany him and I thoroughly enjoyed taking part in this. It was so peaceful high in the sky, with stunning views over Cambridge (I was still living in Bedfordshire).

I was also blessed to go to a conference in Amsterdam, where I met some great well-known speakers and authors such as Lynne McTaggart and Dawson Church. I've seen Deepak Chopra in London and I met Bruce Lipton and others at an EFT event. I travelled to Bali to see a friend who was taking a year out exploring the world. Whilst travelling around Bali I passed my PADI scuba diving certificate, which I had longed to do when living in Doha. I also almost drowned at Tulamben when scuba diving with a faulty mask. This gave me an epiphany about the teaching job-share position I had just accepted, showing me that I shouldn't extend it beyond the agreed time if it was offered (every cloud has a silver lining). I remembered this later when the job was offered on a permanent basis.

Another time, I went to Tel Aviv for training with a colleague in "The Reconnection" with Eric Pearl and then off sightseeing in Jerusalem. I then travelled with two friends to Phoenix. En route to the Grand Canyon, I experienced a past life realisation or "picked up on" the distress of those living in past times. Out of nowhere, I suddenly burst into deep sobs for no apparent reason. I was shocked and surprised at this, as I was mid-conversation with my friend. The driver informed me that we had just passed over the Navaho Native American Indian Reservation. I continued to struggle with my emotions throughout the rest of the way to the canyon. Our next port of call was Colorado for the Festival of Enlightenment conference, to support our Energetic NLP trainer Art Giser who was speaking there. There were many other fabulous speakers I met professionally as well as socially, including Panache Desai, Joel Young and Rikka Zimmerman – who introduced me to Access Consciousness, which I use to this day.

One particularly moving experience was during a pilgrimage led by Tracey Ash (one of my psychic development teachers), where I had a wonderful meditation alone in Karnak Temple, experiencing the feeling of a crown being placed upon my head. I had no conscious understanding of what this meant, but it felt sacred and alchemical. I now sense that this crowning meant I am the sovereign of my life. I felt called to tone whilst exploring the pyramids, down holes at sacred sights and in some tombs, to help clear the stuck energy. Another interesting pilgrimage was in Peru with Davina MacKail. I became discomforted and tearful at Machu Picchu, where I suddenly felt afraid of the height (having released this fear during my early trainings, I was surprised that these feelings arose). According to Davina, it seems that I was a princess in a past life, sent off to die as a ritual sacrifice to the gods. The following day, having had healing from Davina, I climbed Huayna Picchu (pronounced 'Wayna Picchu') fearlessly, almost to its pinnacle. It was merciless and treacherous, especially on the way down in the rain, but was sacred and awesome at the same time. (The useful resources page has Davina's website link, so you can book your own pilgrimage).

India was fascinating too, with all the colourful sights and sounds, but the contrasts of poverty tugged at my heartstrings. The purpose of our group visit was to have a Nadi leaf reading, which was fascinating and organised by Angela Donovan (this is now available online too). During the trip it became apparent that a new friend needed my support and we often spent time huddled up in her hotel room instead of soaking up the sunshine around the pool. She was at the onset of all things spiritual, having downloads and visions that she didn't know how to cope with. We had lengthy discussions on life and all its mysteries. We stayed in touch and it's been fantastic to see her grow into a happier, balanced and more fulfilled lady. There were other retreats where I had interesting past life experiences, such as in the Cathar region in France. Bonn in Germany with Dr Joe Dispenza was amazing and brought about a huge shift in my consciousness and expansion. All of these events and others had their own individual profound effect on me.

Following that, our kids clubbed together for my sixtieth and sixty-first birthdays, paying for me to go to New York with my daughters. This was a wonderful and fun experience, which I will always treasure. It had been a long-held wish of mine, albeit one I'd expected to fulfil as a married couple. A short while afterwards, my brother emigrated to New York, which was wonderful for him but another loss for me. I travelled to Australia to visit my son and family in Brisbane and Moranbah. Due to my property fiasco I haven't had the funds to visit Australia again, so have yet to meet some of the newer family additions. I adore spending time with my children and grandchildren, it is a primary pleasure of mine! They are the most important people in the world to me.

Although this all seems glamorous and I was lucky to meet so many lovely people, I was often seeking information outside of myself. I still couldn't find answers within me. I've had super expansive experiences, but there have been terrible experiences too, such as almost dying from a health condition, which lead to diabetes. I've had and still have ups and downs – my growth has been interesting to say the least. But I'm still here to tell the tale, living life as fulfilled and contented as possible in the circumstances. I am now able to tap into my inner guidance and find the answers I need within myself, occasionally consulting with others to clarify further. As well as my water and snow skiing when married, plus my scuba diving and skydiving post-divorce, I next took surfing lessons. My friend initiated this on her fiftieth birthday (I was sixty), wanting someone to come along and play with her. I'm convinced I swallowed half the ocean, but the laughter at ourselves was so cathartic. Having been paddle-boarding, kayaking and more since then, white water rafting is next on my bucket list.

I have met even more like-minded and interesting people through running my meditation and spiritual development groups, workshops and events I speak at. I am truly grateful for the insightful discussions and joy we have in each other's company. With the help of the processes in this book, I am now loving the simple things in life, such as a beautiful rose with a sweet scent, playing on the swings at the park and seeing the sunshine glinting on the sea. Even more so, I appreciate things like the laughter and the incomprehensible chats of my youngest grand-daughter, the view from the top of the cliffs near where I live and the blessed feeling I receive when getting together with my family, to chat, play and laugh. I am living life one day at a time. My daughter is due to be married in 2021 (after her wedding was cancelled in the summer of 2020 due to COVID-19), which will be the first time I meet two of my delightful Australian grand-children. The future is bright, and I am cherishing every minute of my life.

The following parts of this book are full of suggestions on how you can become an improved version of yourself. At the end of each part I have given you an invitation to fulfil and questions to explore for more insight and awareness of where you are right now. The way you frame your experience is enormously important. As an example, a friend once said to me that she felt like a failure, because she was getting a divorce. I gave her a different perspective – my own divorce was not a failure; it had lasted many years and gave us fabulous children, no one was wrong and it only ended because we were no longer in resonance with each other. Today we live so much longer than at any other point in history, with so many different pressures; it's amazing that people stay aligned for as long as they do. My own divorce became a blessing, and this was a message I tried to impart to my friend too – there are positives and lessons to take from any situation, you just need to be in the right frame of mind to find these. Throughout this book I'll provide you with ways and means to start looking at things positively, powerfully and for the benefit of you. Let's start with some exercises!

- Write a list of what you like to experience and do. What draws you in and makes your heart sing?

- As a contrast, write a list of things you are doing now and how these make you feel. Ask yourself why you are doing things you don't like to do.

- Is there any way you can incorporate more of the things you like to do in your life?

- Are you able to reduce your participation in activities you dislike? What is your overarching soul's desire?

I once had a client who loved pigs. She developed this love when she was very young, after her babysitter took her to see a tealeaf reader who had two pigs. Whilst her babysitter had her reading, my client played with the pigs. She enjoyed this so much that she vowed she would work with pigs when she was grown up, or else have a pig of her own. The realisation of this desire came true when she was in her thirties, where she worked on a pig farm with over two-thousand pigs. Sometimes what we wish for can arrive very quickly and other times we must wait patiently – it's all about having faith, commitment and desire to achieve your goal.

Ask yourself this, reader: what is your genuine desire and passion for your life? Write this down as a call to the Universe to help you co-create. What steps can you take to create your dreams, to fulfil your soul calling?

Another invitation is to write your dreams using the S.M.A.R.T. goal method.

***S**pecific, clear and easy to understand, written in the positive and well defined.

***M**easurable precise amounts and dates, such as aiming to lose 7 lbs in six weeks. What will you see, hear and feel when you reach your goal?

***A**chievable/attainable. Make sure it is realistic – how high or low do you want to go? Ensure that it is possible to achieve your outcome.

***R**elevant and for you. How this may impact others is important, but your goal should be for you, not because others want you to be/do/have the outcome.

***T**ime-Based with a start and end date, so you can measure how well you're moving towards your final outcome in the interim.

On a piece of A4 paper, write your name and the date at the top:

*Then on another line below, write your smart goal.

*Below this, write a heading – motivation. Underneath this, write why you want the goal (the outcome you're looking for).

*On a fresh line, list all the benefits you'll receive when you achieve your goal. Highlight your greatest benefit.

*Next, write what would be your pain if you don't achieve your goal. For example, "If I don't achieve this goal, then…."

*Consider what achieving this goal will enable you to have, be, do in other areas of your life.

*List obstacles and challenges on a fresh line – what may impede or hinder you from achieving your outcome?

*Set a minimum goal, target goal and extraordinary goal.

*Next, write how you will need to be different to achieve your goal. For example:

*I will start doing…

*To achieve this goal I will stop doing…

*To achieve this goal, I will need to be someone who is…

*List what resources you need and what resources you have available to you regarding things, people, personal qualities, information, skills, knowledge and finances.

*Lastly write "Action – three steps I will complete in the next week that move me closer to my goal are…" Follow this up with, "Three steps I can complete in the next month that move me towards my goal are…"

Having completed this exercise, it is important to see yourself in the future achieving your goals. Close your eyes and create a picture of you in the future. Envision what you will see around you when you are achieving it, hear what you will hear and feel the feelings that you will experience as you achieve it. Visualise your timeline. Where is your past and future?

Now float up above into your timeline, taking your picture with you. From your present, float out into your future, above your timeline – still taking your picture with you. Go out above your timeline until you reach the time you wish to achieve your goal. Once above this time, just let go of your picture, letting it drift into place in your timeline. As it snugly fits into place, notice that all the events on your timeline have shuffled and rearranged to accommodate your goal. Float back to your present, above your timeline; come back down into your now moment. Take a long deep breath and gently shake your body.

Insightful Questions

When you have finished the invitation above, take a notepad and pen. Sit quietly, free from any distractions, in a relaxed manner. Look at each of the questions below, one at a time. Allow the question to just flow freely in your mind, percolating if you will. Then, capture your answers on paper, giving you an insight into where you are right now. This will help you shift your perspective, so that you become less stuck.

According to many of my trainings (but particularly in NLP, Clinical Hypnotherapy and Access Consciousness), asking smart questions invites every molecule to contribute to you, whereas "just thinking" can hamper you. The difference between answers and questions is that one locks you into your best idea, whilst the other opens you up to things even better than you could imagine. The questions set your reticular activating system to go on a hunt for the answer, which expands beyond where you are right now.

- What beliefs and challenges can you trace back to your early formative years? If these no longer benefit you, are you willing to release them?

- Do you usually do what others want, instead of fulfilling your own wishes?

- Do you hold others responsible for everything happening to you? Can you see how you may have contributed to this?

- If you have given your power away to others, how could you have done things differently?

- Is there room to improve your self-confidence? If so, what changes can you make to enhance this? You may want to wait until you've read more of the book for further ideas.

- How often do you choose to participate in simple things that give you pleasure and uplift you?

- What experiences have you got to look forward to in your life? If there aren't any, then will you create some? Even if it's only a day trip, or a visit to some place you have always wanted to see or a show, it's worth doing! My mum died having wanted to see a ballet in London and never got to do this, so I made sure I did it for both her and me.

- Write your strengths and weaknesses – what can you do to utilise your strengths and to improve your weaknesses? Can you accept that you will always have things you are better at?

- Where do you want to be in five years' time, in relation to your work, location and lifestyle?

Having completed all the questions, now consider positive ways in which you can make changes. I wrote how affirmations helped me when I was depressed and overwhelmed. Maybe create your own affirmations as a positive statement, then say them out loud to yourself. This would be a really good way to start making change!

Part Two

To Harmonise

One of the most important elements in our heart-led, self-improvement process, is to find inner harmony. With this in mind, this part will show you ways to harmonise, raise your vibrations and help you understand how disharmony can impact your life.

So, what does it mean to harmonise? Here are some dictionary definitions.

Harmonise:

- To combine or cause things to go together in an effective or pleasing way.

- To bring ideas, feelings or actions into agreement or to a pleasing combination of different parts.

- To bring different approaches and outlooks together, forming a unified plan.

- To make different people, plans and situations suitable for each other.

- To play or sing musical notes that blend well together, creating harmony.

If we used the term "harmonise" in a sentence, we might say: 'The garden has been designed to harmonise with the natural landscape.' Or, as another example, 'The plan is to harmonise (make similar) safety standards across all the countries involved.'

You get the drift – it's all about achieving unity, togetherness and seamlessness. But now, we have to harmonise **your** heart.

Harmony

The dictionary defines harmony as balance, congruity, blending, coordination, compatibility, agreement, peace, peacefulness, cooperation, understanding, unity, like-mindedness and oneness. For me, harmony means feeling balanced, in equilibrium, whole and complete. Therefore, this fits with the dictionary definition well. When I am harmonised, I am at peace with myself, free from inner conflict and fears, negative looping thoughts and rampant negative emotions. It means I have good self-love, self-care and self-esteem. I am congruent, true to myself, authentic, feeling good and in tune with my emotions. My mind, body and spirit are all being nourished and integrated as a unit. Essentially, I am whole, on a physical, mental and spiritual level, with all aspects working together to create a sense of wellbeing and nurturing.

Every organism has one aim and that is to survive. Your body is a symphony of cells, that all need to work in harmony to maintain homeostasis (the scientific term for whole body equilibrium).

Taking this into account, your body cells all work together, in concert, to keep you alive. They do this through finely tuned methods of communication. We're all familiar with the sounds that the human body makes – hearts beating, joints clicking, tummies rumbling, throats vibrating when we speak and sing. But what about the tiny sounds you make that you're unable to hear, such as the sounds made by the trillions of living cells that make up your body? According to Dianne Trussell in *The Science of Music,* your cells sing constantly. Their song changes in response to what's going on around them, whether that's pressure, temperature from the environment or their own inner processes.

Just as the instruments in an orchestra produce signals and musical notes, causing the air to vibrate, cells translate signals from their surroundings. When information from the environment, (such as a biological messenger) meets the outer envelope of the cell, calcium ions are released inside the cell. It is these calcium ions which carry signals. In the same way we'd study an orchestral melody, we must evaluate the collective sound of our cells. Studying an isolated note on its own allows no inference of the melody, just as a single cell cannot change the entire body. And yet, together, as a collective, these cells are the power behind your lifeforce. When each individual cell begins to sing, that melody goes out to neighbouring cells, announcing either health and harmony or discord with the illness of the tissue and organ they're part of. The neighbouring cells "hear" each other's songs i.e. information and respond accordingly. In some ways, it is no coincidence that the word "organ" refers to both an instrument and to various body parts.

When we study the sounds that cells are making together, just as we would study the collective sound of all the instruments in an orchestra, we can form logical, medical conclusions. Multiple scientific studies have been carried out, furthering this knowledge by listening in on cell communications. This is done using an "atomic force microscope" and has led to numerous discoveries. As Rudi Balling describes in his essay *How Cells Translate Signals*, scientists have learned that the plethora of calcium impulses vary relatively to one another in a specific relationship. A stimulus from outside doesn't lead to an absolute increase in calcium impulses but to a change in the frequency at which they occur – in the concert hall this is when notes of the instruments rise and fall in symphony. This pattern is the actual signal that leads to a response in the cells.

Cells use their DNA code in distinct ways depending on their jobs, in the same way that an orchestra can perform one piece of music in many ways. The combination of changes in gene expression in a cell is called its epigenome; it is complex and exquisitely arranged like a symphony. Science shows that genes can be switched on and off, that your health, environ-

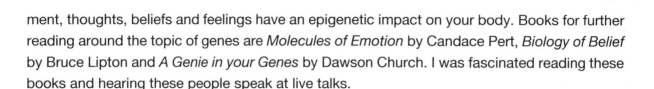

ment, thoughts, beliefs and feelings have an epigenetic impact on your body. Books for further reading around the topic of genes are *Molecules of Emotion* by Candace Pert, *Biology of Belief* by Bruce Lipton and *A Genie in your Genes* by Dawson Church. I was fascinated reading these books and hearing these people speak at live talks.

Disharmony Can Occur From Various Sources

Pollutants, Poor Nutrition and Stress

There is a multitude of things that can contribute to imbalance in your body, including poor diet, addiction, physical or emotional trauma, improper rest or overdoing things. In response to these, your body produces "free radicals", which are unstable atoms that can damage cells, causing illness and aging. As your body ages, it loses its ability to fight the effects of free radicals. This results in more rogue atoms, more oxidative stress (an imbalance of free radicals and antioxidants in the body) and more damage to cells, which in turn leads to even more illness and aging. You can see how the areas I mentioned quickly compound on themselves, building a vicious and negative cellular cycle. There are numerous studies and theories which have linked free radicals with diseases such as Alzheimer's, dementia, cancer, arthritis, diabetes and Parkinson's, as well as age-related vision decline, wrinkles, greying hair and hair loss.

Over time, free radical researchers have begun to focus heavily on the mitochondria. Mitochondria are tiny organelles in cells that process nutrients to power the cell. Research on rats suggests that free radicals produced in the mitochondria, damage the substances that the cell depends upon in order to work properly. This damage causes mutations that produce even more free radicals, thus speeding up the process of damage to the cell. This theory explains why some people age more slowly than others. Although free radicals are produced naturally, lifestyle factors can exacerbate their production. Exposure to toxic chemicals, including pesticides and air pollution, smoking, alcohol and fried foods can speed things up and are linked to cardiovascular disease and cancer. With all this in mind, it's highly likely that oxidative stress is responsible for a plethora of medical issues. The renowned visionary scientist and author Dr Denham Harman, who worked at the University of Nebraska Medical Center, developed the most widely accepted theory on aging that is now used to study cancer, Alzheimer's disease and other illnesses. Harman developed the free-radical theory of aging in 1954, although it took years for additional research to prove its importance. The theory holds that one of the by-products of oxygen utilisation is an adverse chemical reaction in the cells. The results of this are aging and finally death. So, to protect your body and increase your lifespan, be more mindful of what you put into you and onto your skin.

Personally, I use natural products around the home and on my body. These products contain antioxidants, which is the name for molecules that prevent oxidation of other molecules. They lessen or prevent the effects of free radicals, by donating electrons to the rogue atoms, which in turn reduces free radical reactivity. However, what makes antioxidants truly unique is that they donate an electron without becoming free-radical themselves. Just like our cells, no single antioxidant can combat the effects of every free radical, but they work in harmony to counter-act the impact of these chaotic atoms. Below I've included a short list of chemicals/sources for antioxidants, which can help you to start living a healthier life:

- Vitamin C and Vitamin E;

- Glutathione;

- Beta-carotene;

- Plant oestrogens/phytoestrogens;

- Blueberries;

- Citrus fruits;

- Carrots;

- Green tea;

- Soybeans.

As with anything, taking an overload of antioxidants has a negative effect, so be careful to note the recommended daily doses. High glycaemic foods and foods rich in refined carbohydrates and sugar are more likely to generate free radicals, so avoid these wherever possible. Likewise, limit eating processed meat such as sausages, bacon and salami, as they contain preservatives which lead to more production of free radicals.

Dissonance

We have looked at disharmony, so now let's discuss dissonance. This can occur if your beliefs are challenged or when your behaviour is not aligned with your beliefs. Dissonance can manifest itself as stress, anxiety, regret, shame, embarrassment or feelings of low self-worth. There are a variety of social situations where this can arise, but it commonly occurs through forced compliant behaviour in the workplace, particularly when additional information arises that challenges what you knew or thought you knew. In his 1957 essay, *Theory of Cognitive Dissonance*, Leon Festinger proposed that human beings strive for internal, psychological consistency to function mentally in the real world. A person who experiences internal inconsistency becomes psychologically uncomfortable and is motivated to reduce the cognitive dissonance. In essence, you may try to avoid the conflict and facts that bring up your negative feelings. In part four of this book, I'll provide you with a real example of such dissonance occurring.

How Can You Create Harmony?

Every object has a natural vibratory rate, which is called resonance. Resonance is the reverse of dissonance. Your body is in a state of vibration with every organ, bone, tissue and system. When you are in a fit state of health, your body puts out an overall harmonic that reflects this. However, when a frequency that is contrary to your health establishes itself in a specific part of your body, it creates disharmony. This is known as dis-ease. To bring yourself back to harmony, you must restore the vibratory resonance in that part of the body. It's not just cells that work together, but the entire body as a collective. Therefore, this one body part will influence the entire system. Metaphorically speaking, when one instrument is out of tune, the orchestra will be less than perfect and the same is true for your body. Science has shown that music and sound have a significant impact on our health. This is why "Sound Healing" is often used as a way of releasing dissonance. Interestingly, your cells can affect the cells of people around you, as they receive the information too. So, if you're harmonious, other people's cells will be most appreciative of this.

For me, creating harmony is about feeling at peace within myself, being free from inner conflict and having a balance between work, life and fun. It's about congruence, acting with integrity, being true to who I am and to what my values are. It also means having a sense of fulfilment, of serving in some way, whether it's large or small and acknowledging, accepting and letting go of situations, people or other things which no longer serve me. All of this relates to my own sense of self-love and to having a sense of community. I want to feel as if I belong, spending time with people who "get me". Later in this book, we'll delve further into these elements and how they can help you find your own equilibrium.

In the past I've worked too hard, barely giving myself any time to "smell the roses" when I was teaching or when ferrying our four children to after-school activities and competitions at the weekend. I ran purely on autopilot, with little if any downtime to rest or be still within myself. I wasn't aware of what I wanted and who I really was. I just seemed to be on a hamster wheel, doing the same routine things day after day. Often I felt completely out of kilter, but had no time to explore internally what I could do to make life more bearable.

Nowadays I meditate regularly, which allows me to get in touch with my inner feelings and thoughts, receive answers to questions and get guidance from spirit, my Higher Self and the

Universe. I mainly do my own silent meditation, but still use guided meditations too when I just want to relax and be still. In addition, I exercise in one format or another most days, as well as drinking lots of Kangen Water. I am always mindful of what I put in my body regarding food, as my body has some sensitivity. To manage this, I use my Hunter Bio Resonance Machine to rid my body of parasites, viruses and bacteria, which cause most diseases (1 ½ - 2 hours each session). Likewise, I wear Voxx socks and insoles to help bring my body back to homeostasis (see part six with more info on VoxxLife). These products help me have more energy and eliminate my knee pain. When feeling in a low mood, I will do things that make me feel less stressed and more blessed, which has a ripple effect out into the world (see the butterfly effect in part seven).

Summary

So, in this chapter we have looked at:

- ❖ Harmony, which means being in balance mentally, emotionally and physically, with all parts of you working as a cohesive unit. It means that your body is working in tandem with your heart to create wellbeing.

- ❖ Disharmony is because of pollutants and stress, but can be offset with the help of antioxidants.

- ❖ Resonance is when your body is working in harmony.

- ❖ Dissonance means that one body part is out of sync with the rest, causing dis-ease and ill health. It means you are not living a life in alignment with your values.

Write down when you're anxious and upset. What sets you off? This can be a cause of disharmony in your body. Write your triggers down, noticing what happened, when, with whom and at what time of day. Include all your feelings, thoughts and beliefs. Did you get angry, upset, want to run away, hit someone or something else? Have you discovered a pattern? Note the time of day (you may have been more tired and vulnerable) and the time of month (when you may have been hormonal). Or, is it a particular person or situation that causes your distress?

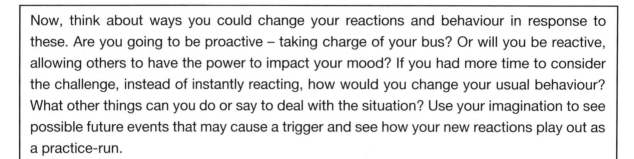

Now, think about ways you could change your reactions and behaviour in response to these. Are you going to be proactive – taking charge of your bus? Or will you be reactive, allowing others to have the power to impact your mood? If you had more time to consider the challenge, instead of instantly reacting, how would you change your usual behaviour? What other things can you do or say to deal with the situation? Use your imagination to see possible future events that may cause a trigger and see how your new reactions play out as a practice-run.

Insightful Questions

When you have finished the exercise above, take a notepad and pen and sit quietly, free from any distractions. Look at each of the questions below, one at a time. Allow the question to just flow freely in your mind, percolating if you will. Then, capture on paper what arises. Your answers will give you an insight into what your thoughts and beliefs are now and will shift your perspective, so you become less stuck.

- *Can you think of any other ways you could make changes?*

- *What does your mind want and need, in order to be harmonious?*

- *What does your body want and need, to feel more in balance?*

- *What can you add to make your life more serene?*

- *What can you reduce or eliminate, to reach equilibrium?*

- *Will you take regular time out, free from any stimulation, to connect with your inner self?*

- *What do you do to feel in balance? Is there anything else you could include?*

- *Are you doing anything that enhances your spiritual side? If not, then what can you add?*

Having completed all the questions, form some positive ways in which you could be more proactive, taking steps to move forward for your benefit.

Part Three

Why Your Physical and Energetic Hearts are Important for Optimal Health

What Your Heart Does

Your heart integrates and balances your physical, emotional and mental body. It is at the centre of your circulatory system, which is a network of blood vessels that delivers blood to every part of your body. Thus, your heart provides blood to every cell and organ. Blood carries oxygen and other important nutrients that all body organs need to stay healthy and to work properly.

Your heart has four separate chambers, two on your right side and two on your left side; it is divided into two separate pumping systems. The right side of your heart receives oxygen-poor blood from your veins, which it then pumps to your lungs, where it picks up oxygen and gets rid of carbon dioxide. The left side of your heart receives oxygen-rich blood from your lungs and pumps it through your arteries to the rest of your body.

How Your Heart Maintains Its Normal Function

As already mentioned, your heart's job is to pump enough blood to deliver a continuous supply of oxygen and other nutrients to your brain and other vital organs. To do this, your heart has to regulate the timing of your heartbeat. Your electrical system keeps your heart beating in a regular rhythm and adjusts the rate at which it beats. When your system works properly, your heart rate and rhythm is normal. In contrast, problems with your system can cause arrhythmia, which means that your heart chambers are beating in an uncoordinated or random way, too fast or too slow.

The four chambers of your heart are made of a muscle called myocardium, which is the main pump. This relaxes to fill with blood and then squeezes (contracts) to pump the blood. Your muscle must be able to relax enough so it can fill with blood properly before it pumps again. The health of your heart muscles affects its ability to relax and contract – both of which determine whether your heart can pump enough blood each time it beats. Your heart has four valves that control the flow of blood in and out of your chambers. There are valves between the atrium and the ventricle on each side of your heart, all designed to keep blood flowing forward only. When each of the chambers contract, a valve opens, allowing blood to flow out. When the chamber relaxes, the valve closes, preventing blood from leaking back into the chamber and allowing the chamber to fill with blood again. Thus, a problem with your heart valves can disrupt the normal flow of blood and cause serious medical issues.

Your heart also serves as a complex information processing centre, because it influences your brain function, nervous system, hormonal system and most of your body's major organs. With this in mind, taking excellent care of yourself is vital. When any part of your body isn't working at an optimal level, your heart has to work so much harder. For example, when you're in a state of stress your heart needs more oxygen, which increases your heart rate. A state of constant stress can fatigue your heart and compromise your ability to reset, leading to inflammation, infections, toxicity and heart disease. What this all means is that your heart is your body's reset button. Without a working heart you are no longer alive in your body, so it's vital you take wonderful care of it.

Inactivity, Stress and Alcohol

Kevin R. Campbell MD, a cardiac electrophysiologist at North Carolina Heart and Vascular (Raleigh) is quoted as saying, "Several activities that people don't think twice about can have a negative impact on heart health. People with an inactive lifestyle i.e. those who don't move enough and sit for five hours or more each day have double the risk for heart failure." (*American Heart Association Journal of Circulation; Heart Failure*). Overindulging in alcohol can lead to high blood pressure, stroke and obesity, all of which increase your risk of heart disease. Just two drinks a day for men and one for women can interrupt your normal heart rhythm and cause heart failure. Likewise, excess stress spurs the body to release adrenaline, which temporarily affects how your body functions. Your heart rate increases and your blood pressure may rise. Over time, too much stress can damage blood vessels in your heart and increase your risk of heart attack and stroke. Dr Campbell says that to minimise the harmful effects of stress, you need to find a release. Thus, sharing your feelings with a loved one, working with a coach/ therapist or taking exercise to relieve mental tension is really beneficial.

Teeth Care, Salt and Sleep

You might be surprised to learn that flossing (or failing to floss) has a major impact on your overall health. A study published in May 2014, in the Journal of Periodontal Research, found that people with coronary heart disease who flossed, experienced fewer cardiovascular problems. Similarly, a study in 2013 in *International Scholarly Research Notices* shows that bacteria associated with gum disease promotes inflammation in the body and has been associated with increased risk of heart disease.

You may be less surprised to learn that salt is a very real and dangerous ingredient when it comes to high blood pressure – which is another risk factor for heart disease. To ensure you're not having more than the recommended daily amount, check for hidden sodium, as many processed foods such as canned vegetables and soups, meats, frozen dinners, chips (crisps) and other salty snacks have the highest sodium content. So, read the labels carefully!

Finally, sleep is absolutely vital. Your heart works hard all day. If you don't get enough sleep then your cardiovascular system doesn't get the rest it needs, which can lead to harmful side effects. Your heart rate and blood pressure dip during the first phase of sleep (the non-REM phase), which is just one indication of how essential resting can be. Chronic sleep deprivation can also lead to high resting cortisol and adrenaline levels, similar to levels experienced in a stressful situation. Seven or eight hours is generally recommended for adults, whereas teenagers should aim for nine or ten hours a night. On a personal note, I drink organic caffeine-free tea and coffee, as the caffeine increases my heart rate. When this happens, I can feel it, and I really dislike the sensation of my heart rate speeding up. Caffeine is a stimulant and therefore will keep you awake if taken too close to bedtime. Caffeine can also increase blood pressure, which is certainly not a good thing. A good bedtime routine signals to your body that it is time to sleep, so by doing the same thing at the same time your body can prepare itself to wind down from the day.

Heart Coherence

By bringing your heart to coherence (which I must add is not the same as relaxation) you support your cardiovascular and circulatory systems, regenerating the structure of your heart, thus helping to reset the homeostatic mechanism for your entire body. Homeostasis of your complete body or as I like to call it "harmonising your heart" should be your daily aim. So, check in during the day to see how your body is, how you are feeling and what your thoughts are. If they are out of alignment and you aren't feeling your "best", then do what you can to counter-act this. Having explored the source to discover what has created the imbalance, you can now take steps to regain your equilibrium.

When I was in Colorado, I was very lucky to meet Dr Howard Martin of the Heart Math Institute. This was where I discovered that we have three "brains": the heart brain, the regular brain and the gut brain. The heart brain is actually more powerful and picks up messages before the regular brain. It was amazing to watch my friend (who has a phD in science) volunteer in a demonstration which showed how fantastic the heart is. Dr Martin wired my friend up to a monitor, which we could all see on a large screen. He then gave her a set of cards, with the pictures face down. Some were happy pictures and some sad. I was so fascinated, because her response showed up on the screen before she had even turned the card over. How awesome is that! It showed that your heart can detect your environment and circumstances incredibly quickly, transmitting to your brain exactly what is occurring. The Heart Math Institute has placed data collection equipment around the world, which is able to detect when emotional surges occur and where. What was interesting is that the data showed a spike in emotions all around the world before news of Princess Diana's death broke, which is the same response as my friend in the demonstration.

Similarly to cells, your three brains are like an orchestra, with billions of neurons cooperating to produce a harmonic symphony, harnessing together an ever-changing network of neurons that work in synchrony. Although the head, heart and gut brains work together, they have obvious distinct physical functions, performing different mental and emotional roles. Your heart brain senses the world through emotions and feelings, memories, visions, images and dreams. Your head brain analyses information and applies logic and reasoning to create details for future plans. Finally, your gut brain is used to understand your identity and who you are in the world. Its role is self-preservation, teaching you to listen and follow your gut instinct. Below is my process to assist you when you have unwanted emotions and beliefs to let go of.

Harmonise Your Heart technique ™

I channelled this technique from spirit, one night early in 2018. It is a combination of things I had instinctively used for a long time but not thought to sequence together. This exercise aligns your three brains to create balance, allowing you to release and eliminate negative beliefs, looping thoughts and emotions that are no longer serving you, bringing equilibrium throughout your mind and body. It helps you to live in the magnificence of you, by harmonising your heart and being in tune with your true essence (Soul).

1) Begin by getting in touch with all your negative emotions and thoughts of the situation or person that you want to change. Rate on a scale from 1-10, with 10 being the highest/ most negative feelings you are experiencing.

2) Place your dominant hand in the middle of your chest, so that it covers your physical heart and upper heart energy centre (thymus). The base of your hand should be between your breasts and the tips of your fingers near your clavicle.

3) Place your other hand on your solar plexus, which is under your breasts, between your ribcage and belly button.

4) Visualise a purple heart sitting on top of a golden infinity symbol (the same as the front cover of this book).

5) Next sing the sound 'AH' for thirty seconds to rebalance your heart, then 'AW' for your gut and finally 'EE' for your brain. This toning synchronises and balances your three brains, bringing them back into equilibrium. Now visualise a white light connecting them, knowing they are now all balanced, synchronised and strengthened.

6) Tap firmly on your thymus saying, 'I love, honour, respect and support myself. I release, resolve and rescind all that no longer serves me, sending it to the sea to be transmuted, no longer to be with me.' (Alternatively, you can be specific and say what you want to let go of…)

7) Take a deep breath in through your nose, then release it like a big sigh out of your mouth, letting go of everything you desire to be free from.

8) Next say, 'I am now free' and visualise yourself with the outcome you wish to have.

9) Inhaling love from the symbol, now say, 'I fill my heart with love, joy and bliss. And so it is. Thank you, thank you, thank you.' You can also add any extra emotions you may need at the time.

10) Finally, anchor the wonderful feelings by crossing your arms in a hug of yourself, knowing that your good feelings are permeating throughout your body down to a cellular level.

I have written about the other energy centres (chakras) later in this part, what they are associated with and how to bring equilibrium to them.

Vibration

According to The Heart Math Institute, "Your heart field is powerfully active; it is what strongly influences your surroundings by generating the largest electromagnetic field in your body. Your heart is the most powerful source of electromagnetic energy in the human body, producing the largest rhythmic electromagnetic field of your body's organs." Our hearts have vast electrical fields, approximately sixty times greater than the electrical activity in our brain. As The Heart Math Institute describes it, "The magnetic field produced by your heart is over 100 times greater in strength than the field generated by the brain and can be detected up to three feet away from your body."

Where Science And Spirituality Coincide

Entrainment

The field of your heart is affected by others within your space. This process is known as "entrainment" and explains why so many of my clients have said they've never felt so calm and relaxed as when they're in my consulting room. This is because it is a tranquil setting and I consciously ensure I am in the right state for them to entrain to. How this happens is as follows: my clients' breathing slows, they let go of their body tension and just relax – sinking into their chairs. My serene energy field influences them, synchronising them with my tranquillity. The gravitational pull towards synchronicity is one of the founding principles of the natural world. According to quantum physics, this is observable in each and every one of our everyday lives. As mentioned in part two, the basic law of physics teaches us that everything in the universe is made up of particles or waves, vibrating like strings at different frequencies, from the cells in our own bodies to the light and sound waves that echo through the cosmos. Within these vibrational phenomena, resonating particles will communicate with and influence each other. In part seven I have written about how "everything is energy" and the "connectivity" of everything.

Entrainment also explains why it's so important to spend time with friends who are positive, rather than negative friends who will drain you and leave you feeling tired and lacklustre. Positive people spark a positive reaction in others, radiating energy. This is especially powerful if you are a highly sensitive person.

Practical Ways to Care for Your Heart

Now that I've explained why it's so important to take care of your heart, let's look at how this can be done:

Essential oils

Studies at Taiwan University showed that lavender, eucalyptus, anise and chamomile are of fabulous benefit to your heart rate and blood pressure. Other oils that also have good properties for your heart are bergamot (which can lower heart rate and blood pressure), cedarwood (which promotes relaxation and temporarily reduces heart rate, so it's good if you're anxious), citronella (helps to ease stress) and frankincense (anti-inflammatory, so can help prevent heart disease). Clary sage and jasmine are also beneficial. There are also others, all related to each of your body's energy centres, which I will describe later in this part.

Yoga

Stretching and moving your body is another way to harmonise your heart. Yoga enhances cardiovascular health in numerous ways, calming your sympathetic nervous system and increasing your parasympathetic system, resulting in a reduction of your heart rate and blood pressure, which creates relaxation in your body. It lessens disease-causing inflammation, calming hypertension and boosting beneficial HDL cholesterol. Yoga also improves your circulation and lung function, with some studies suggesting that it is as effective at reducing the risk of heart disease as brisk walking and cycling. Yogic breathing and meditation are fantastic ways to help soften and ease tension from your body. Below I have written suggested poses, all of which are beneficial. Write them down, then go to YouTube to see how to do these until you are familiar enough to do them alone. Or, better still, join a class where you can have a sense of community and someone to check if you are doing the poses correctly to prevent injury.

- **Easy Pose (Sukhasana).**

- **Mountain Pose (Tadasana)** helps strengthen your heart and improves your flexibility.

- **Standing Forward Bend (Uttanasana), Big Toe Pose (Padangusthasana).**

- **Downward Dog (Adho Mukho svanasana),** a resting position as it calms your system and energises your body.

- **Head to Knee Forward Bend (Janu Sirasana), Bound Angle Pose.**

- **Chair Pose (Utkatasana),** increases your heart and respiration rate. It also increases heat in your body and strengthens it. **Cat Pose (Marjariasana)** is good to do after the Chair Pose, as it allows your heart rate to settle and become soft and rhythmic again.

- **Cow Pose** and **Sphinx Pose** allow your chest to open. This is a mild backbend that gently opens your chest, stretching your lungs and shoulders. **Cobra Pose (Bhujangasana)** increases the stretch to your chest and requires more strength and stamina than the Sphinx Pose. **Tree Pose (Vrikshasana)** calms and brings equilibrium to the mind. Reposing in this way is useful, as a harmonious mind leads to steady and healthy functioning of the heart.

- **Extended Hands and Feet Pose (Utthita hatapadasana)** requires more focus and strength to balance. **Triangle Pose (Trikonasana)** is a heart opening standing posture designed to promote cardiovascular exercise. Your chest expands when breathing deeply and rhythmically. It also increases your stamina.

- **Warrior Pose (Virabhadrasana)** improves balance in the body and increases stamina. It also releases stress, while calming your mind and helps keep your heart rate in balance, **Bridge Pose (Setu Bandhasana)** is less demanding than the Bow Pose. The Bridge Pose facilitates deep breathing, opening and improving blood flow to your chest region.

- **Bow Pose (Dhanurasana)** opens and strengthens your heart region, it is stimulating and stretches your whole body. **The Half Shoulder Stand (Sarvangasana)** pacifies and activates your parasympathetic nervous system and creates space in your chest. It is a restful and rejuvenating posture. As a novice, begin by using the wall as an aid instead of doing the pose freestanding. An easier posture to begin with is just putting your legs up against the wall, with your bottom touching the wall.

- **Sitting Half Spinal Twist (Ardha Matsyendrasana)** works on your whole spine and opens your chest sides alternately. **Two Legged Forward Bend (Paschimottanasana)** serves as a resting posture. **The Seated Forward Bend** brings your head lower than your heart, thus facilitating a reduction of your heart and respiration rates, allowing your system to recuperate. **The Stick Pose (Dandasana)** facilitates good posture and strengthens your back, whilst stretching your shoulders and chest.

Breathwork Brings about Calm

Working with your breath is an extremely reliable and practicable means of bringing about calm. Observe your breath when anxious or under stress, feeling the difference to when you are calm and rested. When you are feeling stressed, you tend to take shallow, quick breaths. In contrast, when you are relaxed and in control, you take longer breaths. I have used the "7-11 technique" for many years and found this swiftly brings my body back into harmony (see part six for the instructions on this). When you exhale, it activates your parasympathetic nervous system, which decreases your blood pressure, dilates your pupils and slows your heart rate. This lowers emotional arousal levels, preparing you for relaxation and is often referred to as "rest and digest". It's essentially the opposite to anxiety and "fight or flight", where your body is getting ready for action, triggering a response in the sympathetic nervous system.

It is important to understand that it is your exhalation that stimulates the response. The reason why it is beneficial to have longer "out-breaths" than "in-breaths", is because the former is more effective at lowering your emotional arousal and calming. So, to reduce anxiety or stress, continue breathing this way for a few minutes or until your body and mind are in coherence. I have taken part in many breathing methods, including box breathing (where you breathe in for the count of four, hold for four, and breathe out for four) as well as other variations – both fast and slow – to either relax or stimulate energy in my body. Research and experiment with different breathing exercises to see what works best for you.

Learning to control your breath and heartbeat can really enhance your sense of connection, your feelings of love and your sense of gratitude. You'll feel connected to yourself, to others, to nature and your surroundings. Breathing, especially diaphragmatically (into your belly as opposed to your chest), is a superb way to balance your body and mind. It has played an important part in my journey during yoga and meditations. I am very lucky to be someone who does this naturally; I do it through my nose, which is very calming. I've often noticed that when my clients shallow breathe they are extremely anxious, so one of the first things I get them to do is to give themselves a "breather" i.e. take a few deep breaths. I also taught my private tutoring children to do this as part of my accelerated learning processes, before we began their lessons (more about this in part six). If you'd like to read about nose breathing, and why it's so beneficial for your health, I highly recommend *The Oxygen Advantage* by Patrick McKeown.

K.I.S.S. – Keep It Simple Sweetie

Cultivate an appreciation for beauty, for the simple things in life, in nature, people or the arts. Practise self-care, have self-compassion, acceptance regarding your body and emotions, engage in activities that make your heart light up and sing – it can be as simple as buying a bunch of your favourite flowers. Practise your receiving – which many women find more difficult, as they are generous givers. Practise forgiveness of yourself and others. Find things to be grateful for every day. In parts four, five and six of this book I'll cover these topics more in depth and also show you further ways to strengthen and bring your heart into harmony.

What Are Your Energy Centres and Their Roles?

Energy centres, also referred to as chakras, play a significant role in your overall wellbeing. They are the concentrated energy centres of your body, with the term "chakra" meaning "wheel" or "disk" in Sanskrit. The function of your chakras is to spin and "draw in" energy, keeping your spiritual, emotional, mental and physical health in balance. They are dynamic, constantly evolving and adapting to change, ensuring that you are functioning at optimal levels. With this in mind, when these energy centres are misaligned, it is vital that we can recognise and correct this. Now, let's look at where these energy centres are located, and how you can keep them in balance.

Heart Energy Centre

Your heart energy centre plays an important part in your body's equilibrium. It is the centre point of the seven main chakras in your physical body. People often talk about the twelve chakra system, with three above your crown, all which have varying names. However the two names that most people seem in agreement with are the soul star and the stellar gateway. There is one below the feet called the earth star and an additional centre in your body commonly mentioned is the higher heart chakra, which is situated at your thymus. Tapping this spot is a great way to keep the gland active, stimulating and boosting your immune system – which is especially important right now due to COVID-19. The tapping on your thymus gland creates vibrations that stimulate an increase in the maturation and release of white blood cells.

The heart centre is situated in the middle of your chest and includes the heart, the cardiac plexus, lungs and breast. It also rules your lymphatic system. This is the centre of the energetic activity in your body. It is the gateway which balances the world of physical i.e. the lower three energy centres (chakras) i.e. the root, sacral and solar plexus, with the world of spirit – which are the three upper energy centres i.e. the throat, third eye and crown.

The heart is the energy centre that the other centres depend upon to achieve balance. Your heart energy centre is often depicted as green – symbolising love, health, growth, prosperity and abundance. Working together with your physical heart, it helps your entire system to function properly. It is the point at which resonance is established and maintained. So, if you have an energetic block in your energy system then it is important to clear this. Never underestimate the power of free flowing energy.

The heart chakra is driven by the principles of transformation and integration, generating love that ripples throughout your life. Qualities associated with the heart chakra are: love for yourself and others, relationships and relating, compassion, empathy, forgiveness, acceptance, transformation and change to grieve and reach peace, as well as the ability to find the centre of your own awareness, integrating your insights into a cohesive, harmonious state of being.

Having an open heart chakra enhances feelings of deep connection and a harmonious exchange with all around you. You'll deeply appreciate the beauty in the world. Your heart centre is associated with your capacity to love and integrate, acting as a bridge between earthly and spiritual aspirations. It will help you to transcend personal identity and limitations of the ego, experiencing unconditional love and connection with all, heart centred discernment and appreciation of beauty in all things. An open heart chakra will ultimately improve your relationship with others, making interpersonal relations deeper and more meaningful. As you might have guessed, the emphasis is on giving and receiving love, depending on how open your heart is. Love is essential in any relationship, particularly self-love. Love experienced through your fourth chakra is about romance, but it's also about going beyond the limitations of your ego, to have compassion and acceptance of all. When living from your heart, with your heart energy centre open and balanced, you will have more clarity of vision to act with discernment and compassion in challenging situations.

If your heart chakra is out of balance, you may experience difficulties in relating with others, feeling jealous, co-dependent or feeling closed down and withdrawn. Other signs of this include: being overly defensive, fearful of intimacy, relying on others for approval and attention, trying to people please at all costs, being a rescuer or playing the victim role, extreme isolation (becoming hermit like and antisocial), holding grudges and being unable to forgive. This can manifest in physical ailments, such as lung infections, bronchitis, circulatory problems and heart issues. When out of alignment you may give way to grief, anger, jealousy or fear, plus dislike of self or others. It is important that you release your negative emotions to make way and open your heart chakra for more love and compassion to enter. When experiencing hurt feelings, it is always best to fully feel them, so they can flow out. Holding on to these feelings can lead to ill health.

EFT and Emotion Code Case Studies

The art is to acknowledge your feelings, accept and sit with them. There are many tools in part six that can help you release and cope with your emotions if they feel "too big" for you, but only after allowing yourself to acknowledge and feel them. EFT (emotional freedom techniques) are a fantastic method. By tapping on acupuncture pressure points to release them, whilst voicing your negative feelings, you can clear your energetic blocks.

My client Daphne had a fear of spiders, which was a hindrance as she wanted to visit family in Australia – a country full of large insects and other such creatures. Daphne was too terrified to even look at pictures of spiders. To help her, I used the EFT Movie Technique, with the outcome being that by the time we'd finished she ended up stroking a spider, which conveniently just happened to be at my front door. And all of this was in one session! Daphne was blown away by how different she felt and she later rang me to say that she'd had a wonderful time in Australia. She thanked me profusely! Of course, not all issues can be dealt with in a single session, but this does demonstrate the remarkable power of such a simple technique.

Another client, Jasmine, was feeling deep anxiety and a strong sense of unworthiness, due to an incident with a friend. Although she was no longer in touch with this friend, the incident had affected her deeply. We used the emotion code to release trapped feelings of unworthiness and other related emotions. Jasmine was delighted with the outcome, informing me of how light she felt at the end of the session. She said that it was as if someone had lifted a boulder from her body. In part six of this book I have included a number of tools that you can use on your own to release negative emotions and looping thoughts, or to generally bring about balance. If your feelings are still unable to soften or if they simply won't disappear, then contact me so I can assist you to move forward and feel good (www.denisedavis.co.uk). ♥

Essential Oils

Earlier I listed some essential oils that will benefit your heart rate and blood pressure. But there are even more oils available, all of which will help your heart chakra to awaken love, compassion and kindness towards yourself and others:

Rose opens your heart, allowing you to feel unconditional love for yourself, coupled with self-compassion. It is both calming and elevating. Geranium and neroli oils are used to ease stress and anxiety to create calm (they also have other benefits). Ylang ylang reduces stress and lowers blood pressure. I have created my own aura and room sprays, one of which is called "Love". This helps to harmonise your heart, bringing it into balance. It is soothing, uplifting and helps to develop your journey of love. It opens and softens your heart, creating greater receptivity to give and receive love. The spray also enhances self-love, assisting you to love and live in the now. I use this regularly and have had excellent feedback from others who continue to use it for its positive benefits. If you wish to make a purchase then contact me (www.denisedavis.co.uk). ♥

Ways to Strengthen Your Heart Chakra

When your heart chakra is open and balanced, you feel full of love and flowing with compassion and you are accepting of yourself and others, forgiving easily. Giving and receiving love will strengthen this chakra. See the world and everyone/everything within it covered with love and kisses – extend this out to the atmosphere, biosphere, ionosphere and geosphere. Pay compliments to others, kiss everyone you care about, smile at everyone you meet. Smiling is contagious – it may brighten other people's days, causing a loving, ripple effect in the world. Stop criticising and judging; choose to be kind not right. Hold green crystals such as emerald, malachite and jade, plus pink crystals like morganite and rose quartz (I used to wear rose quartz in my bra to infuse more self-love and to soothe myself when I was experiencing deep sadness and despair. These two pink crystals are wonderful for assisting you with unconditional love). As stated in the Times of India article *The Science Behind Healing Crystals*, "Holding crystals or placing them on your body is said to promote physical, emotional and spiritual healing. Crystals do this by positively interacting with your body's energy field or chakra. According to experts, crystals act as a power hold for healing, as they allow positive energy to flow into the body and release toxic negative energy. Each crystal has a different vibration which arises from their molecular composition."

Remaining Six Energy Centres (Chakras)

Alongside the chakras we've already discussed, there are six more, all of which are important in having a balanced body, mind and spirit. Please remember the disclaimer at the front of the book, as the symptoms I mention below may require you to consult with a physician.

Root Energy Centre

This chakra is where your sense of stability and security rests. It is located at the base of your spine, your perineum and first three vertebrae. Balancing your root centre creates a solid foundation for opening the chakras above it. Having a solid foundation, without fear of your basic needs being unmet, leaves you feeling grounded, safe and secure. You'll experience less anxiety and stress. According to Milton Erickson, an American psychiatrist and psychologist, some of your current feelings are rooted in how safe you felt as a child. If your needs were consistently met as a young child then you were more trusting of life, happier to believe that your needs would always be met. Conversely, the opposite is true if there was inconsistency or some needs unmet during childhood.

If there is an imbalance in your root centre, then you may experience anxiety, fears or nightmares. Physical problems might occur in your colon, bladder, lower back, prostrate, legs or feet. This could also manifest as an eating disorder. As previously mentioned, meditation tranquilises your nervous system and connects you to something greater than you, whether that's your Higher Self, God or another deity, the Great Creator or the Universe. This connection to universal energy brings about a sense of peace and stability.

The colour associated with the root chakra is red. So, if you want to balance this centre then it's a good idea to wear red clothes, eat red food and use red crystals (like red jasper). Black tourmaline, bloodstone, smokey quartz, hematite and jet crystals are also associated with this chakra. Yoga poses for the root chakra are Standing Forward Fold (Uttasana), Garland Pose (Malasana), Head to Knee Forward Bend (Janu Sirsasana) and Easy Pose. Cedarwood, frankincense, black pepper, patchouli, spikenard, vetiver and sandalwood essential oils are very helpful in opening and balancing the root chakra, as they provide a sense of grounding and centre your mind.

Sacral Energy Centre

This chakra is where your creativity and sexual energy stem from. Creativity is part of your nature as a human and if neglected can lead to stifled and constricted thinking, inability to solve solutions and frustration. Conversely, when this energy centre is balanced it creates a sense of joy, abundance, wellness and pleasure. It is located above your pubic bone and below the navel. When out of balance it can create feelings of emotional instability, fear of change, sexual dysfunction, depression or addiction.

You can balance this centre via creative expression and honouring your body. Using the mind to change from one form to another requires being creative and transformative, so solving problems such as Sudokus, crosswords or brain training conundrums, creating art, gardening, knitting, singing and baking are all good ways of exercising your creative mind. Self-expression is a vital way to honour your inner child; it doesn't matter what the outcome is, it is more about the pleasure derived from the creative outlet itself. So, keep this chakra balanced. Even if it's something simple , like creating a Lego house when playing with your children or grandchildren, do whatever takes your fancy, but do something creative regularly. Honour and respect your body and its needs, including having wonderful sex (when appropriate for you).

The colour orange is associated with this chakra, so wear something orange, maybe a scarf or underpants if it's too vibrant as a top or dress. Beneficial crystals such as orange calcite, orange selenite, carnelian, sunstone and fire agate help to bring balance to this centre. Yoga poses such as the Goddess Pose (utkata konasana), Reverse Warrior Pose (viparita virabhadrasana), Wide Legged Forward Bend C (prasarita padottanasana c), Seated Forward Bend (paschimottanasana) and Reclined Bound Angle Pose (supta baddha konasana) also assist this energy centre, helping you realign to equilibrium.

Essential oils good for balancing this centre are cardamom, clary sage, neroli, orange, patchouli, rose, sandalwood and ylang ylang.

Solar Plexus Energy Centre

This is your personal power centre and is where responsibility for your self-esteem, warrior energy and transformation lives. Your solar plexus influences your metabolism and digestion. If you seek to tap into your strengths, then it's important that this chakra is balanced. You can find it above your navel and under your breastbone. If this chakra is in equilibrium then you'll feel confident, have a firm sense of purpose and be self-motivated. If it's out of alignment then this can result in low self-esteem, difficulty making decisions, anger and control issues. It is important to have logical goals/desires/intentions so you can move forward to achieve them. Otherwise you're just coasting through life, a passenger on someone else's bus. It's time to be your own driver.

Each step you take towards your objectives strengthens this chakra. Tap into your "gut feeling" and intuition when deciding, leaving your mind and body to perform the actions. Close your eyes, relax and ask your question, pose one scenario then the other. Whichever answer feels lighter and brighter, that's the correct one for you. For those of you who are more visual, try to see paths depicting your options – the one that is lit up is your best choice. Anything that feels dark or heavy is taking you away from your right path.

The colour yellow is associated with this centre, so wear yellow clothes and use yellow crystals such as citrine, yellow calcite, amber and topaz. Yoga poses for this centre are the Bow Pose (dhanurasana), Breath of Fire, Prayer Pose (high lunge twist with Anjali mudra), Revolved Triangle Pose (parvritta trikonasana), Vajroli Mudra and Cobra Pose (bhujangasana).

Beneficial essential oils are black pepper, cedarwood, cypress, geranium, ginger, juniper, mandarin and peppermint.

Throat Energy Centre

Your throat chakra is located at the centre of your neck, in your throat, and is also linked to your shoulders. It is the passage of the energy between the lower parts of your body and head. The function of this chakra is the principle of expression and communication. The throat energy

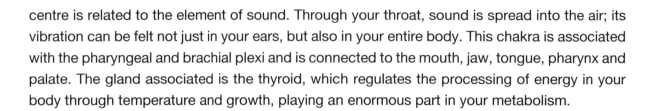

centre is related to the element of sound. Through your throat, sound is spread into the air; its vibration can be felt not just in your ears, but also in your entire body. This chakra is associated with the pharyngeal and brachial plexi and is connected to the mouth, jaw, tongue, pharynx and palate. The gland associated is the thyroid, which regulates the processing of energy in your body through temperature and growth, playing an enormous part in your metabolism.

Because of where it is situated, your throat chakra is often seen as the "bottleneck" of the movement of energy in your body – as it sits just before the upper chakras of your head. So, opening your throat chakra and keeping it balanced can assist you in aligning your vision with reality. Furthermore, by opening this chakra, you can release pressure that may affect your heart chakra. The throat centre is about the expression of your truth, your purpose in life and creativity, with a natural connection to your sacral chakra, which is your main creativity centre. Remember too that the throat is the point from which we express our truths and speak out. Communication, both verbal and non-verbal, including your internal and external talk, is your connection to the etheric realm, realms of spirit and your intuitive abilities. Your propensity to create, projecting ideas and blueprints into reality, comes from within this chakra. It is by balancing and harmonising this chakra that you can realise your vocation and purpose.

While a blocked throat chakra can contribute to feelings of timidity and introversion, an overactive chakra is no good thing either. When this chakra is overactive, it can lead to non-stop talking, gossiping or being verbally aggressive and mean. This indicates that the filter between your thoughts and what comes out of your mouth isn't working well. An imbalance can also manifest in ways such as not being able to listen well to others, excessive fear of speaking, having an imperceptible voice, difficulty keeping your word and other secrets, telling lies, excessive shyness or secretiveness and a lack of connection to your life purpose. With an imbalanced throat chakra you may experience physical symptoms such as hoarseness, sore throat, thyroid problems, laryngitis and neck pain. Emotional symptoms can be depression, an inability to express yourself, anxiety, aggression and lack of self-esteem.

To stimulate or support this chakra, incorporate the colour blue into your environment – wear clothes with touches of blue and eat blueberries. Blue is the colour of wisdom and honesty and is very soothing. Wearing pale blue clothes and using blue crystals are a marvellous way to boost healing of this chakra and balance it. For example, blue crystals such as turquoise, aquamarine, blue lace agate and angelite. Essential oils such as jasmine, rosemary, sandalwood, calendula, eucalyptus and ylang ylang can heal and activate this centre. As well as talking openly with close friends and family, it is important to be open and honest in all you say. Speaking in a heartfelt way can also work wonders in strengthening and balancing this chakra. An alternative is to journal, writing down everything without censorship or editing. Yoga poses such as the Camel, Plow, Bridge, Fish and Standing Forward Bend help to realign and balance this chakra.

Third Eye Chakra

Your third eye is located on the forehead between your eyebrows. It is slightly above the bridge of your nose, behind your eyes. This chakra is your centre of intuition and foresight and is about your imagination and being open. Indigo is the colour associated with this centre – a dark bluish purple. This energy centre is associated with your pineal gland, which is in charge of regulating your biorhythms, including your sleep and wake states. The importance of this centre is its relationship with your perception, the effect of light and altered states of consciousness. It is close to your optical nerves and is sensitive to visual stimulations and changes in lighting.

Psychological and behavioural characteristics associated with this chakra are vision, intuition, perception of subtle dimensions and movement of energy, psychic abilities related to clairvoyance, illumination, connection to wisdom, insights, motivation, inspiration and creativity. Your third eye chakra is an instrument to perceive the more subtle qualities of reality. It goes beyond the more physical sense, into the realm of subtle energies. Awakening your third eye allows you to open up to an intuitive sensibility and inner perception, because it connects you with a fresh way of seeing and perceiving in more subtle and etherical ways, as opposed to your usual physical vision. Visions can appear blurry, ghostlike and cloudy. However, your visions can also appear just like a movie playing out in front of your eyes. Sustaining awareness of your third eye centre requires focus and the ability to relax into a unique way of seeing. When focusing your mind and consciousness, you can see beyond the distractions and illusions that stand before you, thus gaining more insights to help you live and create in a way that is congruent with your highest good.

When your third eye centre is imbalanced, it can manifest as feeling stuck in the daily grind, without being able to look beyond your problems and set a guiding vision for yourself. An overactive chakra may show up as fantasies that appear more real than reality, an indulgence in psychic fantasies and illusion, not being able to create a vision for yourself and realise it, rejection of everything spiritual or beyond the usual, not being able to see the greater picture or lack of clarity. When blocked, you can lose your sense of direction in life and become stagnant. You may also distrust your inner voice. Your perception about life and where you're headed becomes negatively skewed and almost unrecognisable. You are unable to let go of your past, with a fear of what the future holds. This can make you very dogmatic in your beliefs, daily routine and how you view others.

An overactive third eye can also be disorienting and cause psychic distress, where you feel you are getting lost in streams of phantasmagorical visions or bombarded by nonsensical information, which may sweep you off your feet unless you're strongly grounded. A sign of hyperactivity in this centre can be overindulgence in a fantasy world whilst losing touch with reality. When your third eye centre is in overdrive, the constant flow of thoughts can be mentally exhausting. You may feel intimidated by having to make decisions that would normally be simple, with cloudy judgement, lack of focus and an inability to distinguish what is real. Symptoms of an overactive third eye centre can include headaches, vision, seizures, insomnia, nausea or sinus problems. Additional non-physical signs may include hallucinations, being judgemental, anxiety, mental fog, feeling overwhelmed, paranoia and delusions.

A blocked third eye centre can wreak havoc on your physical wellbeing, as it governs your pituitary gland and neurological function, your body's ability to fight infection and regulate sleep, and your ability to maintain a balanced metabolic function. Therefore, you may experience insomnia, develop high blood pressure or be frequently ill. You may suffer from migraines, sinusitis, seizures, poor vision or sciatica. Emotional symptoms could be delusions, depression, anxiety and paranoia. You may experience vivid dreams, nightmares and heightened scepticism.

In terms of clearing a blocked third eye, there are plenty of things that you can do. If the energies you're experiencing are out of control, then anchor yourself in your body and ground. Ask that the experience be more comfortable for you. Issues may also arise from a lack of overall balance in all your centres. Meditation is a lovely way of alleviating blocks in this area and this can really help you embrace compassion and forgiveness. Energy work, such as Sound Healing, is a highly vibrational practice which can balance and unblock your third eye. You can perform Sound Healing on yourself using a drum, tuning forks, singing bowls, gongs or your voice – toning, singing mantras or any song that takes your fancy. Sound is also uplifting, balancing and healing, which you can read more about in part six. Once balanced you will see life with clarity, take things more easily in your stride, go with the flow and be flexible, knowing what you want in life and making plans on how to achieve it. The greatest aspect is that you will have heightened intuition to tap into what you have learnt to trust. To restore balance may require making positive lifestyle changes, eating healthier and taking exercise, but it is absolutely do-able and will benefit you so much in the long-term. Just make sure that the focus of your intention is soothing and calming, helping you to bring equilibrium to this centre.

The colour associated with this centre is indigo/blue, so wear clothes or use crystals of this colour such as amethyst, labradorite, lapis lazuli and sodalite. Essential oils that are beneficial are bay laurel, clary sage, cypress, elemi, frankincense, helichrysum, juniper and marjoram. Useful yoga poses are Candle Gazing (Trataka), the Child's Pose (Balasana), Wide Legged Forward Fold (Prasarita Padottanasana), Alternate Nostril Breathing and Toning Aum/Om.

Crown Energy Centre

This chakra is located at the top of the head or slightly above the head, it sits like a crown radiating upwards. It gives you access to higher states of consciousness as you open up to what is beyond your regular personal preoccupations and visions. The crown chakra is primarily connected to your pituitary gland, secondly to your pineal gland and hypothalamus, both working to regulate your endocrine system. The crown is also associated with your brain and the entire nervous system.

Psychological and behavioural characteristics of this chakra are consciousness, awareness of higher consciousness, wisdom of what is sacred, connection with the formless and the limitless realisation, liberation from limiting patterns and achieving communion with higher states of consciousness such as ecstasy, bliss and presence. The crown chakra is associated with the transcendence of your limitations, whether they are personal or bound to space and time. It is where the paradox becomes the norm, where seeming opposites are one. The quality of awareness that comes with this chakra is universal and transcendent. As you become immersed in the energy of the crown chakra, you feel a state of union with All That Is, of spiritual bliss. This centre allows access to clarity and enlightened wisdom. It has been suggested that this chakra is the gateway to your Divine Self, sometimes named your Cosmic Self and linked to the infinite, the Universal.

When there is an imbalance in this chakra, it can manifest as you being disconnected to spirit, with cynicism regarding what is sacred. Conversely, an overactive crown chakra could show up as a disconnection with your body. You may live totally in your head, disconnected from all earthly matters and your body. You may be obsessively attached to all matters spiritual, ignoring your mind and body's needs. You could experience being very close-minded.

A blocked crown chakra can cause a stunting of your spiritual growth, as it's your gateway to spiritual wisdom, connecting you to the wider universe. Symptoms of blockages can be isolation and loneliness with an inability to connect with others, lack of direction, inability to set or maintain movement towards goals and feeling disconnected spiritually. Physical symptoms may include nerve pain, neurological disorders, thyroid and pineal gland disorders, Alzheimer's, reoccurring headaches, migraines, schizophrenia and delusional disorders, insomnia and depression. An overactive crown chakra can leave you feeling "off", below par and "out of sorts". You may feel detached from your outer world, even from the people around you. Others may see you as appearing "flighty". Your crown centre links with Divine energy and blends the physical and non-physical realms. It governs your consciousness and sub-consciousness, while influencing your spirituality, inner wisdom and ability to relate to your inner self plus others. When out of balance, it affects your functionality and can leave you vulnerable to a variety of physical and non-physical symptoms such as depression, lack of empathy, dizziness, confusion, mental fogginess, seizures and light sensitivity. Other possibilities are feelings of aggression, superiority, criticising and being judgmental of others, being distrustful and feeling "lost" or in the midst of a crisis.

My client Amanda came to me feeling lost, so I used sound therapy to rebalance her body and mind. We then talked about what was going on in her life. Amanda was at a transitory stage; she knew she needed to make changes, as she was unhappy, but was unsure of her next steps. I carried out some clearings and release work using Access Consciousness with her, before doing a "Future Life Progression" session where she could see what she was doing, feeling, seeing and hearing in the future (more info on FLP in part six). By working with me, Amanda gained insight and advice from her future self, and left with a spring in her step – she now had a way forward. When your crown chakra is balanced you'll feel more grounded, in control of your emotions, intuitive and connected to the Divine.

To counteract the over-activity of this centre, maintain a healthy lifestyle – eating wholesome food, with excellent hydration combined with regular exercise. Other things that are beneficial are Energy Healing, tai chi and wearing white or deep purple coloured clothes, as these are the colours associated with this centre. You could also incorporate these colours into your diet. I found that yoga practice helps to balance and heal this chakra (as well as the others). Specific poses for this chakra are inverted poses such as the Supported Headstand and Shoulder Stand. To gain the most benefit, try to spend time in these poses whilst focusing on your breath. It's very important that you practise slowly, particularly when coming out of these positions. Meditating regularly helps clear a crown chakra blockage and can in fact be beneficial for balancing all the chakras.

To assist with opening this centre, visualise a white light tinged with purple pouring in through the crown of your head. Imagine that the light is travelling throughout your body, dissolving and releasing all of the blocks out through the soles of your feet, to be transmuted by Mother Earth. Crystals that also aid this chakra are diamond, clear quartz, moonstone, amethyst, selenite and purple fluorite. These can be held or placed on the body and crown during meditation or Energy Healing, or worn as jewellery. Essential oils to balance and connect with this centre are elemi, frankincense, sandalwood, saffron, lotus, jasmine, lavender, lime, myrrh, rosewood, galbanum, gurjum and helichrysum.

At some time or another, many of you may have experienced energetic blocks, imbalanced or overactive chakras and energy sabotaging habits that have prevented you from accessing your full vitality. This can lead to feeling exhausted, being scattered, dull or even poorly. But, it doesn't have to continue! If you put into practice some of my suggestions and even do them regularly as a preventative measure, then you will surely see things lift.

Return to Love

Whether you look at it from an energetic, physical or spiritual perspective, the heart is the place where you'll return to centre yourself. This is where you must look if you want to find your true connection to the Universe and to feel at peace with the Divine. In spiritual circles and at the end of yoga sessions, we place our hands in a prayer position, at our heart chakra. Then we say, 'Namaste' which means 'I honour the divine in you'. This is a great way of connecting our heart energy centres and bringing good vibrations for all involved, as it invokes a feeling of spiritual connection.

Returning to love is all about taking proactive steps to reduce tension, making the environment healthier not just for you, but for others too. For example, before entering a meeting room where there may be conflict, you could send a pink bubble of love, so people feel kinder, more compassionate and understanding. By doing this, you are creating more of a win-win situation, filled with increased cooperation and collaboration. Another suggestion to get yourself into a positive state, particularly when it is important for you to feel more confident (such as before a presentation or an important meeting) is Amy Cuddy's "Power Pose". Stand upright with your eyes facing straight ahead, place your hands on your hips (like Wonder Woman) and your feet hip-width apart. Then take a few deep breaths whilst in this stance. This preparation should leave you feeling calm, composed and powerful. Science shows that your mind and body are connected, meaning how you hold your body will affect your feelings. Your body language governs how you think and feel about yourself, ergo the way you hold your body has a significant impact on your mind.

Amy Cuddy, who created this pose, conducted a study at Harvard University where participants sat in either a higher power pose (expansive posture) or low power pose (leaning inwards with legs crossed) for a couple of minutes. Those in the high power pose felt more powerful and performed better than their low power pose counterparts. The most astonishing part was that the pose affected their body chemistry, with a decrease in cortisol and an increase in testosterone. Amy Cuddy believed these hormonal effects were further evidence of increased feelings of power. During one of the talks I attended, Dr David Hamilton said that he uses this method too and recommends it to his clients.

When giving talks and workshops, particularly when tutoring groups of children, I always begin my lessons with an accelerated learning process. To start, I ask the children or participants to do a "jelly wiggle", followed by some "brain gym" exercises. Not only does this release tension, but it also gets everyone on the same page energy-wise. Science shows that movement increases your heart rate, pumping more oxygen to your brain, thereby helping the brain to work faster. It also assists your body with releasing helpful hormones, which provide a nourishing environment for the growth of brain cells. Brain gym helps with balance, posture and coordination. More importantly, in a learning setting it improves comprehension, focus, organisation, communication and emotional health.

Following this, I then ask everyone to take three diaphragmatic breaths, which means breathing from your belly instead of your chest. Breathing this way lowers your stress hormone cortisol, reduces your blood pressure and slows your heart rate. It increases your energy, improves digestion, stimulates your lymphatic system and helps to relieve pain and muscle tension. To add to this, slowing your breathing means you use less energy. It sustains your attention – which is important in learning situations.

Next, I get the participants to expand their awareness using their peripheral vision, ensuring that learning happens easily and effortlessly. This state optimises your learning abilities and helps you take in more information from your surroundings whilst eliminating your stress and anxieties. It is a "now state" where no negative emotions are experienced, thus there are no barriers to learning and concentration is ultimately improved. Your open mind is more able to take in all the new information being presented, as well as recalling it later when needed.

My final step before starting a lesson is to ground the participants using a visualisation technique. Grounding is when one is connected directly to earth, and can be achieved by standing barefoot on a natural surface such as grass or sand. In the visual exercise, the participants are like trees, with their roots going down to the centre of the earth and drawing up the energy into their body. The reason I do this, is because many people have become separated from their bond with Mother Earth. Grounding reconnects you to your environment, allowing you to focus in the present, which is important when learning. Other benefits are that it neutralises free radicals, improves sleep, aids pain management and releases stress. It also harmonises and stabilises your body's basic biological rhythms, reduces inflammation and increases your energy and vitality, along with improving blood pressure, relieving muscle tension and headaches, decreasing healing time and protecting the body against electric and magnetic fields. The accelerated learning techniques and how to do them are given in part six.

So, now you have balanced your physical heart, it is a marvellous time to bring equilibrium to your heart energy centre. One of my processes for achieving this is via Sound Healing, where there are unique tones for each energy centre (chakras). I have come across a few distinct sound sets for the chakras, but I use the one that has 'AH' for the heart centre. I always set the intention that my higher heart energy centre (thymus) be included in this heart toning. I tone/sing the sound 'AH' in whatever pitch I fancy. Sometimes I stay in the same pitch, at other times I go higher, lower, louder or quieter, whatever I instinctively feel. Combining this toning with others creates a wonderful overtone and is a fabulous way to raise a group's vibrations. You can tone until you feel more relaxed and harmonious in your heart and body.

On February the 14th, 'AH' is toned around the world for Sound Healing Day (you know it as Valentine's Day – what a wonderful day to honour and love yourself more). When running groups, I ask everyone to sit in a circle. One at a time each person takes a place in the centre and the entire group then sings their name for roughly a minute. This is a powerful, uplifting and healing activity that you can easily do with your family or with a group of friends. Alternatively you could do a "positive word bath", where one person stands in the centre and you all move around to face them, saying one or more things you like, admire or love about them. These are delightfully nourishing and cherishing activities which most people love taking part in. In part six, I'll provide you with some more information about the benefits of sound and mantras.

Other things that help lift my mood are: listening to upbeat music, playing my gongs and other instruments, laughing with friends, a good soak in a bubble bath, singing each month with my song group (then sharing our joy by singing for the residents in care homes), painting, reading, creating in many forms, spending time with family, enjoying a good theatre show, dancing, walking by the sea, forest bathing, swimming, trying new activities, exploring new places and going to sacred and heritage sights. I also love looking at beautiful evocative artwork, the sunrise and all manner of natural beauty.

Summary

So, in this chapter we've talked about:

- ❖ Why your physical heart and energetic energy centre is important.

- ❖ What your heart does and how important it is for life.

- ❖ How your heart maintains its normal function and things that affect its optimal wellbeing.

- ❖ The role of your three brains and how to synchronise them.

- ❖ How your heart entrains to another person's heart.

- ❖ The benefits of yoga and essential oils to harmonise your heart.

- ❖ Diaphragmatic breathing exercises, to calm your body.

- ❖ Creating enjoyable feelings with gratitude and appreciation.

- ❖ Your remaining six energy centres and their roles, what affects them and how to balance them if they're not in equilibrium.

- ❖ The pink unconditional love bubble and Power Pose to uplift your spirits and make you feel safe and powerful.

- ❖ Accelerated learning techniques to use when you are learning additional information, especially for exams and when giving or receiving training.

Invitation

Explore what activities uplift your vibrations.

 Write out a list of the changes you want to make.

Putting goals on paper makes them tangible and creates a guide you can follow. You can use the smart goals from part one, noting what goals have changed since you wrote them.

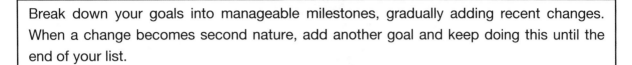

Break down your goals into manageable milestones, gradually adding recent changes. When a change becomes second nature, add another goal and keep doing this until the end of your list.

Check off milestones as you reach them and celebrate by giving yourself a treat. If you experience a setback, don't give up. Remember that as changes turn into habits, you'll be on your way to your ultimate goal i.e. maintaining your healthy mind, body and spirit. As Frank J Sileo puts it, "Lifestyle changes are a process, and don't occur quickly." According to a study in the *British Journal of General Practice 2012*, it takes about sixty-six days for a practiced behaviour to become an entrenched habit.

Insightful Questions

When you have finished the invitation above, take a notepad and pen. Sit quietly, free from any distractions, in a relaxed manner. Look at each of the questions below, one at a time. Allow the question to just flow freely in your mind, percolating if you will. Then, capture your answers on paper, giving you an insight into where you are right now. This will help you shift your perspective, so that you become less stuck.

- *When will you start some of these suggestions, to gain and maintain harmony of your heart?*

- *What else can you do to make your heart feel happy and at peace?*

- *How do you breathe? If through the mouth, will you experiment with ways to retrain yourself to breathe through the nose, thus reaping the benefits?*

- *Can you imagine yourself using the pink bubble or Power Pose, feeling confident and at ease?*

- *Will you regularly tone 'AH' to keep your heart in balance, or at least use it when feeling anxious or sad? This can be very uplifting.*

Part Four

What is Harmonising Your Heart?

In parts two and three we looked at how your heart and harmony perform as separate entities. However, as you might have guessed, I believe that in order for us to obtain "heart coherence", our heart must be working in harmony with our body, melding in an optimal fashion. Being fully harmonised means having an awareness of your mental and spiritual wellbeing, which in itself boils down to one key aspect: self-love.

What is Self-Love?

For me, self-love is about taking excellent care of your mind, body and spirit. As I've mentioned previously, I use 100% natural products on my body, such as those made by Tropic Skincare. Remember that whatever you put onto your skin will be absorbed into your bloodstream. Therefore, if the products you're using are full of chemicals, this can be harmful. I perform all my washing and body-care rituals much slower and with more presence, blessing my body parts with love and thanking my body for all that it does. For example, I might thank my feet for allowing me to walk, drive and swim. The Tropic body cream is suitably named "Body Love". When moisturising with this after a bath or shower, I have the intention and believe that I am giving my body more love. I tell myself, 'I love you; I am loved; I am love; life loves me, God loves me, the Universe loves me, I love life, I love God and I love the Universe.' Using natural products in your home and on your body also reduces your carbon footprint in the world. In addition, I also bless my food and water – my large water container has positive words on it; science shows that this infuses the water with these qualities.

Let me ask you a question, dear reader: do you swallow your feelings to keep the peace with others? If you do not face your feelings, then this is likely to impact your ability to express yourself and you may experience issues with your throat. To help relieve this, you can tone your throat energy centre, (see part six for the note to tone) and spray some colloidal silver in your mouth – this is a natural antibiotic and will ease such problems. The most important thing is that we unlock your ability to be authentic, allowing you to share your thoughts and feelings, thus freeing your voice. This requires vulnerability and being assertive. If you share and open your heart, it allows others to be more openhearted and share their frailties too. Your inner dialogue reflects your relationship with you. Is your dialogue with yourself uplifting and praiseworthy or limiting and critical? Remember that your subconscious mind is always listening to what you say and think. So, it is a good idea to speak out loud, saying some lovely things about yourself.

The Power of Your Mind

Your unconscious mind's role is to preserve your physical body whilst the body runs your physical functions. In NLP (neuro linguistic programming) the belief is that your unconscious mind holds both the blueprint of your body now and a blueprint of your body in perfect health. Go into a quiet space and ask what your body wants for your optimal health. The best time to do this is when you're fully relaxed, just before sleep or upon awakening. The message may not come to you straight away, but could arrive during the following day or a few days later.

According to varying schools of thought, your unconscious mind has the age of a child – somewhere between the ages of three and seven. It requires clear and simple instructions to serve you and takes all directives literally. So, if you say, 'My job is a pain in the neck' then it may create this in your reality, giving you a literal pain in your neck when you're at work. Your unconscious mind communicates through stories, symbols and emotions. If you suddenly feel fear, your unconscious mind has detected a perceived threat to your survival, which may or may not be real. It also stores and organises your memories, sometimes burying your most traumatic ones until it decides that you are more able to process them (whether you consciously believe you're ready or not).

Your unconscious mind doesn't process negatives, so if you say to your friend, 'Don't forget our catch up is on the 9th next month' it will create a picture of you forgetting your catch up. So, it's better to say, 'Remember our catch up is on the 9th next month.' It also makes associations, so if you had a wonderful experience at school achieving excellent exam results, then your unconscious mind will equate learning with success. Conversely, the opposite is true. So, if you had awful experiences at school, then you may feel anxious learning anything new. Just know that you're an adult now and that not all learning is the same.

Self-Love

Self-love comprises self-care, self-respect, self-esteem, loving and appreciating yourself in all aspects of your being. It's about taking responsibility for your own happiness, growing from your actions and behaving in a way which supports physical, mental, emotional and spiritual growth. When you expand your sense of self-love, you become more balanced in your life purpose and values. You become more mature, more focused, more capable. Failing to adhere to your values often creates a dissonance in your life – you feel dissatisfied, unfulfilled and empty. When you fully accept and allow your true natural self to emerge, embracing the unique being you are, fully expressing the unique energy that presents who you are at your core, your life becomes more harmonious and full of joy.

The price you pay for failing to self-love and not being true to yourself, is very high. Some people end up spending their whole lives just trying to please others. It's okay to put yourself first. Drop your mask, allowing the real you to shine through, recognising the divine, magnificent being that you are.

Good Self-Care

Self-care means taking care of your physical wellbeing. According to Maslow, you will love yourself more when you take care of your basic needs. Therefore, it is important to nourish yourself daily through activities like exercise, good nutrition, hydration, quality sleep, meditation, grounding, downtime, fun/pleasure, intimacy and healthy social interactions. This includes having a good support network of friends and family, as human beings naturally yearn for connectedness and shared purpose.

Let's look at these one at a time:

Movement – taking the right amount of exercise or movement is so important. Explore various different activities to discover what works for you, so you can continue to carry them out in the long term. Exercise and movement keeps all your muscles, organs and entire body in optimal working order. Science shows that exercise affects your mind and your body. It increases longevity, reduces depression and elevates self-esteem. I do yoga each week to keep my body supple and flexible – it loves to stretch then end in a relaxation. On leaving the gym class I feel calm and contented, ready to face the day. I perform strength training and conditioning using weights to help my bone density, making it less likely they will break should I have a fall. This also counteracts any aged-related thinning of the bones. In addition, I do low impact exercises, movement and dance to improve my cardiovascular system (making my heart strong so it doesn't have to work as hard to pump blood), firm my muscles and increase my lung capacity. Cardio exercise reduces your risk of heart attack, high cholesterol, high blood pressure and diabetes. It also helps burn fat and calories.

Personally, I adore walking by the sea and in the forest and always feel better once I've done this. Although I knew that negative ions oxygenated your body, I didn't know just how beneficial these can be. Research shows that these negative ions, which can be found in plentiful amounts by the sea and in forests, clear the air of airborne allergens such as mould, spores, pollen, bacteria and viruses. They also clear the air of dust and cigarette smoke. Negative ions perform these functions by attaching themselves to positively charged particles in large numbers, thereby negatively charging those particles. As a result, these viruses, bacteria and spores become too heavy to remain airborne, thus preventing them from entering your nasal passages. The negative ions neutralise free radicals, revitalise cell metabolism, enhance immune function, purify the blood and balance the autonomic nervous system – promoting deep sleep and healthy digestion. Studies have shown that regular mindful forest walks reduce stress, anxiety, depression and anger. Plus, they strengthen the immune system, cardio and metabolic health – thus boosting your overall wellbeing. More oxygen enters your bloodstream and therefore your blood pressure and heart-rate lowers. Humans biologically need to be in nature to connect and so the forest is a fabulous way to do this. If you want to know more about this phenomenon, then *Forest Bathing* by Dr Quing Li is a good read.

In terms of walking, when using a Fitbit that my daughter gifted me for Christmas, I noticed that housework and gardening added to my ten thousand steps per day. People who take ten thousand steps per day are considered "active" with a less sedentary lifestyle. Check out the number of steps necessary for your age group, as it can vary. Walking is a low impact and simple way to get fit, it increases your good cholesterol (HDL) and decreases the bad cholesterol (LDL). Just walking can burn about 200 to 300 extra calories a week if done daily, with a potential weight loss of about 1 lb per week. Each 2,000–2,500 step taken is about a mile. Walking a mile can burn 80 calories for a 150 lb person. Depending on your weight, walking 10,000 steps can burn between 250 and 600 calories. Once you've done the same route enough times, you'll start to get a good idea of how many total steps you're taking in the journey. This is a good opportunity to leave your Fitbit off. Just like your mobile phones, this sends out electromagnetic frequencies which can disrupt your energy systems. If I do have my Fitbit switched on then I'll also carry a shungite crystal to counteract the electric emissions.

Before you move on, ask yourself the following questions:

- How many steps are you taking a day? Is it up to the required amount for your age group?

- What can you add, in order to boost your physical wellbeing?

Books for Exercise Guidance
- *The Women's Health Little Book of Exercises* by Adam Campbell

- *Strength Training For Women* by Marc Mclean

- *Anatomy of Exercise 50+* by Hollis Lance Liebman

- *Fitness over Fifty* by the National Institute on Aging

Nutrition – self-care is also about knowing and eating the right food for your body. This isn't just about your taste buds and preferences, it's more about what food aids your optimal health. For years I had a bloating tummy and a feeling of discomfort whenever I ate certain foods. The problem was, I didn't know which foods were causing the issues. By process of elimination, I finally discovered that my discomfort was caused by eating bread and that my blood sugar levels elevated when I ate this. Even though I love fresh bread from the bakery, I immediately swapped to gluten-free, albeit I still only eat this occasionally now (as it contains more sugar and puts my body out of sync).

If you feel a slump in energy around four o'clock in the afternoon, this usually indicates low blood sugar. So, to normalise, have a snack i.e. a piece of fruit with a handful of nuts/seeds (fruit and protein). You may experience issues after eating onions and garlic, particularly those of you with IBS (irritable bowel syndrome). I went on a low FODMAP diet, which helped me to get rid of my IBS and SIBO (small internal bacterial overgrowth). I did this for about six weeks and then gradually added back a food each week to see if or how it affected my body. I have since been able to eat everything that I ate prior to these conditions, although I know of others who are still unable to eat certain foods.

If what I've said here resonates with you, then I highly recommend *The Complete Low FODMAP Diet* by Dr Sue Shepherd and Dr Peter Gibson. However, it really is about finding what works best for you. A low GI eating regime, including alkaline food, generally suits most people's bodies, but certain foods make some people sluggish whilst energising others. If you're looking for a book with recipes that can elevate your mood, then *Eat Yourself Happy* and *Eat Yourself Calm,* both by Gill Paul are good. Whilst going through this adaptive eating phase, you may need to change the recipes around and make substitutions which work for your dietary requirements. For example, I suggest that you swap sugar for a plant-based substitute such as stevia. You also need to be proactive and methodical. For example, keeping track of which portion size keeps you at your optimal weight and which foods help you weigh less. Generally, I can always tell if I've put on weight by how comfortably my clothes fit. I check my weight now and again, but sometimes I don't do this for months. I have just discovered *The Sirt Diet Cookbook* by Jacqueline Whitehart and *The Sirt Food Diet Recipe Book* by Aidan Goggins and Glen Natten. Sirt foods contain a unique set of anti-oxidants, known as sirtuin activators, that can help with fat burning, protect against disease, promote good health and ultimately increase longevity. Dark chocolate, green tea and pomegranate are all good examples of these. Dr Michael Mosley has various recipe books to reduce your carbohydrates and lose weight, such as *The Fast 800* and also one for people with blood sugar challenges called *The 8 Week Blood Sugar Diet.*

Food "Baddies"

As you'll probably know, in dietary and nutrition terms, sugar is something of a supervillain these days – it's said to be as addictive as heroin, which is why many food manufacturers use it in their products. Often, these manufacturers combine sugar with salt, which makes for a winning combination, because it means that you crave these foods without knowing why! I still put salt on my food occasionally, but I use Himalayan pink or rock salt and black pepper to season my food. Thankfully in recent years the myth of "low fat" has been dispelled. We were previously led to believe that low fat was good for us, but the truth is that manufacturers often load these "low fat" alternatives with sugar and other unhealthy ingredients, which leads to excessive hunger, weight gain and disease. These alternatives are designed to help us reduce saturated fat, but instead the manufacturers just replace it with hydrogenated fat, which is bad for your heart and cholesterol. Low-fat foods may contain carbs, trans fats (hydrogenated) leading to mood swings, cravings and unbalanced blood sugar levels. Your body needs good fats from eating oily fish, avocados, nuts and seeds to maintain healthy blood vessels, to make hormones, and to keep your nervous system functioning correctly. Good fats in your diet also help absorption of vitamins. Research has proven that following a low-fat diet can make you deficient in these vitamins, lessening your immunity, limiting your body's ability to heal itself and damaging your bone health. With all this in mind, when buying food, check the label's total fat content. Anything over 17.5 g per 100 g is excessive. It is healthier to have 3 g or less per 100 g. For saturates, more than 5 g per 100 g is a lot – it's better to have 1.5 g or less per 100 g. Fat eventually turns to sugar in your body. Carbs of which sugar is 22.5 is massive, and 5 g or less per 100 g is fabulous. Always choose the low levels to reduce your carb and sugar intakes. Personally, I mostly cook from scratch, as this ensures that I know exactly what is in my food. I'm not perfect and I do occasionally eat processed foods, but my diet has improved significantly since I became harmonised with my body's wants and needs.

Your gut is an essential part of your body and many of the body's ills can start from here. A leaky gut is proven to affect the rest of your body and your mind, as well as causing a wide range of long-term conditions, such as chronic fatigue and multiple sclerosis. Research suggests that many of the symptoms are caused by the immune system reacting to germs, toxins or other substances that have been absorbed into the bloodstream via a porous (leaky) bowel. Aspirin and non-steroidal anti-inflammatory drugs, such as ibuprofen, can irritate the bowel lining. They can damage the seals between the cells, allowing some substances to pass through the gaps and into the bloodstream. However (as long as you're not taking them long term) the inflammation in your body should reduce once you stop taking the medication, unless you're extra sensitive.

Alongside this, there are other conditions that damage the seals too. Inflammatory bowel diseases such as Crohn's disease, infections of the intestines such as salmonella, norovirus and giardiasis, coeliac disease, chemotherapy medicines, chronic kidney disease, radiotherapy to abdomen, HIV/AIDS, cystic fibrosis, type 1 diabetes, sepsis and complicated surgery,

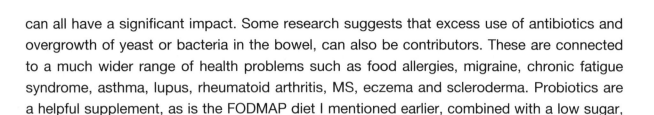

can all have a significant impact. Some research suggests that excess use of antibiotics and overgrowth of yeast or bacteria in the bowel, can also be contributors. These are connected to a much wider range of health problems such as food allergies, migraine, chronic fatigue syndrome, asthma, lupus, rheumatoid arthritis, MS, eczema and scleroderma. Probiotics are a helpful supplement, as is the FODMAP diet I mentioned earlier, combined with a low sugar, fungal and gluten-free regime.

Useful Books

- *Lean in 15* by Joe Wicks, The Body Coach. Use and adapt this to suit your lifestyle – fifteen minutes to make each dish.

- *Healthy Gut Cookbook* to improve your digestive health, by Gavin Pritchard and Maya Gangadharan (based on the GAPS diet to treat gut issues). It explains what has gone wrong, through stages, showing you how to heal using certain foods.

- *Medical Medium*, by Anthony Williams, is another book which suggests way you can help your gut and other health issues.

- *The Journal: What the Doctors Don't Tell You* has many interesting articles for health improvement.

Many people like the Paleo regime, which focuses on reducing carbs plus avoiding grains and refined sugar, whilst increasing nutrient dense whole foods. My GP was an advocate of this lifestyle, which she said was closer to the natural way we ate many years ago. However, unlike the GAPS diet, it doesn't allow dairy products. By now, if you've been experimenting, you'll have some idea of what is working or not working. I've got gadgets in my kitchen, such as nutri-bullet, which help to break down my homemade soups into a smooth mix, as well as helping to make smoothies. I also use a juicer, which helps when experimenting with recipes and finding ways for me to reduce sugar content (often by using more green veg with just a little fruit). I've found that my body works better with protein from fish and meat, although there are still days when I completely omit them from my diet. Instead I eat nuts, eggs or baked beans for my protein.

Hydration – I rarely drink tap water, as in the UK it contains fluoride, which research suggests can lead to damage of the parathyroid gland, resulting in hyperthyroidism. Studies show that too much fluoride can lower IQ levels in young children and cause neurological problems. It can create skin problems such as acne, high blood pressure, myocardial damage, cardiac insufficiency and heart failure, reproductive issues such as early puberty in girls, thyroid dysfunction, joint issues such as osteoarthritis, joint disorders and ADHD. Fluoride is said to calcify your pineal gland, which secretes melatonin and is your gateway to your psychic powers. It also converts signals between your nervous and endocrine systems. Melatonin is said to be a neuro-protector and plays a vital role in the aging process, especially protecting against Alzheimer's. When fluoride accumulates and calcifies, it blocks the melatonin's effectiveness, which affects your wake and sleep cycle and may also cause weight gain. With this in mind, I use non-fluoride toothpaste, thus eliminating it altogether.

In some parts of the UK, chlorine is used in place of fluoride. Research has indicated that chlorinated water has a negative impact on the body. It provides you with relatively low protection against protozoa and it speeds up the aging process (similar to extended exposure to the sun) because it depletes the skin of natural oils that hold moisture. This can lead to dry, itchy skin. Showering in warm chlorinated water may increase THM (trihalomethane) formation through enhanced reactions between organics and residual chlorine, which may cause cancer. A study published in 2002, in the *Environmental Research Journal*, demonstrated that chlorine is associated with heart defects and other medical conditions in infants. As your skin absorbs the chlorinated water and other contaminants, they go into your bloodstream, which may be detrimental to your body – not just the surface but internally too. Chlorine kills the bad bacteria, but unfortunately also kills the good bacteria that your skin relies on. Apart from the supposed health issues, I also dislike the taste.

I keep hydrated by drinking good quality water. At the moment I have a friend who gifts me Kangen Water, but my intention in the future is to buy a Kangen machine for myself. Kangen is alkalising and ionised water, NOT alkaline water – which isn't as good for you. The important component is molecular hydrogen, which is one of most powerful antioxidants, similar to miracle waters in Lourdes, France, Pakistan and Germany. The antioxidants grab the free radicals and then transmute them into water, which is dispersed through your urine. Thus, you are hydrated at cellular level, which brings the body into homeostasis. 8.5 pH and 9-9.5 pH are drinking waters. 7 pH is for pharmaceutical medication and drinking water for babies (use to mix formula), 11.5 pH is a degreaser so it cleans pesticides off your fruit and veg. 2.5 pH is a sanitiser and kills most germs within thirty seconds. It can be swished around the mouth and used to clean surfaces and wound infections. This is why the machine is classed as a medical device, because of its 2.5pH capabilities. 4.5 pH-6.5 pH is beauty water, the same pH as your skin, so acts as moisturiser and toner. To cleanse your face, use 11.5pH then spray 2.5 pH to sanitise. Let it dry naturally to kill bacteria on your face. Then use 6.5 pH to moisturise and tone.

You can use 2.5 pH for spritzing your outside plants to eradicate any bugs, 6.5 pH mist for spraying your acid loving plants and 8.5 pH for your alkaline plants. The same applies for indoor plants. It may be a good idea for you to research healthy drinking water and alternatives to chemicals to clean your house, car and garden. (See useful resources section to make contact for further information from my friend about Kangen Water and Ukon).

During COVID-19, I used the 2.5 as a sanitiser. I would spray myself and my shopping when click and collecting, before placing the food into my bags. For times when I didn't have access to the 2.5 sanitiser, I used an organic product made from seaweed, called "Ishga". Although this contains alcohol, it has no chemicals, unlike many sanitisers on the market. At the end of July 2020, when I was feeling unwell with a bout of nausea, I began taking Ukon capsules – a high quality turmeric surrounded with a Kangen Water capsule – to help boost my immune system.

Remember that the earth and your body are approximately 70% water. According to Masaru Emoto, water is aware of what you say. He conducted experiments showing the effects of both kind loving words and horrible words, using labels placed on water containers. Your unconscious mind is also listening, so it's important that you think kind thoughts about yourself, especially when eating and drinking. Take care not to watch any scary or negative TV programmes or movies when you are eating or drinking, as your emotions will have an impact on what you're ingesting. To ensure you drink enough water each day, there are apps on your phone that you can use to remind you to imbibe. For more information, I highly recommend checking out *Your Body's Many Cries For Water* by F. Batmanghelidj MD and *The Hidden Messages in Water* by Dr Masaru Emoto. Dr Emoto also has other great books on this subject, including *The Miracle of Water* and *The Shape of Love.*

When making hot drinks, I use organic decaf tea and coffee, because caffeine acts as a central nervous system stimulant. When it reaches your brain, the most noticeable effect is alertness. You'll feel more awake and less tired, firing on all cylinders. However, there are numerous and well-documented side effects of taking too much caffeine, including raised blood pressure, increased risk of heart attack, gout attacks and insomnia. The long-term effects include nervousness, difficulty in sleeping, restlessness, irritability, headaches, dizziness, ringing in the ears, muscle tremor, weakness, fatigue, rapid heart rate, rapid breathing and also dehydration – as tea and coffee are diuretics. I use positive visual aids to send messages to my unconscious mind with objects around my home, including mugs with words such as "Morning Gorgeous", "Lovely Lady" (with a heart picture), "Follow Your Dreams", "Hello Beautiful" and "Transformation of Matter". I also have lots of heart mugs and glasses in various shapes and sizes. When people come to visit me for a cup of tea, I want them to feel loved, beautiful and transformed and to this end I let them choose their cup to drink from. I also have heart-shaped plates, bowls and ornaments so that love is spread throughout my home.

Speaking of tea, when it comes to milk I am also careful about which products I use. An overload of dairy milk leaves me mucusy, especially in winter. Prior to changing my milk, a cold would last longer. So now I mainly use oat and coconut milk or lactose free milk, because normal cow's milk contains sugar, which my body doesn't like much. Food for thought – no other animal drinks another species' milk except for us. Cow's milk is for calves and not made for humans.

Good Quality Sleep – one upside to living alone is that I can sleep in total darkness, with no noise or movement from someone snoring or fidgeting. Sleep deprivation was used as torture in the war and was very effective at breaking people's resistance, as sleep plays a vital role in good health and wellbeing. Getting enough quality sleep at the right time can help protect your mental and physical health, quality of life and safety. The way you feel while you're awake depends in part on what happens while you're sleeping. During sleep, your body is working to support healthy brain function and maintain your physical health. In children and teens, sleep also helps support growth and development. The damage from sleep deficiency can occur in an instant – such as causing a car crash or it can be harmful over time, raising your risk for some chronic health problems. It can also impact how well you think, react, work, learn and get along with others. Whilst sleeping, your brain is preparing for the next day, forming new pathways to help you learn and remember information. Studies show that a good night's sleep improves your learning, regardless of the topic. It also enhances your problem-solving skills, focus, decision-making and creativity. If sleep deficient, you may have trouble solving problems, making decisions or controlling your behaviour. You may have heightened emotions and difficulty coping with change. Sleep deficiency has also been linked to depression, suicide and risk-taking behaviours.

Sleep plays an important part in your body's reparation process, as your body heals and repairs your heart and blood vessels whilst you're sleeping. Thus, ongoing sleep deficiency is linked to an increased risk of heart disease, kidney disease, high blood pressure, diabetes and stroke. It can also increase the risk of obesity. For teenagers, each hour of sleep lost increases the risk; this also affects other age groups too. Sleep also helps maintain a healthy balance of the hormones that make you feel hungry (ghrelin) or full (leptin). When you don't get enough sleep, your level of ghrelin goes up and your level of leptin goes down. This means that when you've had little sleep, you feel hungrier.

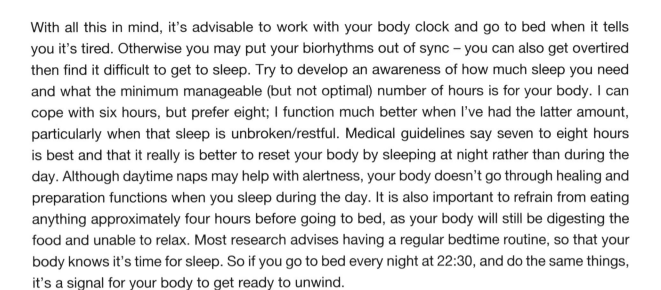

With all this in mind, it's advisable to work with your body clock and go to bed when it tells you it's tired. Otherwise you may put your biorhythms out of sync – you can also get overtired then find it difficult to get to sleep. Try to develop an awareness of how much sleep you need and what the minimum manageable (but not optimal) number of hours is for your body. I can cope with six hours, but prefer eight; I function much better when I've had the latter amount, particularly when that sleep is unbroken/restful. Medical guidelines say seven to eight hours is best and that it really is better to reset your body by sleeping at night rather than during the day. Although daytime naps may help with alertness, your body doesn't go through healing and preparation functions when you sleep during the day. It is also important to refrain from eating anything approximately four hours before going to bed, as your body will still be digesting the food and unable to relax. Most research advises having a regular bedtime routine, so that your body knows it's time for sleep. So if you go to bed every night at 22:30, and do the same things, it's a signal for your body to get ready to unwind.

When I'm finding it hard to fall asleep, I spray lavender on my pillow (or essential oil on a hanky on my pillow), listen to solfeggio sounds or sleep meditations on YouTube and take long slow deep breaths whilst saying in my mind 'relax or sleep'. These help get my mind and body into a relaxed state. Every night when I get into bed, I switch on my self-healing and self-sooth by placing one hand on my heart and the other on my solar plexus. Alternatively I just cross arms across my chest (heart) embracing each shoulder or put my hands under my boobs (solar plexus) with crossed arms in a hug before I sleep. I also give gratitude for the day and do similar activities to my morning practice.

Tooth and Gum Care – as I mentioned in part three, many people don't connect the importance of regular dental/hygienist appointments for teeth and gum care and how this can affect your health. According to research, gum disease can cause health issues in the body such as diabetes, heart and kidney disease, Alzheimer's, asthma, osteoporosis and cancer. If left unchecked, it can also lead to tooth loss. One explanation suggested for this, is that bacteria in infected gum tissue can enter your bloodstream and travel to other parts of the circulatory system, causing inflammation and arterial plaque.

Eliminating Pathogens – my Hunter NLS 4025 bio resonance machine works remotely using your DNA. It analyses the energy in your body with significant detail and precision. A gentle restorative energy is then applied, working with your body to improve health in those specific areas. It is non-invasive and completely pain free. It also recognises and helps combat bacterial, viral, parasitical and fungal infections, many of which go undetected in your lives, but can significantly affect health.

Each element of your body has an energy field with a distinct natural frequency pattern. When there is dis-ease or stress, the pattern de-stabilises and the Hunter can detect it. Using DNA, the Hunter NLS signals your body, using specific frequency patterns from its database relevant to that organ or part of the body. The pattern is then reflected back and any distortion shows dis-ease, infection, inflammation or stress. The more stable the frequency pattern, the more energetically-balanced that section of the body is. The Hunter's software displays the results on a detailed diagram of the body and gives the option to analyse with greater detail. At this point any bacteria, fungi, viruses or parasites warrant further investigation. The programme also analyses a selection of the most appropriate frequency patterns to restore health. Using all the information provided, the Hunter then applies an energy frequency to de-stabilise the bacteria, fungi, viruses and parasites. Additionally, it sends multiple signals back to stimulate your healing process. Areas of interest where your body is inflamed are automatically identified and displayed on the computer screen so you can see it in "real" time. We then delve further down with significant detail and precision to discover the causes of your body's distress, such as which pathogens are the perpetrators causing dis-ease and stress in your body. Then, between us, a decision is made on which areas to treat during your session.

This diagnostic method has proven very effective for a large range of conditions, especially for long-standing chronic pain, illness and injuries. It helps you to understand what is going on in your body and how your systems are affecting each other. Please refer back to the disclaimer – this is not to replace any medication prescribed by your physician.

Meditation and Down Time to Just "Be" – if you fail to give your body time to rest, by reducing how much you do physically and mentally, then your body will decide this for you – giving you a cold or something else to enforce you being still. I often meditate first thing in the morning, especially when feeling below par, to set myself up for the day. At stressful times I sometimes meditate twice or more a day. If I haven't meditated in the morning, then I will meditate as and when it suits me best. There are occasions when I don't meditate at all, such as when I'm visiting my grandchildren, as I have so little precious time with them. I have been meditating since the age of seventeen, when I first did yoga. I was meditating every day, until my mother died, after which point I got scared as I had spirit visitations and stopped for a while (as I mentioned during my story). In any case, I highly recommend doing it daily. Since James left, over sixteen years ago, I've found the benefits of daily meditation to be extremely far-reaching.

According to Matthew Thorpe MD PhD, "Meditation is a habitual process of training your mind to focus and redirect your thoughts. Meditation reduces stress, controls anxiety, promotes positive health, enhances self-awareness, lengthens your attention span, increases memory and generates feelings of love and kindness for yourself and others. It also helps to develop beneficial habits and feelings such as a positive mood and outlook, self-discipline, healthier sleep patterns and even increased pain tolerance." As Dr Joe Dispenza told me when I was at his week-long retreat, 'Your telomeres shorten when you're stressed for any length of time. But with regular meditation they lengthen, which increases your lifespan.' To read more, see his blog "Telomeres: The Biological Clock in Our Genetics".

A study (PubMed Central Goyai M et al. JAMA Intern Med 2014) with 3,500 adults showed that meditation lives up to its reputation for stress reduction. Normally, mental and physical stress cause increased levels of the stress hormone cortisol. This stress hormone can disrupt sleep, promote depression and anxiety, increase blood pressure, contribute to fatigue, brain fog and for some people (like me) increase blood sugar levels. An eight-week study called "Mindfulness Meditation" reduced the inflammation response caused by stress (Brain Behaviour and Immunity vol. 27 `Jan 2013). Research has shown that meditation can also improve symptoms of stress-related conditions such as irritable bowel syndrome, post-traumatic stress disorder and fibromyalgia, as well as helping to reduce anxiety, depression, phobias and stress-related issues such as panic attacks.

Grounding – continuing on from part three, grounding is when your bare skin is in contact with natural ground, such as grass, dirt, sand or water. Growing up, I spent most of my life walking around barefoot at any and every opportunity. As a teenager I would often walk to Hemel town barefoot – I suppose I was classed as a "hippy" for doing this. It was a natural instinct for me and obviously my body wanted me to ground – even though I had no conscious understanding of grounding back then. The human body is a sponge, soaking up negatively charged electrons from the earth. This concept was given wider attention when Clint Ober released his book *Earthing: The Most Important Health Discovery Ever?* Almost twelve years before his book was published, Ober discovered that the same system of grounding used to stabilise telecommunications and wires could also stabilise the atoms in the human body. During my very first psychic development group, over sixteen years ago, I was taught how to ground by doing a visualisation process (I share this process in part six). When you have a solid connection to the earth, it helps you connect more easily with the higher realms. It was also really useful for me when learning Reiki Healing and during my other trainings.

Even though this might seem like a new concept, grounding has been practised since the beginning of time, when your ancestors walked barefoot or wore conductive leather moccasins or sandals. However, since the invention of rubber-soled shoes, this has created a non-conductive barrier between you and the earth's electrons. As your direct contact with the earth diminishes through the routine use of synthetic flooring and shoes, electromagnetic instability threatens your health. All your cells are made of atoms, which possess unique positive and negative charges that are based on the number of negative electrons or positive protons they carry. Many healthy atoms have a negative charge because they possess more electrons; however, these atoms can have electrons "stolen" from them, making them highly reactive and damaging. They then become free radicals, which we have already discussed in great detail. As free radicals infiltrate your cells and tissues, your health declines. To stop this destructive process, you must supply your body with neutralising antioxidants via your food and other such means. Grounding provides this, as it gives you a large dose of negative electrons.

Earthing (grounding) also improves your sleep and reduces pain, inflammation, cell damage, stress and trauma when walking barefoot outside, and can be carried out when sitting, working or sleeping indoors. When we are indoors, we are generally surrounded by appliances which give off harmful frequencies. Earthing ensures that you are connected in a way that transfers the earth's electrons from the ground into your body, thus reducing the impact of these frequencies. I have an earthing mat that I hold when watching TV or using my laptop to counteract the EMFs. My mobile phone case has a shungite crystal dot and I have organite crystals to reduce Wi-Fi electromagnetic frequencies in my lounge and bedroom. Likewise, I sleep on a grounding half-sheet placed over the lower half of my bed. In part six I have given you a grounding visualisation that you can do, if you're unable to get out and do it in nature.

Pleasure and Fun with Intimate Social Interaction – spending time with others is very important to me, as I live and work alone. Whilst writing this book I often took myself out to write, allowing me to be in the presence of others, because sometimes I felt isolated and lonely. I made sure I had regular close encounters with those I love, creating a good work/life balance.

Social support and social interaction are one of the most important factors in predicting the physical health and wellbeing of everyone, including the very young. Having good, social interactions is vital to human health on a mental and physical level. Many people find it difficult to open their hearts and share their feelings and problems. However, social interaction, where people can express their feelings and share their problems with others, has a hugely beneficial outcome. It helps in coping with stress and major life changes like divorce, redundancy and moving house. I was so grateful for the emotional support of my children after my husband left. I had loving people to listen to my woes, allowing me to vent and just holding space for me. This was especially important, as I had to make new friends; divorce can make you a pariah, as some women perceive you as a threat – suddenly you fancy their husband (which you never did before and still don't!) Again these were people I could talk to who'd had similar experiences or at least compassion, to go out and have fun with. I found that during COVID-19 it was even more vital to keep in touch with those I love via video calls. Although it wasn't the same as being with them in person, it was better than having no visual contact at all. I was fortunate to regularly take socially distanced walks with a friend, thus getting out in nature for fresh air and company.

According to "Psychology Today UK", studies show that lonely people often suffer more from cardiovascular problems, stress and depression, compared to those with a strong social network of friends and family. Knowing others value you is an important psychological factor in helping you to forget the negative aspects of your life and helping you to think more positively about your environment. Social support not only improves your wellbeing but also affects your immune system, where lack of social connection can lead to the onset of anxiety and depression. When carrying out research for my clinical hypnotherapy studies, I discovered that with life-threatening conditions such as cancer, a strong social network aided recovery faster and improved quality of life. Sometimes the "wrong" sort of social network can have a negative influence, especially if this involves "drug taking" or excessive consumption of alcohol. In these cases the social interaction can have a devastating impact on physical and mental health – when leaving behind the unhealthy behaviour you lose your network of friends too. Therefore, it's imperative to find friends who are supportive of your new positive habits and behaviours.

A Sense of Purpose – studies suggest that having a sense of purpose in life is associated with a lower risk of death. A sample of nearly 7,000 people, which included a psychological wellbeing evaluation and a questionnaire assessing purpose in life, showed that stronger purpose in life was associated with decreased mortality and that purposeful living may have health benefits. In their 2003 essay *The Development of Purpose during Adolescence*, Stanford psychologist William Damon and his colleagues defined purpose as "a stable and generalised intention to accomplish something that is at once meaningful to the self and of consequence to the world." Purpose is about more than just completing simple day-to-day tasks like going to work or feeding the family; it's about reaching beyond one's self to progress or complete your goals.

Leaders in the growing, evidence-based field of positive psychology believe that finding your sense of purpose is the key to happiness, flow, optimal experience and a life well lived. When you find your purpose, you'll open yourself up to new opportunities, awakening to goals and ideals that are personally meaningful, reaching beyond and progressively defining your existence. Purpose doesn't have to have specific definitions or boundaries. Whether you experience a sense of purpose as a volunteer, receptionist, carpenter, teacher, maintenance worker, parent or physician, it doesn't matter. It is only the **sense** of purpose that matters. Your sense of purpose can be large or small and it is okay if you're still striving towards your goal or even if you've reached your aim already. Having a sense of purpose or meaning is the motivation that drives you towards a satisfying future. It also helps you to get the most from the things you do and achieve – large, small and right now. A sense of purpose helps you to prioritise your life, make plans, get the motivation to keep going in tough times, identify things that truly count when circumstances change and become more resilient as you grow. Good examples could be a short-term goal like finishing a work project or a long-term aim to achieve a promotion or do some voluntary work. For me, writing this book fulfilled the criteria – it gave me a sense of focus and productivity during the enforced time I was alone (due to COVID-19). A sense of purpose will often reflect the things you value, such as safety and security, pleasures such as family gatherings, financial stability, fun and laughter, along with qualities you respect, such as honesty, integrity, authenticity and justice.

My sense of purpose has changed throughout my life, as I've learned additional aspects about myself and the world. I've met new people and experienced different things. Primarily, you must identify what matters to you. When I was younger, my aim was to stop working in an office, as it bored me to tears and didn't feel purposeful. I got married and had a family, which was always part of my personal long-term plan. I combined family life with study, which resulted in my degree and becoming a teacher, which was my ultimate career goal back then. However, after teaching for many years, I became disillusioned with our education system. So, I decided to change and the coaching I had before my divorce gave me my vision for my new career. Ask yourself this, dear reader: are you living your life with a sense of purpose? If not, then can you contemplate what you want to be/do/have as your sense of purpose?

Sometimes life throws curveballs, in the form of accidents or illness, which may impede your journey towards your goal. Your sense of purpose will help you when things go wrong. Having purpose helps you to overcome your challenges, making you resilient and motivated, able to put things into perspective and capable of focusing on what's important to you, so that you can move forward and enjoy your life. As your needs change over time, you may end up redefining your purpose – and that is absolutely okay. Before writing this book, I felt lost and without a sense of purpose. My kids were all grown up, with families of their own, and had no "need" for me – as they're perfectly capable of taking care of their own lives now. Although I was still coaching, which was fulfilling, it didn't occupy much of my time. This all changed once spirit gave me the nudge of inspiration to write my book. I felt my next purpose was to leave this book as a legacy, making my life worthwhile by sharing my message and useful tips with others. My next purpose might be to create a set of oracle or coaching cards…

Good Quality Downtime – making time for yourself is important in any relationship; your relationship with yourself is no different! On that note, make time to enjoy all the things that really feel good to you. I disliked my own company after my ex-husband left and it took time to get used to it, because for forty-nine years I had lived in large and frenetic households. I spent time learning to feel happy in my own company and now I enjoy it. If you haven't yet learnt how to be on your own, it's time to start! Take yourself to the movies, do some arts and crafts, cook your favourite meal or simply curl up on the sofa with your favourite book. The point is to make time for **you**, in whatever way you enjoy. Be really honest with yourself about what must be done in order for you to satisfy your own needs. As I said in part one, my ex-husband was brilliant at taking care of himself and ensured he took care of his needs. I didn't realise at the time how important this was for everyone. I should have done the same for myself. Ask yourself the following questions, dear reader:

- Do you need time to yourself? Do you need to take some time to just "be"?

- Do you need more adventure?

- Are you feeling the need for more security and stability in your life? How can you give yourself what you need?

Self-Care

Self-care is also about resilience. Monitoring your emotions and thoughts can help you to remain as positive as possible. Take time out to regroup and re-energise by listening to your body's needs – if you're tired then take a nap. If you're feeling sluggish, then move! This oxygenates your blood, energising you. If I spend time in places with lots of other people's energies, like at a conference, a wellness fair or even at the supermarket, this can sometimes fatigue me as I feel the energies of those around me. To counteract this, I need to spend time alone to rest and re-energise myself. As I mentioned earlier, the opposite is true too. If I'm alone for too long then I want to spend time with friends and family, as I need personal human interaction – talking, hugging and laughing.

Guidance From Your Feelings – it is worthwhile for you to take a moment to check-in internally before saying yes to the requests of others. It's important that you feel able to say no, without compulsively pleasing and rescuing. Don't give justification either, you don't need to. Otherwise it just becomes a verbal tennis match, with the other person offering suggestions on how you can still fulfil their wishes.

It is extremely beneficial for you to have an awareness of which people make you feel energised and which people make you feel drained. This will allow you to allocate exposure to them accordingly – this applies to immediate family members too. As I've changed and grown, I've learnt to spend less time with people who sap my energy. I realised that certain relationships were very one-sided, with me giving time and energy to listen during their challenges, but leaving me feeling exhausted and low, whilst they were happy, energised and rejuvenated. Likewise, those same people weren't ever available when I needed support. So, be kind to yourself and make sure you take time out to stop for your own replenishment. Allow yourself space for contemplation and inspiration. See failure as a form of discovery – you have learnt how not to do something; now you can try again but differently. Keep experimenting with encouraging positive self-talk, because the more you practise, the easier and more natural it becomes. When catching your negative thoughts or statements, say, 'Clear, cancel and delete' then replace them with thoughts of how you'd like it to be/what you want to have instead, ensuring what you say is in the present tense not the future.

Remember, in any situation, to treat yourself how you would treat your dearest friend. Stop judging – be caring, especially in times when you have "slipped up" and not been your perfect best. After all, no one is perfect – it is human to err! Eliminate the idea that self-development is important and urgent. Just allow yourself to be in flow. Focus on how far you've come, how resilient you are and how kind you are to yourself and others. Celebrate you!

It's also really important not to force yourself into situations which feel too vulnerable. I made this error when in Tarragona, Spain, at Dr Joe Dispenza's retreat. We were guinea pigs on his first week-long retreat, with the additional challenge of an unknown physical task. The purpose was to "move beyond the unknown". We had no idea of what the challenge would be, although my body had "sensed" it would be something I wasn't happy about. I briefly did some calming exercises, but as a sizeable group of one hundred people there was a collective fear, which I felt too. The tasks were aerial "walkways", similar to "Go Ape" in the UK and were extremely challenging. I didn't check in with my body to see what its fears were or whether I should participate. Instead, I just forced myself to do the exercise, which took absolutely ages. I felt the stress hormones rushing around my body, which was so unhealthy, as it raised my blood sugar levels. After the event I was in such a state that I was incapable of going to eat with everyone. I had to give myself a soothing bath, go to bed and eat a little snack whilst there. My body wanted rest. On reflection, I should have given myself time to tune in and make the right decision for me, trusting my feelings, senses and intuitions, before making my decision. However, one of the silver linings from the event was that I learnt lessons and gained insight – it was the instability of the walkways that distressed me and not the height aspect.

Obviously, there are some scary situations in life that may be unavoidable. So, unlike me in Spain, have a brief chat with the one inside you who feels scared. Ask questions on how the situation could be made easier and negotiate to find things that will reassure your inner you. Take the necessary time to complete the task in a manner that suits you. Listen to your body's needs – your body needs reassurance and protection and **you** are the best person to provide this. If your body says no, then heed that!

Spiritual Aspect – catering for your spiritual side means carrying out anything that you regard as sacred. It could be listening to or making music and art, performing rituals and ceremonies, going to sacred sites, going on pilgrimages or retreats or just being in nature – anything that uplifts you and connects you to your true self, the real inner you. Taking time for spiritual self-care is soul fulfilling, as it encourages introspection, clarity and comfort. It calms your inner turbulence by quietening your mind, leaving you space to feel and honour what your heart yearns for. When you're truly happy and thriving, you will know it, deep in your core.

Fulfilling your spiritual self can really help improve your relationships with others. You'll experience more inner peace, clarity on your needs for happiness, enhanced feelings of oneness and universality, as well as a deeper, more introspective relationship with yourself. As previously mentioned, there are multiple things that you can do to enhance your spiritual self-care, such as meditating, mindful walking, decluttering, connecting with community, journaling, reading inspiring materials, having periods of unplugging from technology and achieving forgiveness of yourself and others.

Self-Esteem

Self-esteem means having confidence in your own worth and abilities. It means that you've got self-respect, dignity, high morale, confidence, assurance and assertiveness. It's about how much you like and appreciate yourself, accepting your weaknesses and your strengths. As mentioned earlier, words are energy, and your body listens to your negative self-talk, so speak lovely things to yourself! If you have high self-esteem then you are able to self-validate, celebrating your achievements, without feeling the need to explain your shortcomings to others. You have more compassion for yourself as a human. With high self-esteem it is more likely that you will take care of yourself and explore your full potential, having a balanced but accurate view of who you are and what you can accomplish. Remember this – you are a good person who deserves respect, but it's also important to give respect to others in return.

The causes of low self-esteem and lack of confidence vary between people, but often this is the result of an unhappy childhood, where carers/guardians or teachers were extremely critical. Thus, poor academic performance in school is a common denominator in many people who suffer from this. Relationship troubles are another common factor in people with poor self-esteem. Prior to my divorce, all of these things applied to me. I was frequently low and unhappy, with no concept of my own self-worth, because my husband seemed more interested in spending time with others than with me. Immediately following the divorce, I was at rock bottom. It was only through taking the time to learn about who I am and what I am truly capable of, that I was able to get through this time and emerge as the slimmer, more confident and harmonised person that I am today. Academically, I have tested myself, by continuing my studies up until the present day. This has built my confidence, continually presenting me with challenges to overcome, to degree level and beyond. Ultimately, in pursuit of improvement and education, I have put myself "through the mill", and in doing so I have proved to myself that I am more capable than I could possibly have imagined. I am a person who embraces change and likes new experiences – being far happier as a result.

Validation – many of you will have devoted your lives to receiving validation. If you didn't receive this from your caregivers early in life, you may have looked elsewhere. Some people say that validation is an essential developmental need. However, from my experience, this can easily turn into an unhealthy and damaging obsession, which ultimately causes more harm than good. Depending on how deep your need for validation goes, your search can shape every aspect of your life, from your relationship patterns to your career choices. It's important to remember the old adage, "You can't please everyone all of the time". Not everyone will like and respect you, and that's okay, just as long as you are capable of self-validating. Never underestimate the power of self-acceptance and acknowledging how far you have come.

As an example, I once had a client named Samantha, who was stuck in a place where she was always looking for love and acceptance from others. She didn't realise how much her need for validation ruled her. Samantha did not understand that she had to find a way to **give validation to herself**. Together, we worked on a plan to get Samantha back in the driving seat of her own bus. I assisted Samantha with the validation exercise in part six of this book, which enabled her to have greater feelings of self-worth – permeating throughout her body, right down to her cellular level. It was interesting to note that, after this, her body posture and language changed. Samantha now walked upright with her head held high, denoting a self-confident air.

Once you have fulfilled your need for validation, you can then move on to the next developmental stage – self-possession. You're no longer concerned with how others perceive you, because your choices emanate from your own inner compass. You feel called to express all that you are, not because you want someone else to take notice, but because it is a natural manifestation of your being alive. You are aware of your value, offerings and your self-actualisation demands, so that you can express them fully.

I have paid attention to this distinction between validating-seeking and self-possession throughout my own personal journey. I found that my creative expression was entirely different depending on where I was coming from. If I was motivated to talk or write by the desire to get attention or to be seen in a particular light, it hampered my output. The words were there, but it came across as stilted and inauthentic, leaving me feeling like a "try hard" and empty. I was talking or writing for the wrong reasons. Yet when I wrote from a place of true self-possession, with no concern for how it would be perceived, something magical happened. Speaking or writing became a kind of healing elixir, one that nurtured and nourished me from the inside out. It was like I was in tune with my inner being, one that I was born to commune with, to share my wisdom from my heart and soul. Let me ask you this, dear reader: when you sit down to create, to relate or to manifest, where does it come from – a quest for external validation or a need to express all that you are? What fuels your steps forward?

Some Signs of Low Self-Esteem

There are numerous indicators that a person has low self-esteem. To start with, you may have the belief that others are more capable or successful than you and could experience difficulty accepting positive feedback or help. You may fear failure, which can hold you back from success at work. Mental health issues such as sadness, anxiety, depression or even feeling suicidal are a common side effect of this, alongside negative thoughts and emotions, limiting beliefs and unhelpful habits that compromise your lifestyle. You might have fewer expectations from life, ignoring or neglecting your own needs whilst possibly fulfilling everyone else's. Perhaps you feel awkward and lacking confidence in social settings. I have been there, done that and worn the t-shirt! Now and then I still have a wobble, as a human being I am imperfectly perfect, but on the whole I have moved on from this place. And the most important thing to note, is that you can move forward too. You are strong and capable – I believe in you. Now, you must learn to believe in yourself.

Ways to Improve Your Self-Esteem

One way to improve your self-esteem is to think positive thoughts and say positive statements to yourself on a daily basis. Learn to accept compliments and gifts with graciousness. This may feel uncomfortable at first, but it will become easier as time goes on. Eliminate negative self-criticism and don't use self-deprecating language. Be kind to yourself and have more self-compassion. You believe in the ability of others to make decisions, so now stop being their rescuer. Know and understand that it is okay to make mistakes – these are just lessons to be learned. Practise holding yourself erect and upright in a positive pose, reinforcing to your mind that you have self-respect and are feeling good. Treat criticism not personally but constructively; checking in to see if there is any truth in what they've said and if not then dismiss it. Allow yourself to shine and don't dim your light to make others feel comfortable. I did this constantly during my school years, as I was brighter than most of my friends, but I was more concerned about having good social connections than passing tests and exams/being classed as a "swot" – all of which was unconscious behaviour (on a side note I lacked self-belief around my abilities too). Act assertively, knowing the importance of taking care of yourself first (plane analogy – use your own oxygen mask before helping others) and don't feel guilty for being assertive. Learn to become more at ease when communicating with others, expressing your likes and dislikes, asking for your needs to be met. Surround yourself with the right people. Get to know yourself and be your own best friend. Acknowledge where you need change and what changes would be good to make. Pay it forward or give back by supporting others.

If the self-healing processes that you are using to conquer anxiety, stress or hurt are not working, then be proactive and seek support. You can contact me to book a coaching session (www.denisedavis.co.uk). ♥

Self-Respect

Self-respect is a gift you give yourself. It comes when you are less motivated to please others, just to get their approval. Instead, you are motivated to live a life of authenticity and personal integrity, regardless of what anyone else thinks about you. If you have self-respect, then this shows others how to treat you. Receiving respect from others may help you feel part of a community, feeling safe to express yourself. This is especially important when we are young. If you haven't had the right role models to show you how to be respectful to others, then your own sense of self-respect may be low. Let me ask you this: is there dissonance in your life? Could this be because you're not living in accordance with your values? For example, if you place a high value on spending time with family, but your work is taking up more and more of your time, then this may cause dissonance and dissatisfaction.

Luckily, there are plenty of ways in which you can gift yourself with more respect. These include:

- Being confident in your own opinions, interests and beliefs;

- Believing you're capable of making your own decision, regardless of group opinion and what others are doing;

- Not allowing other people's thoughts about you to shape your own view of yourself;

- Reminding yourself of your strengths, instead of focusing on the negative things in your life;

- Forgiving yourself for your mistakes, they are just lessons – helping you to learn what works and what doesn't;

- Surrounding yourself with positive people;

- Having pride and confidence in yourself;

- Always behaving with honour, dignity and integrity, being true to you;

- Refraining from self-judgement and avoiding comparing yourself to others.

So, reader, it's time to start moving forward. Make positive affirmations and 'I AM' statements. Celebrate your wins. Love and embrace the things that make you different and special. Realise that beauty is in the eye of the beholder and will differ for most people – don't compare yourself to photoshopped models. Follow your passion, do things that make your heart sing. Be mindful and treat others with love and respect. Have daily gratitude. Ask for help and don't go through your challenges alone. Humans are herd animals and are here to support each other. Learn to say no without explanation. Journal, even if it is just doodling patterns to release swirling thoughts. Know that you are not your feelings and that rejection is not as meaningful as it feels – every rejection is a learning experience, every mistake an opportunity to grow stronger and more vibrant. Understand that your value doesn't lie in how your body looks, nor in your achievements. It's about who you are and whether you feel good on a soul level.

Summary

In this chapter we have looked at:

- ❖ How to reach harmony with your body, mind and spirit.

- ❖ How self-love and its components such as self-care, self-respect and self-esteem are important in creating peace and equilibrium between your mind, body and spirit.

- ❖ Symptoms of poor self-care and low self-esteem.

- ❖ Ways you can create self-love for yourself and celebrate you.

Invitation

You will need a notepad, a pen and a mirror. Look into the mirror and say to yourself, 'I love you' whilst making direct eye contact. The eventual aim is to see beyond your physical body and really see yourself, your inner being, your energy and life force – to really feel love for yourself. If you're unable to say 'I love you', then begin with 'I like me' or 'what I like about me is…'

When doing the above exercise, notice what thoughts and feelings arise. Make a note of them, so you can focus on reinforcing the positive ones and re-framing the negative ones, so that they don't prevent you from achieving self-love. You can journal about them, adapt the Ho'oponopono statement below, use the EFT short form in part six or say the "Access Consciousness clearing statement" (Google this, as no one is allowed to share it). Fold an A4 sheet of paper in half, draw a picture of you with your issue on one half and your desired outcome on the other half. Release the unwanted half of your picture to the rubbish bin, in pieces, or burn it. Now, say this:

'Dear body, I'm sorry I often look at you and think you are too … and not … enough. Please forgive me for devaluing you and making myself feel unattractive and insecure. Thank you for grounding me in the world, carrying me through life, enabling me to do many amazing things, being the support and basis of my life. I love you.'

Next, write a list of ten positive things you like about yourself regarding your looks, personality and skills. Following this, write ten things you dislike about yourself. Look at the negative points from a fresh perspective. For example, if you've written stubborn as a negative, think about when and how being strong-willed benefitted you or could be of benefit to you. It could indicate that you are determined and persist with tasks that everyone says will fail. There are positive and negative aspects to the majority of traits, it's just a case of re-framing your perspective and learning to appreciate the benefits of you. Instead of asking 'what's wrong with me', you could ask yourself:

- 'I wonder what a successful version of me would feel like.'

- 'I wonder what it would take to create the abundant version of me.'

- I wonder what the version of me that's healthy would look like.'

- 'Where is my greatest joy?'

- 'What makes me happy?'

- 'What books in the bookshop should I gravitate towards?' or 'Which TV programmes would assist me?'

- 'What would provide me with the most uplifting, exhilarating and freeing experience? I want to find it!'

Make positive statements such as:

- 'I love the thought of having optimal health.'

- 'Excellent health is my birth-right.'

- 'I am always taking excellent care of myself.'

Now create some more of your own…

Insightful Questions

When you have finished the invitation above, take a notepad and pen. Sit quietly, free from any distractions, in a relaxed manner. Look at each of the questions below, one at a time. Allow the question to just flow freely in your mind, percolating if you will. Then, capture your answers on paper, giving you an insight into where you are right now. This will help you shift your perspective, so that you become less stuck.

- *How have you stopped yourself from using your wings and flying? What is preventing you from being the best possible version of yourself, from doing things you love and being the person you'd like to be?*

- *When will you give yourself permission to be your full expression of you, warts and all?*

- *Do you suffer from inner conflict? If so, what are you going to do to eradicate this?*

- *Are you willing to be vulnerable?*

- *What you resist persists. When will you face your feelings, fears and stop self-rejection and sabotage?*

- *In what ways can you love yourself more?*

- *Are you fully showing self-care?*

- *Are you willing to meet yourself where you are, to understand yourself and be present with yourself?*

- *Are you open to sharing and being intimate with yourself?*

- *Are you honest with yourself?*

- *Are you "with" you in ways that matter? Do you take time to know what matters to you and make that a top priority in your life, willingly wanting to, as a natural act of love for you?*

- *If you give yourself acts of love, are they dictated by others or things you truly want for yourself?*

- *Have you stepped into your own power, driving your own bus, on the journey of life that **you** wish to experience?*

- *Do you give time to truly **be yourself** and **with you** in your world?*

Having completed all the questions, now think of some positive ways in which you could make changes. Return to your proposed changes and see if you can think of any other ways you could improve your life, by moving forward positively.

Part Five

More Ways to Love Yourself

This part will give you more suggestions on how to increase your self-love. Self-love is the starting point for being able to love others unconditionally, accepting them for who and what they are. However, before you can give love and respect to others, as well as receiving it, you need to give it to yourself first. Remember that your life is a gift to enjoy, so it's good to put your needs first. This isn't selfish or wrong, as society would lead you to believe – it's about becoming the best possible version of you. The best possible version of you is better equipped to help others too.

Being Mindful

Being mindful means that you are totally present, knowing what you think, feel and want. Whatever activity you are doing, you exude focus, excluding everything else from your mind. You are mindful of who you are and act on this knowledge, rather than on what other people want for you or from you. It is about connecting with yourself. The easiest way to do this is to become free from all stimulations, completely connected to your inner being. I perform most of my regular meditations in my bedroom, but mindful walking in the forest or by the ocean also helps, as does swimming.

In order to get in touch with my inner being, I start by turning off all stimuli and relaxing, putting myself into a calm, peaceful state. When I first started mindfulness meditation, I found that using a mantra really helped. I would repeatedly tell myself to relax, as this helped to quieten my monkey mind. I also created a metaphorical balloon above my head, where I placed my thoughts as they came in during the relaxation, reassuring them they'd be retrieved after the meditation. This made it easier for me to stop focusing on them. When you begin the exercise, you may like to think of a place where you felt happy. Try visualising your ideal space – seeing, hearing and feeling what comes into your awareness.

Initially, I spent maybe only ten minutes (which felt like an hour at the time) laying or sitting still without movement, ignoring an itchy nose or other such irritations (according to Dr Joe Dispenza, your body is unused to such stillness and will give you reasons to move, but it's about over-coming your body through your mind). Eventually, after much practise, I now regularly spend an hour without moving – time just seems to fly by. The longest meditation I have performed was at an event in Bonn, when 1,500 of us took part in meditation for over four hours. It was truly magical, cosmic and fascinating. The scientists measuring the energy in the room said it rose immensely. During the week of the retreat, many of us also took part in having our brains scanned and having our heart coherence monitored during the meditations. The results showed that we all went into heart coherence and the theta relaxed state or higher.

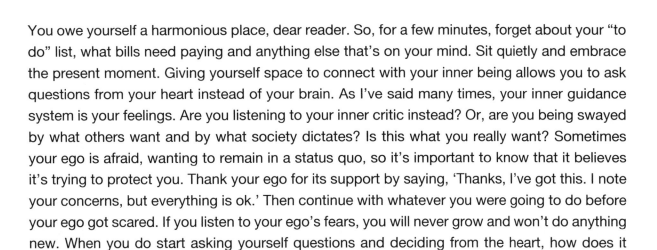

You owe yourself a harmonious place, dear reader. So, for a few minutes, forget about your "to do" list, what bills need paying and anything else that's on your mind. Sit quietly and embrace the present moment. Giving yourself space to connect with your inner being allows you to ask questions from your heart instead of your brain. As I've said many times, your inner guidance system is your feelings. Are you listening to your inner critic instead? Or, are you being swayed by what others want and by what society dictates? Is this what you really want? Sometimes your ego is afraid, wanting to remain in a status quo, so it's important to know that it believes it's trying to protect you. Thank your ego for its support by saying, 'Thanks, I've got this. I note your concerns, but everything is ok.' Then continue with whatever you were going to do before your ego got scared. If you listen to your ego's fears, you will never grow and won't do anything new. When you do start asking yourself questions and deciding from the heart, how does it feel? Do the choices feel light or heavy? If your choice feels light, then you are in alignment with what your Soul and Higher Self wants.

Another mindful activity I like to do, is to journal all thoughts and emotions that are present. I find the process of putting words to paper both cathartic and freeing. If I'm feeling yucky in my solar plexus chakra when I wake up, then as part of my morning practice I will include a brain-dump of my thoughts and feelings for ten to thirty minutes before I get up. Journaling encourages mindfulness and helps you to keep things in perspective. It helps you remain present and provides an opportunity for emotional catharsis, helping your brain regulate your emotions. It also provides a greater sense of confidence and self-identity. According to studies, such as *The Health Benefits of Journaling* by Maud Purcell, journaling reduces stress and thus improves both your physical and mental condition. In particular, it lessens the impact of physical stressors on your body, lowering blood pressure, improving liver function and boosting your immune system – thus decreasing your risk of illness. It has also been reported to help wounds heal faster and reduce depressive symptoms.

A study in New Zealand, conducted by James W. Pennebaker, found that when you translate an experience into language by writing it down, you make the experience graspable. In 2013, researchers found that 76% of adults who spent twenty minutes writing for three consecutive days in the weeks before a biopsy, were fully healed one day later. Conversely, 58% of the control group had not recovered in that time frame. Journaling also keeps your memory sharp, boosts your comprehension and increases your working memory capacity, which may be reflected in improved cognitive processing.

A unique social and behavioural outcome of journaling is that it improves your mood, thus giving you a greater sense of overall emotional wellbeing and happiness. It also strengthens your emotional functions. As your journaling habit develops in the long-term, you become more in tune with your health, inner needs and desires. It can provide a greater sense of confidence and self-identity, helping you to cope during times of personal adversity and change, whilst emphasising important patterns and growth in your life. Research has shown that writing can also assist you to develop more structured, adaptive and integrated schemes about yourself, others and the world. It unlocks and engages right-brained creativity, giving you access to your full brainpower.

If you have no idea how to start journaling, then you could begin from there, even just writing down that you have no idea of where to start or writing anything you've recently experienced, just to get yourself in the flow. A quick way to engage your brain, is to give yourself five minutes to write down however many words you can think of that start with S – begin with "success" and go from there. Have fun!

Once I have filled my journal, I shred the contents. If this seems surprising, it's because I don't want to have the energies of old thoughts and emotions in my home long-term. Once every-thing has been written, I release it to the fire. Some people buy a beautiful journal to write in, but if like me you write it on paper, then it is easier to dispose of. Alternatively, you could have a journal for joyous things and paper when you know you wish to get rid of the contents – which I find is the best option for me.

Follow Your Needs and Stop Distractions

It's important to recognise and stay centred on what you need. This increases your ability to focus on the positive aspects of yourself, hence why turning away from distractions is vital. Stopping automatic behaviour patterns and habits that may get you into trouble or keep you stuck in the past, increases your self-confidence and your self-love.

Trusting **yourself** to look after your best interests is paramount. After all, no one knows you as well as you do. During my first hospital appointment with a dietician after my diabetes diagnosis, she gave me nutrition advice. I had already cut out bread, rice and pasta, but she informed me that it was important to reintroduce and keep these in my diet. In my heart, I knew this was wrong, as I know my body's requirements, but I grudgingly handed her the steering wheel to my bus. After all, she had trained for years; she had the qualifications and was adamant that she knew better than me. Subsequently, I gained weight and my blood sugars rose. Now I always listen to my own inner knowing – no one knows my body as intimately as me. When I omit these foods, my body is healthier, slimmer, without bloating and IBS. My lifestyle is gluten-free. My mouth likes bread, but my body does not and I treat the latter with the kindness and respect that it deserves.

Never sacrifice your needs for the needs of those around you. This used to be something that I really struggled with. Having been told all my life that we must put others first, I found it difficult to put myself first. I thought I was being selfish, and in large part this was a result of how others treated or perceived me on the few occasions where I didn't put their needs before my own. My beliefs changed for the better when my first coach explained to me that life is a gift – if we live it for others then we aren't really treasuring our own presence. The truth is, if you take care of yourself first, then you are best equipped to serve others. As a working mother of four, I needed to be well to look after our large and busy family. Yes, I exercised and ate wholesome healthy foods, but I had factored in little down time just for me to relax. So be badass, honour and prioritise the commitments that you make to yourself. Stop your distractions, so you can live in balance, with work, rest and play, in a way that suits your needs.

After James left me, I didn't exercise enough self-care. I continually filled my diary, ensuring it had few gaps, because I hated being on my own all the time. What I didn't realise, is that I was doing this so I didn't have to face my thoughts and feelings. I couldn't deal with them. Soon, my busyness became monotonous, and I finally realised that I needed time to rest. With this in mind, it's important to ensure you take regular downtime, thus preventing burnout or dis-ease. Today, I am much better at listening to my own needs. This was reflected during the writing of this book – after having a brief spell of illness I visited friends instead of getting straight back into writing (which I would have done in the past), in order to regroup and uplift myself. I wanted to honour my basic needs for human connection before I got back to writing. Throughout this project, my principle has been only to write when I am feeling in flow. I like to give myself space to just "be" – after all, we are human beings, not human doings. This also helped me to recognise my distractions, ensuring that I stopped unhelpful habits, staying disciplined and motivated. It's all about balance and recognising your own distraction patterns and behaviours, particularly the ones that hinder your progress.

Set Boundaries

In the past I didn't have any boundaries; my life was very reactive, run by other's wants and needs. Setting limits is a good way to love yourself more. It's okay to say no to extra work, love or activities that deplete or harm you physically, emotionally and spiritually. My boundaries were poor, because I allowed others to continually drive my bus. A good example of this is from the story I told in part one, where I was given a tennis racket for my eighteenth birthday, only to be told by James that I'd never be able to play well because I had small, weak wrists. He was older than me and very sporty, so I believed him and duly put the racket away without protest. I gave up before I had even begun, putting another person's opinion before my own dreams. If this happened now, my reaction would be very different; looking back I can see that small signs of this "rebellion" were already beginning to take hold during the later stages of my marriage. I recall James telling my daughter that she didn't have the right temperament to study law and that she shouldn't pursue it as a career. Mainly, we were a united front, but here I felt so strongly that his beliefs were wrong; I went against him and told her to pursue it. Fortunately, she listened to me and is now an excellent solicitor who gets wonderful feedback from her clients. The bottom line is this: we can only really know what we are truly capable of if we test ourselves. You have nothing to lose by giving yourself the chance to succeed. So, be proactive and make sure you are in the driver's seat of your own bus.

Since I began to treat myself with more respect, I have noticed that friends in my circle now treat me with more respect, as I have stronger boundaries. In the past I've had relationships with people purely on the basis that I didn't want to hurt their feelings, but in reality I was only hurting myself and them in the long-term too – because a relationship can never work under these circumstances. Now, I look out for my own needs first, which puts me in a better position to treat other people in the right way, with kindness and respect. If anyone who previously treated me poorly continued to do so, then we simply wouldn't be friends, as there wouldn't be any resonance between us. On the flip side, if you are in a similar situation, then it's important to remember that everyone is doing their best. We all make mistakes and sometimes people are late or forgetful or even rude without meaning to be. But, if you think that someone really isn't serving your personal needs any longer, it's time to let them go – with love, light and blessings. Letting go makes space for new people and experiences to enter, ones which are more suited to you and provide a better vibrational match. However, before you cut anyone from your life, try and take a moment to put yourself in their shoes. Perhaps there's a reason they are behaving this way, perhaps they have received awful news or were experiencing a terrible problem. This compassion doesn't mean forgoing your boundaries and condoning the behaviour of those who continually inflict hurt without remorse, but it does mean that you can be more understanding of those who are having problems right now.

Ask yourself the following questions:

- Are you easily swayed to do what others want you to do? In what ways have your boundaries weakened?

- How would you deal with this differently next time? Can you think of ways to better enforce your boundaries at work and in your personal relationships?

A common scenario where this problem arises, is when people are asked to work overtime. This can be tricky, especially if the extra hours will interfere with an important event, such as a family function. In these cases, it's time to be polite but firm. Where you might once have immediately backed down, now you must develop the strength to stop being fearful about losing your job and politely decline. A good example of this was with my client, Jennifer. Jennifer was frequently being asked to take on extra work and this was interfering with her personal life. She found that when she eventually stood up for herself, her boss seemed to have more respect and stopped making unreasonable requests. Another client, Selena, was fed up with her partner always choosing where they went out to eat, but didn't have the required self-care to stand up and take charge herself. I asked her what changes she felt she could make. We discussed various scenarios, and Selena ultimately decided to pre-empt her husband by booking a venue of her choice. When telling her husband about their date, she said that she thought it would be a wonderful surprise for him if she took charge. He was a bit disgruntled at first, but then realised it was nice having her make the arrangements for a change.

One way to consider your boundaries is by drawing two hearts on sheets of A4 paper. Write the title "Acceptable" on one page and "Unacceptable" on the other. Then make your lists. As usual, I like to decorate mine to make it more personal. Once you have finished writing, you could even draw a red line across the unacceptable heart, to further emphasise what isn't ok for you. Then, dispose of this in whatever way you choose.

Find Your Precious People

My relocation to Dorset led me to feel a powerful sense of belonging, a sense of community. Here, I've met like-minded people who are reliable, trustworthy, honest, caring, thoughtful, understanding, compassionate, loyal and spiritual. I finally feel understood and accepted for whom I am, with a sense of being in the right place, of coming home to where I want to be right now.

However independent you are, thinking you can do everything for yourself can be lonely, so it's important to have nurturing, like-minded people that you can also have fun with. It also helps to have the support and love from people around you to stay motivated and keep on track. Positive energy is contagious, so it's imperative to surround yourself with a community of people that you value. Release all so-called friends who take pleasure in your pain and loss, who are jealous when you do well or who are draining you with their constant moans and complaints. In the past I had friends who, when I had high blood sugar levels, would still buy me alcoholic drinks – even when I specifically declined. They didn't really care, because they wanted me to be more like them, as I had been before. They now deemed me as boring. They didn't appreciate the latest version of me, who took more care of what I put into my body. If you are familiar with the term "crab buckets", which is where an escaping crab is pulled back into the bucket by its chums, then you might know what I mean! I am now blessed to have people in my life who fully accept me as the quirky individual I am. We have mutual care, understanding and support. No more crab bucket chums.

Surround yourself with friends who have a positive mindset. Develop and maintain relationships where you are mutually supportive and uplift each other. No one is perfect and you all have your low times. So, accept these, but don't wallow in them. Take steps to solve your challenges and overcome issues. My client Paula had friends who would frequently designate her as the driver on their outings. This meant that she had to forgo drinking and be vigilant, as her friends would get roaring drunk and behave irresponsibly, knowing that she would always take care of them. Paula got to the point where she no longer wanted to socialise, as she didn't enjoy it anymore. After coming to me for a couple of sessions to address her dissatisfaction with life, she became more assertive and informed her friends that she wouldn't be ferrying them around any longer. Paula also widened her social circle, finding friends who appreciated her company and who didn't take advantage of her generous, caring nature. Act with integrity and authenticity to be the most impeccable person you can be. Remember that when you love, respect and honour yourself, others will know to treat you that way. Open your heart, feeling full of love, then radiate it out into the world. When you do this, other like-minded people will be drawn to you.

Forgive Yourself and Others

Do you treat yourself harshly when judging your behaviours and actions or do you treat yourself like your own best friend? In the past, I was definitely my harshest critic. Now I know that taking responsibility for my actions is important, but berating myself for my mistakes serves no purpose and only culminates in me feeling sad and ashamed. Think about a time when you've judged yourself harshly; can you now forgive yourself? As mentioned in part one, until I was in my early fifties I judged myself harshly about an incident when I was thirteen, where my married science teacher kept me behind for detention after school and took me out on many dates, because he fancied me. I believed this was entirely my fault, despite only being a child. However, I eventually realised he had abused his power of authority. As a fully grown adult, he was the irresponsible one. So I finally forgave myself. Funnily enough I never really held negative thoughts or emotions towards this teacher and I continued to see him over the years with James and our family until he moved away to Scotland. So, it wasn't necessary for me to perform a forgiveness process in regards to him personally.

After James left, I forgave him and was grateful, because it led me to finding the strength to overcome my challenges. My belief is that James and I agreed to marry and divorce **before** incarnating on earth, for my soul's expansion. All of your so-called "mistakes" are a gift leading to your learning and growth. Interestingly, when I was teaching, this was an idea that I fully promoted to my students; and yet it wasn't until I underwent NLP practitioner training that I realised I was treating myself differently. I still expected to instantly know how to do something perfectly, without any practice. NLP showed me that there is no failure, only feedback – meaning that you haven't yet learnt how to do the task properly, so try again with some changes. Instead of being unkind and inconsiderate to yourself, be gentle, kind, cherishing and forgiving as you would to a young child or your best friend. Accept that you are human and are imperfect and that you are always a work in progress. Mistakes can teach you to clarify what you really want and how you want to live. So, ask yourself this: what do you want to be, do and have? How can you forgive others for their simple, human mistakes?

By forgiving others, you release all the negative thoughts and emotions in your body. This doesn't mean condoning other people's poor behaviour, it just means that you are ready and willing to let go. Remember that forgiving is healing; all your negative emotions are like a poison in your body. I have used various forgiveness processes but love the simplicity of Ho'oponopono – 'I'm sorry. Please forgive me. Thank you. I love you.' In *Zero Limits*, Joe Vitale says, "The process is about cleansing your thoughts and living a purposeful life." He explains that it helps you to forget bad memories, because you have less feelings of upset towards these memories, further stating, "The four steps involved in this practice make you realise the fact that you are responsible for everything that happens to you and that is in your mind. Once you understand this fact it becomes easier for you to start practicing the steps." (See part six for more on this process!)

As Joe puts it, "Ho'oponopono makes you stronger and gives you the courage to face the truth and tell the truth. You will feel better when you know that your request for the forgiveness has been granted and people are going to trust you again. There are no human beings in the planet who do not commit sins, either knowingly or unknowingly. The ones who have the courage to see their mistake and who come forward to seek forgiveness, are the successful ones. Live your life with no grudges and you will be the happiest one. The practice makes you love everything that belongs to you. Life is not about yourself but everyone and everything that is connected to you as well. It is necessary you take life as one beautiful chance given to you by the Creator and handle it with care."

I used Ho'oponopono over and over every day when on my Cathar pilgrimage in France to help heal the distress caused by one of the facilitator's assistants, who was hurtful to me daily. My continued repetition of the sentences and faith in the process was apparently successful, because by the end of the trip he had asked to be friends and connect on Facebook. A brief explanation of how this works is that I say to the person or situation which has brought me suffering: 'I recognise that what I see in you is mirrored in me, and vice versa. I'm sorry that I had not recognised the flaws in me, so I had to see them in you. Forgive my ignorance, the fear underlying that, keeping me blind to the truth. I love and recognise the Divine at the core of your being and thank you for the opportunity to become more aware of that in me, I can now better see mirrored in you. The more I uncover and release my ignorance and fear, the more of the Divine I can recognise in you.' For further inspiration and exploration, read Joe Vitale's book *Zero Limits* (his online certified practitioner and advanced courses take the four statements into a greater depth too).

In short, it's time to stop living in the past, causing depression and letting the future make you anxious. Live in the now! This has been invaluable to me during COVID-19. I remind myself that for today I have a roof over my head, food in the fridge and water to drink. So, I am okay! For more understanding of what this means, you can read *The Power of Now* by Eckhart Tolle.

Ask yourself the following questions:

- How can you be more kind to yourself?

- Who can you forgive? Can you forgive yourself?

- Write a list of your achievements and things you like about yourself.

- What is the best thing that could happen?

Living Intentionally

Before getting up in the morning, you can set your intentions for the day. This ensures that you feel good before your day begins. Visualise how you would like it to be and what you will see, hear and feel. Although I don't do this every single day, I do it often, and especially when there are times when I have specific outcomes in mind that I feel may need some extra support. When I was attending a conference in Amsterdam, I met Lynne McTaggart, who discussed her "Intention Experiment". This experiment revealed that the universe is connected by a vast quantum energy field and that thought generates its own palpable energy, which you can use to improve your life. Lynne's findings make you rethink what it is to be human, proving that everything and everyone is connected and show why you need to pay better attention to your thoughts, intentions and actions, as they impact your life on a grand scale. Lynne has written numerous books on the subject, including *The Intention Experiment*, *The Field*, *The Power of Eight* and *What Doctors Don't Tell You*. In part seven of this book, I'll go into more detail about connections and energy.

During the moon phases, I set powerful intentions when conducting my ceremonies. Science tells us that the moon affects our moods, especially during full moons (more people commit crimes and suicide or are admitted to mental health facilities than at any other time of the month). During full moon phases, the first thing I do to prepare for my ritual is to clean my home, then I cleanse and clear it to freshen the energies. To cleanse and clear, I use one or a combination of basilica, white sage, my space clearing aura/room spray, palo santo or incense. I especially like frankincense. I often use sound too, mainly utilising my drum or celestial tuning forks and occasionally my big gongs, but you could tone, sing or clap your hands if you don't have these. By releasing the negative energies of my home I am also letting go of what I no longer need, such as old programming, negative emotions, limiting beliefs or any issues that are holding me back. These are excellent practices to carry out, as they remove accumulated negativity from my surroundings and myself, making space for the new to enter.

Next I take a bath with Epsom salts, rose essential oil or whatever takes my fancy, sometimes adding in rose petals, rosemary or other natural flowers or herbs. Epsom salts pull toxins from your body, reduce inflammation, promote weight loss and are relaxing. They also reduce stress, improve circulation, provide relief for achy and stiff muscles and improve sleep, psoriasis, fibromyalgia, ingrown toenails and insulin sensitivity. Note that if you add lavender essential oil or eucalyptus oil, it can soothe irritated skin (another option is to add some apple cider vinegar to soften your skin and rebalance your skin pH, or baking soda which also softens skin and has antibacterial properties useful for foot fungi). When I have no access to a bath, I rub my body with a mix of oils and salts before having a shower, with the intention that they do the same as when I bathe in them.

During my bath or shower I visualise my energy being cleansed, cleared and revitalised, allowing the latest vibrant energies to enter. I see all my "blocks" being drawn from my body by a large magnet at the bottom of the sea near where I live, to be transmuted by Mother Earth (*this is adapted from Art Giser's "Energetic NLP" Lake Process. See the links to his website in my useful resources page if you wish to train with him). Some declarations I make are:

- 'I now leave my past behind.'

- 'I immerse myself in the energy of my rebirth.'

- 'I am a new me and tomorrow is a fresh and wonderful day.'

Then, I create an altar. While I vary what objects I use, I will generally utilise items or pictures that symbolise the four directions:

North is the earth element, so a crystal and stones, flowers, herbs, seeds, soil, a salt candle holder, my twisted hazel twig or my money plant is used.

East is the air element. I often use incense, especially frankincense, a feather and a wand (I am blessed to have a clear quartz wand encrusted with crystals for each chakra, a copper one with a pointed clear quartz and a wooden one with a clear quartz point).

South is the fire element, so a candle, written notes of what I wish to release (to be placed on the fire afterwards) or burning herbs.

West is the final direction, and represents the water element. So, I use a small heart dish with water, pictures of lakes or oceans, a goblet, my miniature cauldron or a small mirror. I also display statues of angels, dragons, unicorns and the ancient deities Isis, Quan Yin, Buddha, Hanuman (the monkey god as I was born in the year of the monkey), Lakshmi (for abundance) or others. I also include some relevant oracle cards.

Following this, I light the candles. I may add other crystals, fresh flowers, a pine cone to represent the pineal gland, symbols or pictures representing what I wish to let go of. Then I call in the four directions – inviting my Ancestors, Star Family and others to be part of the ceremony.

The next stage is where I make dedications and invocations. I write a list of everything that I consciously know to release, adding as an addendum, 'I am open to releasing all that isn't for my highest good, even though I may have no idea what they are.' I then read my list out loud to the Universe/God, in order to fully embrace and feel that everything is leaving. After that, I tear my list into pieces, add the pieces to a metal container I have at home and light them with a match. I add some frankincense to the fire (keep a jug of water nearby in case of an accident) and give thanks for the transformation taking place, plus all my lessons from my experiences. I then return my ancestors and the others from higher realms with thanks. I have also carried out ceremonies in my garden, on the beach (using driftwood and other beach artefacts), as well as making many pilgrimages to sacred sites – particularly for moon ceremonies, solstices and equinoxes.

A wonderful reverential way we honoured Mother Earth, when I was with Davina MacKail and her friends (who are Peruvian Shamans), was by holding a Despacho ceremony at Lake Titicaca. It was lovely, as the locals dressed us in their traditional clothing. This is a prayer offering ceremony, which helps with healing physical and emotional ailments. A prayer offering can be made for many things, whether it's for gratitude, healing emotional and physical ailments, birth and death or restoring harmony and balance. Gifts are offered and placed in the fire for thanks and gratitude. Many times, in different gatherings, I have presented the fire with my "giveaways" and thanked it with gifts. At other times I have placed my "giveaways" into a crystal and buried it in Mother Earth, the sea or a lake, returning it to its origin. The key focus is on releasing during the full moon. Having completed my ceremony, I change focus, contemplating my intentions for the life I wish to lead – as this changes the energy to the positive.

In contrast to the full moon, the new moon's focus is about bringing **in** your desires. The new moon is an auspicious time to begin something new; I use it to reaffirm, with more impetus, my daily faith and trust. I renew my commitments and focus on what I want to bring into my life. I begin the same as with the full moon, by cleaning, cleansing and clearing my home. Again I bathe or shower with Epsom salts and essential oils, visualising my body and my energy as being clean, clear and revitalised, thus allowing the latest vibrant energies to enter. Some affirmations I use to anchor my intentions are:

'I am open to accepting and receiving new beginnings now.'

'I am renewed, revitalised and re-energised with this new moon.'

'My world is full of opportunities and potentials.'

'I am open to more abundance and possibilities unfolding in my life.'

Affirmations are a great way to anchor your dreams. Other ways I anchor are by using sound, smell and movement. I finish my bathing by toning my chakras to balance them (part six has the tones for each chakra).

As with the full moon, I create my altar – lighting a candle and adding some crystals, a fresh flower, items or pictures that represent my intentions, plus anything else I feel guided to add. I call in "my team", welcoming them to join the ceremony. I make dedications and recite invocations. Then I write down all my desires as specifically as possible, placing the words and symbols inside a large heart using different coloured pens. After that I read my list out loud, to speak it into existence, for the Universe to hear and fulfil my dreams. On some occasions I also create a mini vision board using words and pictures of my wishes (my main large vision board I make on my birthday when I start my new year). I then close my eyes and see myself as already having my desires. Finally, I thank the Universe for my abundance in advance, feeling blessed.

According to Maslow and his hierarchy of needs, you can love and accept yourselves more when you live your life with a purpose, regardless of whatever is happening. Maslow theorised that we all have a need to feel there is a purpose to our lives. This doesn't have to be a huge mission/vision, although it can be. Perhaps your intention is to live a healthy and meaningful life and to be the best person you can be, by spreading love, joy and inspiration within your family. Conversely, it could be to spread this love and joy out globally – through setting up an organisation to do this.

Upon having an intention, you will then make decisions that support this intention and feel good about yourself when succeeding in this purpose. A good example of this was when I opened a nursery school in Doha. Most people (including James) thought I was crazy, because I was shortly due to return to the UK to give birth. Despite James's initial misgivings, he fully supported me and helped me set it up. I employed two members of staff whom I trusted, who kept it going whilst I was back home to give birth. My nursery was a fantastic success, running for five years. Couples put their children's names on my waiting list once they knew they were pregnant. On leaving Doha I gave it away, attracting huge interest from potential new owners, as it had been so successful. I felt strongly guided to implement my intention, and thus it had a brilliant, positive outcome.

Conversely, without a purpose you may just be drifting through life on a day-to-day basis with no plans or goals. I felt a bit lost when I moved down to my new home in Dorset, as I didn't know anyone. I joined in lots of activities and met new friends, but was unsure whether I would create a coaching practice, as there were so many others doing the same thing. I felt I had little purpose, which left me feeling like a log in the sea, just drifting along aimlessly. It felt uncomfortable not doing anything, especially in comparison to my previous career as a teacher when I rarely had time for myself unless in the bath (even then when the kids were young they wanted to join me). However, when talking with a friend who was selling her positive living group, I suddenly found my purpose! Another friend and I bought the business together, which involved co-hosting speakers who talked on wellbeing and spiritual matters. I immediately felt galvanised to take action and began to organise events. I felt more alive, worthwhile and elevated, with something to focus on that was good for my community as well as for me. All this creativity came from my sacral chakra, which as a manifesting generator in human design is how I live and create in flow, free from forcing situations.

My intention has been to be stay true to myself, in alignment with my inner guidance. I have often made decisions and choices in life that have made me scared, but I have still carried them out. This included moving to the Middle East with a young family, leaving private school for state school to teach and relocating from Bedfordshire to Dorset – far away from anyone I knew. My life has been lived by the maxim to *go beyond my fear and just do it!* This has led me to an enriching life, full of growth. Most of my experiences are without regret, even the negative ones usually have a silver lining. For example, my divorce has enabled me to travel, study, and live where I wish to, with more self-awareness and an increased ability to tap into my own resources. I see many people whom I knew over thirty years ago still living the same life over and over, like groundhog day. Some are happy, which is great, but some wanted change and were too afraid. Thus, they've lived only half the life they wanted for themselves. It's time for you, dear reader, to be a badass. Start living your life with intention! Before you move on, ask yourself the following questions:

- Are you living a life you love? If not, what can you do to change that?

- How can you be truer to you (authentic)?

- Do you have a vision and purpose for your life? If so, what is it?

- As you have grown, has your purpose changed?

Morning Practice

I have created a daily routine, which I do before I get out of bed every morning. This puts me into a good vibration and sets me up for the day. I repeat this before I go to bed too, so that I can dream and wake up in a good frame of mind. Worrying about things that went on in the day or what will take place the next day, can make you agitated, which leads to poor quality sleep.

The first thing I do, is to sing a little ditty: 'Every little cell in my body is happy, every little cell in my body is well (repeat). I can tell all is well, every little cell in my body is well (repeat).' I sing this whole song twice or more, as it informs my body that everything is working well and healthy (on my YouTube channel "Denise Davis Harmonise Your Heart", one of the clips is me singing the song, so you can hear the tune). Remember that your unconscious mind is always listening to your thoughts and what you say, so it's important that you tell it positive things.

The second thing I always do before I arise is to express my gratitude. I do this at other times of the day too, whenever I feel called to express it. Gratitude is an essential part of my daily life. Even when circumstances have been challenging, I have always found things to be grateful for, such as my body – that allows me to experience life, my eyes – that see the surrounding beauty, for everyone I love having in my life and for fresh running water. Recently, I did a thirty-day challenge of appreciation. Each day I had to write ten new things to be grateful for and say why. Nearer the end of the period, when it was more difficult to find new appreciations, I thanked my eyelashes for protecting my eyes from dust and dirt and other thanks went to the support services such as nurses, firefighters and police officers. Ask yourself this, dear reader: what ten things can you be grateful for today – including things about yourself?

As I mentioned in part four, I was blessed to see Dr Masaru Emoto in Amsterdam at a conference I attended, where he discussed his many experiments and showed us evidential pictures showing how words affected water. The contrast between the positive and negative words was dramatic. Remember, your body is made up of roughly 70% water and your brain is 90% water! Your words are like spells that affect your body, hence you can appreciate the importance of good self-talk (that's why word tests in schools are called spelling tests, because words are important!). In line with this, I often repeat Access Consciousness statements such as 'Everything in my life comes to me with ease, joy and glory', 'What else is possible?' and 'How does it get any better than this?' I also make positive statements, which I learnt when doing smart goals in my NLP and Time Line Therapy.

Wayne Dyer calls his sayings "I AM" statements and has many wonderful books and YouTube videos on this topic. I often use this when making my own statements, including:

- 'I AM abundant.'

- 'The Universe has my back, always, in all ways.'

- 'I AM love, loved and loveable.'

- 'I AM always safe, secure and protected.'

- 'I AM vibrant, vital and healthy.'

- 'My life is a gift and I am grateful to be alive.'

- 'I AM that I am.'

- 'I give myself my own love.'

- 'Why is my life rich and fulfilling?'

- 'Why does everyone in my life treat me with love and respect?'

(Noah St. John is the creator of the why sentences, which are called "Afformations"– see the link to his website on the useful resources page.)

When making these declarations out loud or in my mind, I make sure I am in a relaxed state, so that the suggestions are going directly to my unconscious mind. During my clinical hypnotherapy lessons I was told that self-suggestions are potent and that they are even more effective than directives given by others. I vary the statements and questions I use. One statement I like to make often is, 'Everything is always working out for me.' Sometimes I set intentions and visualise the day as I would like to experience it, as mentioned in the living intentionally section.

When I am feeling below par, I do a brain dump by journaling. I may also listen to wellbeing YouTube clips, such as the Solfeggio frequencies, Esther Hicks or other videos which channel information. One thing that always lights me up and makes my heart sing with feelings of great love and joy, is looking at photos and videos of my grandchildren – this is a wonderful and uplifting way to begin my day.

Daily Feel-Good Exercises

Give yourself permission to feel your emotions, as they're part of your humanity. One of my clients, Dana, was feeling disappointed and unhappy – as her business venture wasn't going to plan. She had sat with her feelings for a while, but they didn't dissipate. So, she came to me for a session. I used the Emotion Code to release her trapped emotions around her business. I finished up the session using some Access Consciousness, leaving Dana feeling lighter, brighter and more flexible to go with the flow. During our next session I did some hypnotherapy to enhance Dana's self-esteem, leaving her more inspired and motivated. She then felt more able to think outside of the box and see things with a brand new perspective. I regularly use the Emotion Code and Access Consciousness on myself and with others, which requires me to give myself permission to release my unwanted thoughts and emotions (further info in part six). You can do these yourself or book a session with me (www.denisedavis.co.uk).

Chanting mantras is a really good way to help you shift your energy and manifest desires such as love and abundance. Specifically, it's good to focus on sacred sounds, formed by speaking ancient Sanskrit syllables. These sounds profoundly influence your subconscious mind and are used to help heal and transform your mind, body and spirit. Neuroscientists with advanced brain mapping tools have quantified and confirmed the benefits of chanting, demonstrating that it can free your mind from background chatter and calm your nervous system. In the *Journal of Cognitive Enhancement*, researchers from Linkoping University in Sweden measured activity in a brain region called the "default mode network", which is the area active during self-reflection and mind wandering, to determine how practising mantra meditation affects your brain. Over a period of two weeks and six sessions, students recited the Sat Nam mantra (true identity) whilst placing their hands over their hearts for eleven minutes. In contrast, they were also instructed to do a slow-based button pressing exercise. The subjects' default mode network settings were suppressed when chanting the mantra, in comparison to the finger pressing exercise, meaning that relaxation and calmness was more present. The more practise of the mantra meditation was conducted, the more pronounced this became. Other research showed that it doesn't matter what you recite, whether a sentence or word in any language – if you repeat something with focused attention then you will get results.

By using the power of vibrational sound, mantras can bypass your conscious mind's programming, to reach the deepest layers of your subconscious. While working to harmonise and balance, they also help to instil new, more positive beliefs. I have chanted in groups and alone. Some mantras I particularly like are as follows:

"Om Mani Padme Hum"

- Om is the sound of the Universe.

- Ma removes the attachment to jealousy and establishes ethics.

- Ni removes the attachment to desire and establishes patience.

- Pad removes the attachment to prejudice and establishes perseverance.

- Me removes the attachment to possessiveness and establishes concentration

- Hum removes the attachment to hatred and establishes wisdom.

"Nam Mayo Renge Kyo"

- This is a vow, an expression of determination to embrace and manifest your Buddha nature, a pledge to never yield to difficulties and to win over one's suffering.

- Nam means devotion and dedication,

- Myo is mystic or wonderful.

- Ho means law.

- Renge means lotus blossom, which is pure and fragrant, unsullied by the muddy water it grows in.

- Kyo means sutra and is said to be like a thread which represents the basic reality of life.

Other mantras include:

- "Sat Chit Ananda" – existence, consciousness and bliss.

- "Aham Bramasmi" – I am the absolute.

- "So Hum" – I am that identifying oneself with the universe.

- Tina Turner's version of "Sarvesham Svastir Bhavatu" (peace mantra).

- "Aham Prema" (I am Divine Love). There is a version where someone has written the lyrics so you can join in or you can just listen. Find ones that resonate with you – there are many on YouTube.

In my living intention section, I mentioned how you can do visual rehearsal for your desires by closing your eyes and imagining your wishes are happening right now – with all the feelings, sights and sounds as accompaniments. You can do this whenever you have the time or need for it.

You Are The Map

Never forget that the roadmap to finding love begins and ends with you. A powerful form of freedom is letting go of everything extraneous and only focusing on what matters to you. Energy flows to where attention goes, so be mindful of where you focus (more in part seven on this). I have trust and faith, but that doesn't always mean that I think things will be beautiful all the time with rainbows and unicorns. I know that sometimes the Universe will not stop the storm, but I trust that it will strengthen me as I walk through it.

When it comes to sensitivity, in the past I was always told by my family and friends that I was "over-sensitive". Therefore, it was refreshing to discover (in my fifties!) that I wasn't alone in this, and that there was even a term for how I felt. As an empath and HSP (Highly Sensitive Person), which apparently makes up 15-20% of the population, I feel things more strongly than most people. However, there are things that I do myself to prevent negative influences on my mind and body. For example, I've stopped watching soaps and the news, because as a sensitive person I found them upsetting and distressing. Because they were negative and I was unable to impart any change on them, they lowered my mood and vibrations. So, it seemed prudent to stop hurting myself. I would hear what was really important anyway, as some of my less esoteric friends would share what was going on in the world. I also take great care when choosing movies, television programmes and books, for the same reason. If you want to find out more information on signs of a sensitive person, Google search "Psychology Today – 24 signs of a sensitive person".

If you are ever feeling overwhelmed, then it's a good idea to take a moment and understand that it's okay to do just one thing at a time. At the beginning of my divorce, I became extremely distressed; my thoughts and emotions were all over the place, and I was overwhelmed by the sheer number of things that needed to be taken care of. I just didn't know where to start. However, I swiftly realised that in order for me to remain calm and in control, I needed to focus on just one thing at a time. On the really bad days, instead of taking one day at a time, I would split my day into three. I would think *thank goodness I have survived the morning,* which really helped reduce my feelings of being incapable. Many years later, I came across a book about the Japanese tradition of "Kaizen", which is about breaking big tasks down into small steps and doing them one at a time. The book *One Small Step Can Change Your Life* by Robert Maurer, Ph.D., does a fantastic job of explaining why focusing on one thing helps reduce anxiety.

Again, to reiterate, always listen to your body. Be guided by your feelings on when you need to rest, recuperate and heal. In the past, when I've pressed on and continued to work, without heeding the signals, circumstances were more prolonged – as my mental, emotional and physical health required more downtime than if I had heeded the call to rest earlier. My intuition is so vital and I almost always follow it now. As mentioned earlier, if you listen to your inner guidance and follows the signs, you will instinctively know which decisions to make and which actions to take.

Earlier in the book I suggested that you wear certain colours, such as yellow, to serve as a reminder of sunny cheery days and to balance your solar plexus energy centre, which is your power base. You can also make a plate of food using a wide variety of colours – eating the rainbow. Including colour in your diet can ensure you're getting enough fibre, minerals, vitamins and antioxidants to help you prevent bone density loss, digestive issues, blood pressure and assist with weight management. Red cabbage, red onion and beetroot are packed with polyphenols, which are an antioxidant. Yellow fruits and vegetables are substantial sources of vitamins and antioxidants, which some say can help combat certain kinds of cancer and are good for your heart and eyes. Mangos and bananas are beneficial to your skin because of the high amounts of vitamin A in them. Pink food, such as pink grapefruit, is high in antioxidant lycopene and vitamin C, folate and potassium. Green foods get their colour from chlorophyll, which helps your body eliminate toxins. Orange foods can support eye health and reduce risk of macular degeneration, reduce blood pressure and lower cholesterol. They may help prevent diabetes, boost your immune system, fight free radicals in your body and support healthy bones and joints. Purple foods are rich in anthocyanins, which are natural plant pigments that help brain health, lower inflammation, fight cancer and heart disease. Blue foods are antioxidants and anti-inflammatory. Apart from protecting against oxidative cell damage that can lead to Alzheimer's, cancer and heart disease, they have been linked to reducing chronic inflammation. Blue foods, especially blueberries, have other health benefits too – including urinary tract and vision health.

As a future life progression and past life regression practitioner, I often have sessions with a colleague to gain insights from my future self on how to move forward and what possibilities my life holds. When having past life progression sessions, I have discovered what was affecting me now from a past life. With this knowledge it was easier to clear blocks and move forward (more info on this in part six, plus a case study of my client Jonathan's experiences in part seven).

Now dear reader, it is your turn. Ask yourself the following questions:

- What will you do today to harmonise your heart?

- Will you have fun creating your own positive "I AM" affirmations? Can you consider how you would like your day to be and set your intentions?

- Will you journal your positive and negative thoughts as a catharsis and a record of your joy?

Be Kind and Gentle With Yourself and Others

It's so important that we are kind to others. A good way to do this, is to *listen* consciously to understand, *not* to think about your reply. Choose your words wisely when speaking to others, as words are like spells and can have a big impact. Spread love and compliments where you can – pleasant thoughts are wasted in your head and could be used to brighten up another person's day. Have good manners, thank people and let them know when you enjoyed spending time with them. Whether it's family, friends or an exemplary service you received – you can text, write a Facebook post tagging them, send a card or a little gift.

Give the people you love space to make mistakes. Be compassionate of their challenges and appreciative of their efforts, remembering to give yourself understanding while you learn how to truly love yourself. Since kindness is a key to love, extend kindness to yourself every day. Ultimately, your relationship with yourself is like any other in life: it takes time and effort to build trust, learn to communicate and create a loving connection. Maybe you've heard that to love someone else you must first learn to love yourself. But in order to really love yourself, sometimes you may have to recognise all the love you have around you. I was blessed to meet Dr David Hamilton at a few of his talks, who says that when we extend kindness to others, we also feel the benefit. According to him, kindness is a fabulous way to extend your lifespan. Dr Hamilton talks about this extensively in his book, *Why Kindness Is Good For You*.

When feeling low or sad, go within and acknowledge what's working, then make a "What's Working for Me" list. Once you see it on paper and accept all the positivity in your life, it will make it that much easier to love yourself.

Use affirmations to reaffirm how you want to be (you can use as below or tweak and create your own):

- 'I release all limiting beliefs of who I am.'

- 'I am worthy and deserving of love and respect.'

- 'I meet my own needs with love.'

- 'I teach others how to love me, by how well I love myself.'

- 'It's safe for me to say yes to my needs.'

- 'I love being healthy and balanced.'

- 'I am deeply supported in my wellbeing.'

- 'I am whole and complete and more than enough.'

- 'Self-care is selfless, and I honour myself.'

- 'The more I give to myself, the more I have to give.'

- 'My self-love gives others permission to love themselves too.'

In what ways can you give kindness to yourself today? Read a book, spend time with a loved one, forgive yourself for some supposed misdemeanour – you will find your own unique way to be kind to you. How will you be kind to others? Pay it forward by smiling, buying coffee for someone in need or assisting others with chores.

Feng Shui

So, we have discussed clearing your energetic systems, mind and emotions, which are important to your wellbeing. Another way to carry this out is to physically clear out stuff from your home you don't need anymore. This can include anything from unused clothes, shoes, jewellery or paperwork you don't need anymore – essentially anything that reminds you of a particular negative time in your life.

In certain Feng Shui disciplines, where you place things makes a difference. Bearing this in mind, I take special care as to where I place certain objects around the house, such as my citrine crystals and my money gratitude jar, which are in my money corner. As I would like to be in a committed relationship, I have placed little statues of a couple in each room.

When I consulted a Feng Shui practitioner, they plotted the heart of my home. Using your house plans, you can work out where your centre is. I discovered it was in two places for me, because my home is quirky and upside down on three floors. The top part of the heart of my home has a window opposite my front door and my lounge window. Apparently anything that comes in, such as money, will speed out through the glass. I was advised to place voile curtains on the window to slow down the chi (energy). At the same spot there is a radiator, and I was told it wasn't good to have fire in the heart and so to leave this radiator off. I followed the advice and added pretty voile curtains at the window. I am chuffed, as it looks softer, as well as slowing down the chi. I changed my usual cover over the radiator to match the curtains, as it looked so stark and ugly being the first thing you see when you enter my home. Now the window and radiator look more feminine and pleasing to my eye, as well as giving an improved energetic benefit.

The second heart of my home is directly below the front door, in a cupboard which previously housed loads of my art supplies. According to the Feng Shui expert, there was no space for the chi to flow freely. It was suggested that I take the cupboard doors off and completely empty the cupboard. I was also advised to place something natural inside, like a large stone Buddha or large pink quartz crystal. As you come in through my front door, you would look down and see the Buddha/crystal with lots of space surrounding it, allowing energy to flow. Apparently this is a marvellous way to increase your abundance.

Of course, it's not always easy to let go. Many people hold on to sentimental objects for personal reasons – such as items given to them by deceased relatives. If this is the case, then it may be that you just need to build up your ability to release. Items from your past can drain, weigh heavy on your soul and contribute to low self-esteem. Although you may be holding on to protect yourself from hurting, you are holding yourself back from moving forward, from reaching optimal self-acceptance, loving who you are and realising your full potential in life. There's no better feeling than finally realising you have a deeply loving, unconditional, mutually fulfilling relationship with yourself.

Explore Life

I have always loved learning, exploring new things and experiences, preventing boredom and stagnation. It also helps my expansion and growth. When I got divorced, I discovered spirituality and what it means for me. Believing in something greater than yourself opens up your soul to the beauty of belief and trust in a benevolent world, one which is conspiring with you rather than against you. It builds your intuition and helps you decide based on your heart, head and gut – your three brains. When you explore your spirituality, it also takes you on a journey to learning things about yourself, with new thoughts, feelings, passions and raw emotions; you'll learn to appreciate yourself for being authentically you.

When you choose just a few of these self-love actions to work on, you will begin to love and accept yourself more. Imagine how much you will appreciate you when you utilise some of the suggestions, and how wonderful you will feel as a cup half-full person! To recap, it's important to fill your own cup first before giving to another. Remember, some say that we can only love another person as much as we love ourselves, or as Polonius said, "This above all: to thine own self be true." If like me you love new experiences, then go to other countries and explore their culture, visit new places, meet new people and learn things that interest you.

By loving yourself more, you set a marvellous example to others in your life. This allows and encourages them to express themselves in the same way. You can live with others more inter-dependently than co-dependently, thus enriching everyone's lives in an expansive, fulfilling way, instead of a needy, constricting way. Being congruent with yourself means that you are energetically raising your vibrations and attracting more people and circumstances that support your wellbeing and life. The Law of Attraction states that like attracts like – if you are in harmony, then this will spread to others, sending positive ripples out into the world (see more in part seven).

Summary

In this chapter we have looked at more ways to love **you**:

- ❖ Being mindful and aware in all you do.

- ❖ Avoiding distractions that prevent you from moving forward.

- ❖ Setting boundaries so others know how to treat you with respect.

- ❖ Stop giving your power away – be the driver of your own bus.

- ❖ Finding your precious people, so you can uplift and support each other.

- ❖ Being forgiving towards yourself and others, so you feel lighter.

- ❖ The power of intentions and how they help you focus on your desires.

* ❖ Moon rituals to bring in the new and release the unwanted.

* ❖ Being kind and gentle with yourself, as if you are your own best friend.

Invitation

To create a self-love ritual, write down your ideal scenarios, describing in detail how you will feel, what you will see, hear and smell. Focus on what you find luxurious, uplifting, relaxing or exhilarating. If at home, close the door, switching off all distractions. Take part in activities that feel nourishing and cherishing to you – such as having a delicious meal with wine, lighting wonderful scented candles and listening to music, watching a happy movie in your pyjamas or pampering yourself with a manicure or pedicure. Maybe you'd just like to have a few beers whilst watching sports on TV, slobbing around in your trackies or play some video games. Whatever works best for you!

Alternatively, do something with friends, like a karaoke, a quiz night, games evening or something altogether different and energising such as a physical outside activity. Go fully into your imagination. Once you've written your list, make a date night for yourself once a week where you can put some of your ideas into action. Make sure you put this in your diary!

Insightful Questions

When you have finished the invitation above, take a notepad and pen. Sit quietly, free from any distractions, in a relaxed manner. Look at each of the questions below, one at a time. Allow the question to just flow freely in your mind, percolating if you will. Then, capture your answers on paper, giving you an insight into where you are right now. This will help you shift your perspective, so that you become less stuck.

* *What will you now add into your life to harmonise your heart?*

* *What insights and silver linings have you received from your challenges?*

* *Do you have strong boundaries? If not, will you allow yourself to be more assertive and strengthen yours?*

* *Do you listen to your intuition/gut instinct and follow its guidance?*

- *In what ways do you love, honour and respect yourself?*

- *Have you found your precious tribe? If not, then what will you do to find additional supportive friends?*

- *Are you being true to yourself and authentic? If not, are you going to start right now?*

- *When have you celebrated being wrong? Have you come to appreciate that mistakes are learning opportunities?*

Before reading this it is important to refer to the disclaimer at the front of the book, which applies to everything you have read and will read.

Part Six

Activities to Harmonise Your Heart,

Mind and Body

In life, people tend to spend a lot of energy worrying about "what if's", many of which will never happen. This only depletes your energy – it's much better to deal with problems as and when they occur, rather than worrying now and reducing your capacity for harmonious living. As a fellow human, professional coach, and healer, I have taken part in numerous activities and exercises designed to help my own heart harmonise and find equilibrium. Now, I want to share many of these exercises with you. Some of these have been mentioned earlier in the book, but here I will go into more depth, to help you practise in the right way.

Solo Processes and Activities

Below are things I use when I'm feeling stressed, upset, unbalanced, fearful or overwhelmed. These are in addition to the ones I use as part of my morning practice. Please explore and find out which ones you prefer.

Awareness

Your first port of call regarding awareness is to notice, acknowledge and accept what you are feeling in the moment. Accept your feelings of anxiety, sadness, anger or other emotions. Sit with them and be the observer, allowing your feelings to flow through you. When you notice anxiety, for example, rate its level from one to ten, with ten being the highest. Then take deep diaphragmatic breaths down to your belly, with a longer exhalation. Inhale, holding your breath for the count of five, and then exhaling for the count of eight (you could also add a pause and hold for three before exhaling). Diaphragmatic belly breathing calms your nervous system, whereas shallow breathing in the chest increases your anxiety. Experiment with your inhalations and exhalations to discover what numbers work best for you. Act normally, as if you're just sitting taking a rest. Repeat the above steps until your rating level has decreased. Look for a positive to place your focus on once you have calmed. Hold intentions and expect the best outcomes.

The Importance of Allowing and Accepting Healing

Consciously you may think you want to change, but sometimes there is an unconscious desire to hold on to your issues. My client Clarissa was very surprised to find that, although she really wanted to change her feelings and reactions, initially she could only reduce them by 40%. She'd been impacted terribly by the pain and upset of another person's behaviour; subconsciously she wanted to keep this pain and upset as a reminder that she wouldn't fall for the same treatment again. On the face of it, this may seem like a perfectly justifiable reason. However, holding on to pain and angst and reliving it over and over again was creating strong feelings and emotions, all of which were affecting her everyday life. I explained the importance of giving herself permission to heal and asked if she could think of other methods of reaching the same outcome (not being taken advantage of), but in a way that was kinder to her.

Clarissa realised she was more knowledgeable now and could trust her own instincts, knowing that she knew the signs and would stop any relationship with similar patterns. We then released all her negative thoughts and emotions using Access Consciousness.

Clearing Box

Two of my friends went through a divorce. As a result, their children experienced distress, which was made more difficult by having to cope with moving away, settling into a new area and school. To try and help the situation, I bought each of the children a worry doll. This enabled them to draw or write what worried them that day and put the note in the dolly's pouch. The dolly took the note with their worries away each night. If you want to do the same, you could create a clearing box in which you place all your concerns and upsets, then at the end of the week have a fire ceremony to release them.

Validation Process

I created this validation exercise by adapting one of Art Giser's energetic NLP techniques (see useful resources section for his website link if you wish to train with him). Art has wonderful courses and workshops, and is great at allowing us to make adaptions. During one of my trainings I recall doing a floor timeline exercise, where my "client" was struggling somewhat. So, I sang my little ditty, 'Every little cell in my body is happy' to her, helping her to move on. Art overheard my singing and mentioned it to our entire group, saying that they too could adapt and include whatever they felt guided to.

If you look for validation from others, you won't ever feel completely happy – it's almost impossible to please everyone all the time **and** be true to yourself. To self-validate, visualise a purple heart right in front of you, with the tip sitting in a sparkly, golden infinity symbol. Feel, see, hear and sense a cord from this symbol going down into Mother Earth and another cord extending up to the Universe (Cosmos). The symbol is filled with unconditional love, validation and acceptance coming up from the earth and down from the Universe. Notice that a translucent cord is emanating from the symbol to you. See, sense, feel or hear this cord filling your body and aura with love, acceptance and validation of the magnificent, unique and magical being you are, throughout your body right down to your cells. Every time I see this symbol, I use it as a chance to self-validate. Likewise, if I ever have self-doubt, then I imagine the symbol and immediately sense my body filling with fabulous feelings. It's definitely a good idea to take the photo from the front of this book, cut it out and place it somewhere that is visible to you daily, as a visual reminder.

Ho'oponopono

As mentioned, Ho'oponopono is based on the four sentences:

- 'I'm sorry.'

- 'Please forgive me.'

- 'Thank you.'

- 'I love you.'

A good example of this in use, was when my client Derek came to see me. He was feeling angry and unhappy with his ex-wife. Initially we did some tapping, but his distress only released a little. When I mentioned it would be beneficial to forgive his ex-wife, he was emphatically against the idea, because he believed it would condone her behaviour. I explained that he was only hurting himself by holding on to these emotions. Again, Derek was quite indignant and reluctant. However, with the use of humour, I managed to persuade him that it would only benefit himself if he could be free of his upsetting thoughts and emotions. To aid this, I told him about the four forgiveness sentences, all of which he could use himself should something else arise at a later date. Dr Joe Vitale's explanation of these sentences is below, and can also be found on his website: www.joevitalehooponopono.com:

Repentance

The one thing that you'll need to realise first of all is the fact that your mind is responsible for everything that has happened to you, or anything that has affected someone else. This is because your mind has generated everything, all the thoughts which might have ended up being toxic to you or to someone else you talked to. Either way, your mind is responsible for all the things that you think it is not. You might find other things to blame it on, but at the end, your subconscious is responsible for almost anything.

The right way to become a perfect Ho'oponopono practitioner is to start saying *"I'm Sorry"* after understanding all the places where your mind has made mistakes, where your mind has caused damage to you or someone else. You might find that ignoring this is easier, that it is easier to blame this on something else, but the acceptance is what will help you realise where you're wrong, and will also make you humble. Repent for every single place that you've gone wrong on. The first step asks you to say sorry for everything that has happened or any wrong thing that you have witnessed. It makes it easy for you to move ahead in your life. Once you know the fact and have the courage to say sorry for anything that was wrong, you will feel better. *'I'm Sorry'*.

Seek Forgiveness

After step one, you might end up with a lot of occasions where you hurt someone, or where someone was affected badly due to your actions or words. In that case, you'll find that you won't really feel light unless the concerned person has forgiven you. That is exactly what you're supposed to find in the second step. It doesn't matter who you're going towards, who you're standing in front of, just ask for forgiveness.

Go up to them and tell them you're sorry for whatever you did, and then ask them to forgive you. You'll find that most of the people will end up forgiving you if you ask sincerely enough. If you put your heart right in front of them and let them see how perfectly honest you are with your apology, they will accept it at all costs. This will instantly make you feel lighter, and you will start to feel better after the person forgives you. You can then move on and continue with the next steps. You will already start to feel free and light, but the next steps will take you about ten times higher. If you cannot say sorry and *'please forgive me'* to them in person then you can still say and believe it knowing that somehow it will still reach them, even if on an unconscious level. Once you are able to say sorry, this step requires you to ask for forgiveness. You will be seeking forgiveness for everything you felt sorry for in the first step. While doing so you are asking to forgive everything from you and your past memories that may have been involved in the wrong doing. This may sound weird for many of us, but once you mean what you say, the process is magical. *'Please forgive me'*.

Gratitude

The third step is basically the happier part of the practice, which includes thanking. Every single day, so many things create so many favours; helping to make your lives easier and better. Make it a habit to thank each and every one for what they do for you. Start off by thanking your own body, for how it carries out all the functions to help you survive and to keep you healthy. Thank yourself for whatever you have done for yourself, thank God who has stayed with you till now. Minute things like thanking the plants for providing you with the oxygen you breathe, without noticing, count too. It doesn't matter who or what you're saying it to, just keep saying *'Thank You'*. Not only will this make you and the others around you feel good, it will also help you count all the blessings you have, and all the blessings that go unseen without you even realising how much everything around you cares about you. How much you care about yourself, how much God cares. This will just give you that extra boost of motivation to keep going, no matter what. The third step that you must go through is showing your gratitude for everything that has happened to your life. This way you will learn to appreciate everything that is big or small in your life. You might get an unexpected response for this thank you, but you need not worry about the result or response. In the right time, the correct result will appear in front of you. This step will help you to have patience as well.

Love

Last but never the least, comes love. Definitely the most effective part of the whole practice is looking around at all the things or the people that make you feel good and instantly light you up. This is all about admitting your love for all these things. You can say *'I love you'* to almost anything, any inanimate object, for example, your house, your car, your favorite ring. It doesn't matter. This way, you'll be able to count all the things you love, all the things you care about, and then you'll be instantly thankful for having these things too. Spreading love and getting love in return is the entire point of this particular step, and this is the perfect way to finish off your practice. The last step that you need to follow is to show your love and say *'I love you'* to every-thing that is yours. This way you will learn to love everything related to you.

Heart Meditation

Find a quiet place where you will not be distracted. Focus your attention on the area of your heart, imagining your breath flowing in and out. Breathe more slowly and deeply than usual. Breathe in for five and out for seven, finding a smooth, easy rhythm, and continue to do this until you feel your heart soften and open. Then create a positive feeling by thinking about or visualising someone you love or care for, such as your children, partner, pet or a special time or place, just so you can get a genuine sense of love and appreciation or calm and ease. Continue with your heart-focused breathing and draw your mouth up into a smile, smiling into your heart. Allow your smile and loving feelings to spread throughout your body down to your cells, through gaps between and out into your auric field. Now place your hand on your heart to anchor these feelings, knowing you can generate them any time you want to. When doing this, you could even allow the feelings to spread throughout your home. You can expand and send this smiley love out into the world or a situation.

This process aids equilibrium, especially when you're under stress, because it calms your heart rhythm. The benefit of this is that you feel more centered, deeply connected to your own heart and connected to others and the planet. It increases order and harmony in your mind, emotions and body, thus creating a greater sense of wellbeing throughout.

Traffic Lights Process

This is a quick method to bring about calm when you're feeling stressed:

- Red – stop what you are doing and stop your thoughts, by placing them into a treasure box that you imagine dropping deep into the ocean.

- Amber – get ready, placing your hand on your heart and your tummy.

- Green – go, breathe slowly and deeply seven times, then hum your favourite tune.

Feel yourself relaxing with your breath. Sense the sound moving throughout your body, uplifting and energising you.

Inner Child Healing

This is something you can work on alone or with a coach. The aim is to resolve negative emotions and experiences that your inner child still holds on to. It can also be used to harness your joy, innocence and confidence. Inner child work is a self-discovery process, helping connect you with the child you once were, along with experiences and emotions that you've learnt to swallow down and repress. The premise is that you access your inner child, listening to and nurturing them. This helps you to heal any root issues that you're undergoing as an adult.

We all have a childlike aspect within our unconscious mind. The inner child can often take over when you face a challenge in life, sometimes causing you to regress in the face of conflict or difficulty. It's a mix of both negative and positive aspects – all your unmet needs, suppressed childhood emotions and childlike innocence, creativity, and joy are still waiting within you. The repressed emotions represent all the things you were taught not to feel as a child if you wanted to be loved. So, if you were only offered attention when you were "good", then you may find that your inner child holds rebellion, sadness and anger. If you experienced trauma or abuse, you possibly learned to hide your pain and fear to survive.

This exercise allows you to find the roots of your issues as an adult, helping you discover and release any repressed emotions that are holding you back and helping you recognise your unmet needs. It assists with resolving unhelpful patterns, offering an opportunity for increased self-care, aiding your creativity, playfulness and raising your self respect.

Repressed or unresolved emotions related to childhood can often cause problems for adults, as they result in people seeking the parenting that they feel they missed out on; disappointment and rejection sets in when other people are unable to fulfill your needs and demands. Your inner child can influence your decisions, as it is part of your beliefs about yourself. Each of us has the desire to be cared for, loved and nurtured. Your inner child is a free spirit: emotional, fun-loving, joyful, imaginative and creative. Your childhood spirit may have been tamed, lost, or forgotten, but it is still somewhere inside you. Believe that you and your inner child deserve respect. Give yourself the nurturing, caring, love, forgiveness, and respect needed to heal. Let go of all negative emotions associated with your childhood and take the wheel of your bus.

Inner Child Process

This is a process I needed during my change to a singleton, because "little me" felt rejected and betrayed, just as I had felt as a child when those whom I loved hurt me emotionally and physically. So, practise the following:

Go somewhere quiet where you won't be disturbed and where you can sit or lay comfortably. Visualise a safe place. You could imagine a beautiful garden or any place in which you feel safe, empowered and whole. Begin by going into relaxation, inhaling deeply with your eyes shut. See yourself walking down a staircase. At the bottom of the staircase is your safe place. In this place you feel strong, safe and supported. Spend a bit of time in this space. Notice what it looks, feels, smells and sounds like. Having acquainted yourself with your safe place, imagine that your younger self has entered, perhaps through a door or another suitable portal. Ask your younger self if it's okay to hug them. If yes, then this may help to make them feel safe and loved. If not, then ask if it's okay to spend time with them now, to get closer and bond.

You can plan a dialogue by asking, 'When was the first time you felt sad or scared?' Await their response. If appropriate, you can reassure them by saying, 'I love you, I'm sorry for...' Ask them what they need today to feel happy and loved. Maybe they want to play a game together in this space – or it could be they want you, the adult, to engage in fun activities. Reassure them you'll carry out their wishes, that you will always love them and that any incidences that upset them, making them feel neglected, unloved, unworthy, small and unheard, will never happen again – as you are stronger and wiser now. Hug them, thank them, and tell them how much you care about them. Say goodbye, letting them know that you will return to check they're okay. Leave your safe place and ascend up the stairs. Take your safe place into your heart, knowing you can return at any time to your heart to reconnect with your inner child. Return to normal consciousness, back into your environment in the present. I keep a painting my brother did of "little me", on my dressing table to remind me to check in regularly. You could use a photo as a reminder, placing it somewhere you will see it every day.

This is the basic process, which will definitely help you, but should you wish for a more comprehensive session then please contact me and book yourself in for an Inner Child Healing session. (www.denisedavis.co.uk). 💜

For those of you who prefer to talk out loud instead of visualising, place a stuffed toy or cushion on a chair to represent your inner child. Begin a two-way dialogue, with you playing both aspects. Another alternative process, for those of you who like to be more "hands on", is to look at photos of yourself as a child. Then journal or write a letter in your inner child's voice. Years ago, when I was taking part in a spiritual development group, I was introduced to a practice where we used "automatic writing". This involves writing with your non-dominant hand, helping you to access deeper levels of communication and connecting with higher realms. On other occasions we also used this to help connect with our inner child, as it allows your younger self to express what they've never had the opportunity to share.

Write a Letter

In a few trainings, I've been asked to write a letter to my future self about what I intend to do and achieve and put it away for say, twelve months. This helps to see how many of my desired changes and wishes have been fulfilled when I open it in the future. Sometimes I create a large heart shape, drawn on paper, with words and symbols inside it or around it and other times I write this as a proper letter on beautiful paper. Before you write your future letter, you could write what you desire to "let go of" beforehand on a mini whiteboard. Then, once the exercise is done, erase it all. Or write what you want to let go of on a piece of paper, then burn or release to your rubbish bin.

Another way of uplifting ourselves was when we were told to write a future letter, elevating the excitement and anticipation of an event we were due to attend. Writing a letter like this makes positive suggestions to your subconscious mind, showing that you have happy expectations of the event. To consolidate this, you then visualise your event turning out brilliantly, which shows your unconscious mind all the enjoyment you had at the event. So, when the event arrives, your unconscious can "recall" what happened and make sure it turns out well.

Walking in Nature

Sometimes when walking and feeling below par, you can say (out loud or in your mind) all the things you wish to let go of on the outward part of the journey. On the return leg you can state the things you have gratitude for, maybe including some affirmations too. At other times you can just enjoy the present moment and your surroundings, like a peaceful, mindful meditation.

Crystals

I love crystals, and have plenty of them in my home, especially in my bedroom. I also keep some in my consulting room, large quartz, rose and green quartz in my lounge and a large quartz in my bathroom. When meditating or self-healing I may place crystals on my chakras to realign and balance them. I use a shungite crystal dot on my mobile phone cover to counteract electromagnetic frequencies and a palm crystal when using my laptop, as well as organite crystals. I also ensure my WiFi is off when sleeping.

After James left, I often carried some of these crystals in my pockets, as I was extremely over-whelmed and in distress. I wanted to excel in my exams, but because I was studying and working, with loads of unwanted thoughts and feelings flooding my body and mind, as well as feeling very sad and unloved, I wore rose quartz in my bra – the crystal which represents unconditional love. Likewise, during my floristry exams, I kept crystals in my pockets and used Bach Flower Rescue Remedy, which enabled me to remain tranquil, focused and with full access to my memory. Another brilliant help was the NLP strategy for visual recall, which I then consolidated further with Empowering Learning. To this day, I use this to help people with dyslexia spell well and to help people with dyscalculia improve their number skills.

Below I've listed useful crystals which I used during that time, some of which I still use to this day:

- Fluorite – focus, a stone of discernment and aptitude;

- Clear quartz – a master healer;

- Tiger's eye – stone of the mind;

- Sodalite – a harmonising stone;

- Amazonite – stone of hope, abundance, courage and truth;

- Smokey quartz – stone of cooperation;

- Hematite – a stone for the mind;

- Blue sapphire – stone of wisdom, abundance and uniformity;

- Blue scapolite – a crystal of support.

Memory is often associated with third eye and crown chakras. Other useful crystals include pyrite, clear quartz, rhodonite or fluorite plus amber, emerald, rhodochrosite and calcite. If you're looking for a stone that will inspire confidence and courage, then blue lace agate, carnelian, diamond, malachite, purite, bloodstone, aventurine and sunstone are all very useful.

Crystal Grids

When creating a crystal grid, crystals are chosen for the purpose required and then are usually laid out in a geometric pattern. Once they are spread out, you can programme them to bring about your desired outcome. You can create wonderful crystal grids for many things, but I have focused on one for healing and one for manifesting. Research what crystals are good for the area you want to improve. A simple grid exercise would be to print off a flower of life circle from the internet and then place a large dominating crystal in the centre. I often use odd numbers, as I was told to use odd flowers during my advanced floristry training. Really, it is a personal decision on what numbers you will make each time you create a grid.

To create a grid to heal your heart or attract a new love (remember intention is the key), place a medium-sized morganite crystal in the middle of your grid. This attunes to the heart and heart chakra, bringing in a frequency of the Divine to attract an abundance of love into your life. Morganite encourages loving thoughts and actions, compassion, consideration, responsibility and being receptive to love from others. Since it's a crystal of the heart, you can use it to attract your soulmate or to deepen your current relationship. It inspires joy and reverence for life, also increasing opportunities which allow you to experience the unconditional love of the Divine. Wearing it may evoke a sense of peace, joy, and inner strength. When worn for an extended period, it can encourage growth of confidence, as well as a feeling of power, coming from a constant awareness of your connection to the Divine – imparting a sense of fairness, effective loving communication and expression.

For the rest of the grid you can use smaller crystals – if using the flower of life symbol for your grid, then make radiating circles around your crystal in the middle, placing nine rose quartz crystals – the stone of unconditional love, compassion, peace, tenderness, nourishment, healing and comfort. This crystal speaks directly to your heart chakra, dissolving emotional wounds, fears and resentments, circulating a divine loving energy throughout your entire aura. It reawakens your heart to its own innate love, providing a sense of personal fulfillment and contentment, allowing you to truly give and receive love. These crystals encircle the morganite.

Next, create another circle around the rose quartz, using seven clear quartz crystals. This is one of the most powerful healing crystals, able to work on any condition. Clear quartz is a stone of power, amplifying any energy or intention. It protects against negativity and attunes you to your Higher Self, relieving pain. The crystal also enhances and strengthens your aura, helping your Higher Self to assimilate in the process of your spiritual growth. This crystal is often used to cleanse, open, activate and align all of your chakras. It radiates its energies outward into the surrounding environment. If including one or two more circles, you could use five moonstone for your next circle and three garnet for your last circle. Or any from these other love crystals – amber, lapis lazuli, opal, red agate, rhodochrosite and rose tourmaline. Sometimes I like to place other crystals outside of the circle grid, but still on my A4/A3 base. I may even add symbols, sometimes words – I really do what comes to me intuitively when creating. So, find out what works for you, as it could be different each time. Follow your own guidance regarding numbers and placement. Keep the grid until you feel you don't need it anymore or change some crystals when you feel called to.

If you wanted to create a crystal grid for abundance, you could put a sizeable piece of citrine in the centre. This gem stimulates the brain, strengthens the intellect, promotes motivation, activates creativity and encourages self-expression. It enhances concentration and revitalises your mind, releases negative traits such as depression, fears and phobias, and is said to be an exceptional healer of your spiritual self, because it is a regenerator.

For your next circle, use smaller pieces of clear quartz, and in the circle after that you could use pyrite. This gem is a powerful protector, which shields and protects you against negative energies affecting your physical, etheric and emotional levels. It stimulates your intellect and enhances memory, helping you to recall relevant information when you need it. Pyrite assists with bringing in money, grounding and opening you up to prosperity – especially financially. It is a heart-opening stone and widely used as a crystal of luck and good fortune. This is one stone that you don't cleanse with water. Following this, use green aventurine on your next circle, which is the gem known as a stone of opportunity. This is thought to be the luckiest of all crystals, particularly in manifesting prosperity and wealth. It is a healing stone with benefits for your lungs, liver, sinuses and heart, releasing negativity and energy blocks. It enhances your intelligence, perception and creativity. For the rest of the circles use one or more of these abundance crystals – green jade, green moss agate, selenite, rose quartz, emerald, ruby or amazonite. As I said earlier, you will choose instinctively each time you create a grid. Often, the crystals you use will be different each time.

Cleansing and Programming Your Crystals

It is important to clean crystals by regularly placing them under running water. Let them dry naturally. Check the crystal's property, as some have to be cleansed differently using smoke, incense, sage or salt. You can also charge your crystals by leaving them in the sun and moon (the crystals I use in my aura sprays gather the sun and moon energies combined with sound). To programme your crystal is to tell it what you want to use it for. Most crystals have a special crystalline structure, which is believed to hold energy, thoughts and information. One way to programme your crystal is to take it in both hands and hold it up in front of you, just above eye level, in the middle of your brow (your third eye). Focus on your crystal and say, 'I programme this crystal for…' Alongside this, crystals look stunning when worn as jewellery – a lovely bonus!

Bach Flower Essences

Bach Flower remedies are a mix of water and brandy containing dilutions of flowers, developed by Dr Edward Bach in England. They have the quality and ability to change a negative emotion into a positive one. For instance, if you have low self-esteem, then taking specific flower essences can help you believe in yourself again. You will be more self-confident when dealing with your day-to-day life. Negative emotions aren't suppressed by these essences, but are instead turned into the opposite positive emotional states. For example, fear of failure is turned into self-confidence or impatience is turned to tranquil peace. The Bach Flower essence gently restores the body and mind by casting out emotions such as fear, worry, hatred, indecision and more, all of which interfere with your body's balance. Once these emotions are released, your body can heal itself. Every flower has a particular healing attribute, in the form of a vibrational frequency from the flower used.

There are thirty-eight Bach Flower essences in total, which adults and children can successfully use because they're 100% natural, safe and harmless. They're non-addictive, without side effects and you're unable to overdose on them. They can be used in combination with other medications and treatments, including homeopathy, without interference. Each essence acts on a specific emotion for all aspects of your psychological and emotional health. You can mix up to six unique essences to create a bespoke treatment for yourself. So, think about the type of person you are and how you are feeling, to determine what flower remedy would be most suitable. Alternatively, you can consult a practitioner who specialises in working with the essences.

Immediately after James left, I was deeply upset and in shock. So, my spiritual development teacher suggested I took "Star of Bethlehem". This eased my symptoms of extreme unhappiness and despair around the loss of such an important person in my life. Since then, there have been many times when I carried rescue remedy spray or pastilles in my handbag to help when I was feeling extremely anxious, panicky or fearful during times of extreme stress, to calm myself or to soothe pain.

Here are some other essences that you may wish to use if you are feeling out of sorts:

- Agrimony is good for anxiety, insomnia, unhappiness, and addiction.

- Aspen can be used for fears and worries.

- Centaury for tiredness, lack of energy, timidity and passiveness.

- Cerato for not trusting your own wisdom or advice and wanting confirmation from others.

- Cherry plum when you feel as if you are "losing it" and in deep despair.

- Chestnut bud for learning and to stop repeating mistakes.

- Clematis for lack of concentration and daydreaming.

- Crab apple for poor self-image, cleansing and being obsessive.

- Elm for depression, overwhelm, exhaustion, and feeling despondent.

- Gentian for feeling depressed and discouraged.

- Gorse for pessimism, despair and hopelessness.

- Heather for disliking being alone/feeling lonely.

- Holly for insecurity, needing compassion, feeling envious and jealous.

- Honeysuckle for grief over bereavement and nostalgia.

- Hornbeam for needing strength, doubting your own abilities, and procrastinating.

- Larch for lack of confidence, feeling inferior, discouraged and depressed.

- Mimulus for feeling sensitive, having a lack of courage, fears and shyness.

- Oak for feeling overworked, being an overachiever and feeling fatigued.

- Olive for lack of energy, fatigue and needing to convalesce.

- Pine for feeling unworthy, undeserving, apologetic and guilty.

- Rock rose for feeling terror and frozen fear.

- Rock water for self-denial, self-perfection or being overly opinionated.

- Star of Bethlehem for trauma, shock and post-traumatic stress.

- Sweet chestnut for extreme mental anguish, feelings of hopelessness, despair and immense sorrow.

- Walnut to assist with change, menopause, moving on and letting go of past protection that is no longer needed.

- White chestnut for sleeplessness and insomnia.

- Wild rose for apathy, lost motivation and lack of ambition.

- Willow for self-pity, resentment, bitterness and complaining.

More often than not, if I feel in need of more guidance or support, I consult my lovely homeopath, who has assisted me with my physical and emotional challenges.

Body Care

I mentioned earlier in the book that I only use natural products on my skin, as they are absorbed into our bloodstream. I don't want unhealthy chemicals racing around my body. "Tropic" offers delicious skin care, hair care and makeup, freshly made in the UK from purely plant-derived ingredients. The products are so effective and have won 170+ beauty awards. You can't find the products in the shops, so if you wish to learn more or order from my website then check out www.denisedavis.co.uk under the products tab "Tropic" ♥.

Wellbeing Through Socks, Insoles and Patches (Voxx HPT human performance technology)

Voxx HPT is a very specific sequence and pattern of neuroreceptor activation on the bottom of the feet and other areas of the body, that triggers a signal to the brain. This aids the brainstem with reaching homeostasis. VoxxLife weave the Voxx HTP pattern into the socks and mould into the insoles. As their company website puts it: "The documented results and benefits arising from the products incorporating the Voxx HPT pattern includes enhanced pain relief and management, especially painful Diabetic Neuropathy, enhanced postural stability and balance and improved mobility and overall energy levels. Remember, you need to wear the socks, insoles or neuro patches 24/7 – that is all day every day, so that the message is constantly being sent to your brain." Recently released products are the eSmart Sleeve, Neurovax patch for your immune system, Metapatches for your metabolism, and Rempatch for sleep, as well as VoxxMagic shapewear under garments. New products are continually being launched, so keep up to date by looking at my website products tab "VoxxLife".

Recently, an exciting business opportunity arose for me to become an independent associate of VoxxLife products. The "magic" socks and insoles, as I like to call them, help create optimal health and improve human performance, allowing people from all walks of life to enjoy an enriched quality of life and achieve their true potential wellbeing. Independently scientifically tested, VoxxLife products have been proven to reduce pain, improve strength and endurance, increase stability and balance, enhance range of motion and improve athletic performance by boosting reaction times. Some people have had profound changes and others (like me) more

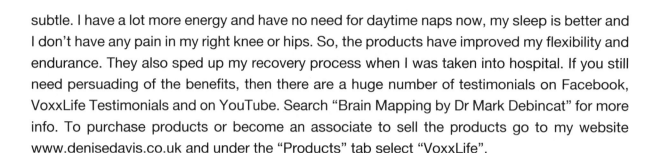

subtle. I have a lot more energy and have no need for daytime naps now, my sleep is better and I don't have any pain in my right knee or hips. So, the products have improved my flexibility and endurance. They also sped up my recovery process when I was taken into hospital. If you still need persuading of the benefits, then there are a huge number of testimonials on Facebook, VoxxLife Testimonials and on YouTube. Search "Brain Mapping by Dr Mark Debincat" for more info. To purchase products or become an associate to sell the products go to my website www.denisedavis.co.uk and under the "Products" tab select "VoxxLife".

Water Clearing and Cleansing

One way you can release negative emotions, looping thoughts, or limiting beliefs, is to stand in an imaginary waterfall, where you envision the water releasing everything that no longer serves you, cleansing your body and aura, washing it down to the earth for transmutation. Should you wish to have an even more thorough cleanse in your waterfall, you can visualise taking off your head, giving it a rinse inside and then returning it to your body. This can help you feel clearer and lighter. Then repeat this by taking off your arm and cleansing it, repeating this with all body parts until you feel you have had a deep cleanse inside and outside of your body. Finally, submerge your entire body in the pool, swimming around to ensure that your whole body is thoroughly cleansed and refreshed with a complete reset. In my waterfall I see/feel/hear/sense that there is a wooded outcrop nearby, where I sit under an oak tree to dry off, with the sunshine streaming through the leaves bringing in vitamin D, light and anything else I may need. You can add and subtract to your waterfall – it could be a lake or river, whatever body of water you prefer. I love my tools and process, but I also love and adore the beauty of Mother Nature in all its wonder and gloriousness! Another technique I use, as mentioned before, is to see/sense/hear my blocks releasing from my power centre (solar plexus) to the sea, drawn by a gigantic magnet. The sea cleanses and transmutes them – again it could be a river, lake or stream. The above exercises are expanded from an Energetic NLP technique created by Art Giser (go to the useful resources page for his website, if you wish to undertake his trainings).

If the above techniques don't appeal, then you could imagine a white sparkly light going in through your crown and flowing down throughout your entire body, taking with it any tension, negative emotions and fear, to be released through your feet for transmutation. For those that may feel uncomfortable using water images, then imagine a hoover sucking everything out from your body that no longer serves you, leaving your body feeling lighter and brighter, both inside and out. Fill the empty space with whatever emotions you need at the time.

For those that prefer more practical ways of doing things, there are numerous other methods and places that you can take advantage of. A good example is during your daily shower –

visualise, hear, feel and sense all negative thoughts running down and out of your body into the drains, to be transmuted by Mother Earth. Once you've cleansed and cleared your body, then send in pink unconditional love to replace all that has been let go, as the universe dislikes a vacuum. You can add anything else that you wish to accompany the love, such as courage, joy and wisdom.

Future Visioning with Future Life Progression (FLP)

Quantum physics proposes that all times are running simultaneously. In simple terms, this means that past, present and future all occurring right now. Our linear view of time is an illusion. A wonderful novel that covers this subject is Richard Bach's *One.* If you are struggling to get your head around the above, then don't worry – as humans we have been conditioned to use only 5% of our conscious minds. The reality is that 95% of your daily thoughts come from your subconscious mind. If you want to make a significant positive change, then the best way to do this is to go beyond your critical conscious mind, changing your thought patterns while in an altered state of consciousness. FLP is a great way to do this. It's a form of hypnosis that relaxes you into a deep but alert state that opens your mind to potentialities. Its creator, Anne Jirsch, is a wonderful trainer and very generous. She regularly gifts practitioners with exercises that she has created (see the useful resources page for the link to her website, if you wish to train with her).

One of the biggest benefits of FLP is that it enables you to align to the correct vibrational frequency to glimpse your future and bring forth that which is for your greatest good. Your mind will open up to the wonderful potential you possess and you'll be taken forward in time, to a place where you can explore the possibilities that extend from your own creation and the paths you choose to examine. You'll contact your future self and be gifted with the knowledge you need to create your best possible future – bringing insights, advice and answers about your current life. Crucially, you'll learn what steps must be taken in order for you to move forward.

FLP can help you find answers in areas such as health, property, investment, trends and forecasting, business, family, your ideal partner, life's purpose, how to relieve stress and anxiety, confidence, goal setting and other areas. It can help you explore distinct life paths, allowing you to determine which decisions to make and the lessons needed to be learned, ideas worth pursuing, potential opportunities and what you need to do to ensure these opportunities come to fruition. FLP can also take you on a journey into your next or other future lives, providing you with knowledge that may be useful for moving forward in a better way.

If you want to experience FLP, then please contact me to book a session – we can work via Skype or in person. (www.denisedavis.co.uk) ♥

Accelerated Learning State and Exam Success Techniques

During my exams, I used a visual recall technique which I had initially come across in my early NLP practitioner training. Later I trained in an expanded version of this strategy, helping kids with dyslexia by improving their literacy, particularly in regards to spelling – people suffering from dyslexia are usually extremely visual or generally have a tendency to access their "feelings" instead of the recall area of their brain. However, aside from the pleasure I took in helping others, this exercise also had the added bonus of helping me with my own exams. I found that, when studying, this method helped me to "see" my revision papers in detail, regularly helping me to achieve results of 100%. I combined this with the use of crystals for exam success – green tourmaline, clear quartz, honey calcite, tiger's eye and amazonite. Just before the exam, I would spray some Bach Flower Rescue Remedy on my tongue, to ensure I eliminated any fears, anxiety or nervousness.

Whilst learning and revising, I also used the other methods that I put together for my students when teaching at "Flying Start Tuition" and privately at home. As mentioned, at the beginning of the class before lessons started, I would get the children to do a jelly wiggle movement with some Brain Gym. When the children were sitting down, they would take a few diaphragmatic breaths to release stress and muscular tension, lowering their blood pressure and reducing their heart rate. This was followed by grounding, which helped them to feel centred, solid, strong, balanced, relaxed and connected to their environment, focused and in the moment. Lastly, the children would expand their peripheral vision, creating a state of calm and focus, enabling them to "download" information to their memory effortlessly (learning directly through their subconscious mind), and delight in their improved recall, whilst bypassing any negative thoughts and self-sabotaging beliefs they might have had. I recommended the children did the same at home too when revising, to ensure the conditions were similar and optimal.

Throughout every lesson I got the children to anchor their success when praised using funky shape bands, which I purchased specifically for this purpose. This was also a good way of creating community bonding. For details of "Flying Start Tuition" online or in person classes, see the useful resources page.

Jelly Wiggle and Brain Gym Exercises

We would start with a jelly wiggle which meant wiggling and wobbling like a jelly. This was followed by Brain Gym exercises, which can make you smarter and sharper, boosting your confidence levels and self-esteem. They also help to revitalise your natural healing mechanisms, increase creativity and improve communication skills. There are numerous Brain Gym videos on YouTube (for more info I have put a link in the useful resources page to the UK Brain Gym website). However, below I have listed some of the most important and most-used exercises:

Marching on the spot to warm up your muscles. Repeat thirty times.

Cross Crawl improves coordination between your right brain, your left brain and your entire body. To begin, lift your right hand above your head. Lift your left leg off the floor and bend your left knee. At the same time, bend your right elbow and try to touch your left knee with your right elbow. Then swap and repeat on the other side. Do three sets of eight repetitions.

Ankle Touch is similar to the exercise above. Lift your right foot off the floor and touch your right ankle with your left hand. Place your right foot on the floor and lift your left foot off the floor. Try to touch your left ankle with your right hand. Do fifteen to twenty repetitions. A variation of this is to touch your ankle behind your back with the opposite hand to foot, which also improves your balance.

Step Touch is like a dancer's warm up and is good for lateral or side-to-side movement coordination. Stand with your legs close together. Take a step towards your right, with your right leg. Place your left foot next to your right leg. Take a step towards your left with your left leg. Place your right foot next to your left leg. Do this thirty times at a slow to moderate pace.

Neck Circles decreases tension in your neck and shoulders. Roll your shoulders back and close your eyes. Lower your head and gently tilt it to the right side. Gently roll your neck from the right to the back, from the back to the left, and then down in the centre. This completes one neck circle. Do ten of these before doing the same on the left side.

Cooks' Hook Up helps to calm your nerves and improves hand and brain co-ordination. Sit straight in a chair. Cross your right ankle over your left ankle. Extend your hands in front of you. Cross your right hand over your left hand and link the fingers. Twist the forearms internally and form a hook, taking six deep breaths. Release the hook and join your fingertips. Take six more deep breaths. Repeat three to five times.

The Brain Button helps improve the flow of electromagnetic energy, relaxing your eyes, shoulders and neck, whilst promoting body balance. Place your left palm on your belly. Place the thumb and index finger of your right hand an inch below your collarbone. Move the fingers in a circular motion. Do this ten times. Place your right palm on your tummy and your left fingers an inch below the collarbone. Massage in a circular motion ten times.

Diaphragmatic breathing

Sit in a comfortable position or lie on a flat surface. Relax your shoulders. Put a hand on your chest and a hand on your stomach. Breathe in slowly through your nose for the count of seven. You should experience the air moving through your nostrils into your abdomen, making your stomach expand outwards while your chest remains relatively still. Exhale slowly for the count of eleven. Repeat for a few minutes until your body and mind is feeling calm and your tension has released.

Grounding

Grounding, also known as earthing, is a practice that is said to help you dispel flashbacks, unwanted memories, and challenging emotions. It connects you to your environment in the present. There are many ways you can do this:

To begin, find somewhere comfortable to sit, with your feet on the floor. Close your eyes, then take three deep breaths and relax. Now imagine roots growing out from the bottom of your feet, going down through the floor, through the foundations of your building, through the soil, through the rocks, through the molten layer right down to the crystalline core of Mother Earth. Let your roots connect and wrap around the crystal. If you have difficulty keeping your roots on the crystal then you could imagine tying a bow or using spray glue to help them stay on. Draw up earth energies (negative ions) through your roots, up through all the layers of the earth, through your feet right up to your heart area. Release anything out of alignment. See, hear, feel and sense these earth energies permeating throughout your body, right down to your cellular level. Allow the wonderful energies to continue coming up from the core for a few minutes, until you feel more harmonious, with a greater connection to your environment. At other times I also include a connection with the cosmos, seeing, feeling, hearing or sensing a silver cord to the universe. Allow the energies to enter your head through your crown, going down to your heart where they mix with the earth energy, filling your entire body. If you wish then you can also release any unwanted beliefs, programming, emotions or thoughts via the same channels for Mother Earth and the universe to transmute.

A very practical way to ground is to put your hands in water, focusing on the water's temperature and how it feels on your fingertips, palms and the back of your hands. What do you notice – does it feel the same on every part of your hand? You could alternate with hot and cold, noting what differences you're experiencing.

Touch items near you. What are the textures? Are they soft or hard, heavy or light? What other things can you feel? What other things can you notice? Is the colour vibrant or pale? If you hold some natural items, such as a stone or a pine cone, what can you notice about them? These are from the ground, so will still have the energy from it. Consciously eat some food, particularly something like chocolate, which you can savour. Again, notice how it feels and smells, the texture and how it changes as it melts in your mouth. You can do the same with your favourite drink. Water is great for grounding and refreshing, as it's something your body is made of and needs a lot of. Hold a piece of ice. What are your initial feelings holding it? How long does it take before it melts? How does the sensation change as it melts?

Take a brief walk, concentrating on the steps. You could count them, noting the rhythm of your footsteps and how it feels when you put your foot on the ground and lift it again.

Inhale your best loved scent, maybe a herb or spice, favourite soap, scented candle, wine or perfume. Breathe in the fragrance slowly and deeply, noting its qualities. Is it sweet, sharp or spicy?

Move your body by stretching, doing jumping jacks, skipping with a rope or jogging on the spot. Pay attention to how your body feels before you start, during the process and when your feet are on the ground or in the air.

As mentioned in other places in the book, taking deep breaths will relax but also centre you. You could "box" breath – breathing in for four, holding for four, breathing out for four and then repeating.

Listen to your surroundings. What noises can you hear? Can you distinguish the pitch and tone? Let the sounds wash over you and remind you of where you are in the moment. Make a list of things you notice around you too. For example, five things you hear, four things you see, three things you can touch from where you are, two things you can smell and one you can taste.

If you're still not feeling grounded, having completed just one of the above exercises, try combining them.

Peripheral Vision

Peripheral vision is an excellent exercise to do when you want to learn and recall important information. This is a short and sweet exercise, taking around thirty seconds.

While facing straight ahead, pick a spot above eye level to direct your attention to (in my private tutoring class I made a flower head for the children to use as the focal point). Focus on this spot for five to ten seconds before expanding your focus to the periphery whilst keeping your eyes completely still. Loosen the back of your jaw, as this is where you may hold on to any unhelpful self-talk. Continue to expand your awareness. Notice that as you stare at the spot you can see both sides of the room and a large part of what is behind you.

Notice any movement that may be going on in the periphery. Be aware of the distinct sounds around you. Stretch your hands out to each side of you and wiggle your fingers. Can you see them moving? Well done. See how far back you can move your hands whilst still being aware of the wiggling of your fingers. Observe the relaxation in your body and the stillness of your mind. When you return to normal vision, make sure to look straight ahead.

Ancestral Healing

I loved having Ancestral Healing, as it left me feeling free, with a positive outlook. I signed up for this because I was experiencing upset from the aftermath of my divorce. During a shamanic soul retrieval session, I gathered aspects of me that were "lost" due to the distress of our separation. Since then, I've had ancestral coaching/healing in many different formats such as Shamanic Healing, The Journey, Past Life Regression, Hypnosis, FLP, all rolling back into the past and then into the future. All of these I use on my clients too, to help release the negative patterns of the people who came before them in their lineage (their ancestors), which affected their present lives. The added bonus is that it also cleared issues from their descendant's lives. This healing allowed my clients to reclaim their power, so that they had more control of their bus journey, both now and in the future. In fact, most of the processes I use can assist you to release any ancestral issues holding you back from reaching your full potential.

Music/Sound and Movement

Listen to uplifting music and dance freely for a few minutes. Science shows that music releases dopamine, the feel-good chemical in your brain. Music can influence your thoughts, feelings and behaviours, relaxing your mind, energising your body and even helping to reduce pain and enhance memory. It can also lead to improvements in production when played in the background, as long as it is simple, such as instrumental tracks without complex lyrics (which can be distracting).

Likewise, movement oxygenates your body. Your body dislikes being static for too long and appreciates regular movement throughout the day, so take regular five-minute dance breaks or walk around the block. Movement can increase your brain size and make it healthier, prevent memory loss, improve sleep, reduce anxiety and depression, and boost your mood.

Toning Your Energy Centres

There are twelve major chakras (three above the head and one below the feet, plus the higher heart chakra/thymus in your body). But most people only focus on the main seven centres in the body to tone. As well as your voice, you can also use tuning forks, tingsha bells, drums and other instruments to balance all twelve of your chakras and cleanse your aura. You can combine the use of white sage or incense to clear and cleanse your aura. I have come across at least four ways to tone with varying distinct sounds, but these are the ones I mainly use, as briefly mentioned in part three of the book:

- Crown   EE as in see

- Third eye (forehead)   IH as eye

- Throat   EH as bed

- Heart   AH as in ma

- Solar plexus   AW as in saw

- Sacral   OH as blow

- Root   OO as in zoo

Protection

When I started taking psychic development classes, I was told that I needed to protect myself. Subsequent mediumship teachers and healing trainers said the same – all except one. When I was training for Reconnective Healing, Eric Pearl told me that no one needs to protect themselves. This resonated with me, as I had reached fifty years of age without protecting myself and hadn't felt I was harmed by not doing it. Again, this is a matter of preference – some clients feel happier using protection and others don't. I did however use protection when I was in spiritual development classes and was told it was a necessary part of the training. I would visualise a pink bubble around myself filled with love and health, with a reflective layer returning to sender anything that wasn't for my highest good. Sometimes I would place a shield or put myself in a pyramid. Find what suits you best, if you feel you need protection at any time.

NPA Process (Non-Personal Awareness)

I met Joel Young, the creator of NPA, at the Festival of Enlightenment 2011 in Colorado. At the time I was attending one of his workshops, where he gifted the audience with his process and guided us on how to use it with each other. I was fortunate to meet him socially too. He is a lovely, generous man with a wonderfully powerful yet simple technique for letting go of blocks and living your dreams. On a practical level it's a six-line spoken transformational tool, that helps you stop taking things personally. As Joel explained, 'It may not be your first thought, but I realise that the mechanism of "taking things personally" is responsible for a huge amount of unnecessary suffering. When you learn how to reverse that mechanism, it will bring you a huge amount of relief.' If you want to learn this process more in depth, the link to Joel's website is in the useful resources section of this book.

The NPA Process

Q1. What are you experiencing, that you would like to allow to pass?

Q2. What are you not experiencing, that you would like to allow to come?

Your responses to the above questions should be a "spew". Let your answer be a natural, unedited and unfiltered expression. Notice what pops out when you let this happen and let that be your answer.

Now, say the following sentences out loud, using your answer to fill in the blank in the statements. Stay present to your experience, as you say the words.

- This ....
- This Energy of ....
- This Pure Energy of .... is not personal.
- This Pure Energy of .... is not personal.
- This Pure Energy of .... is not personal.
- And I am willing to experience it.

Now, be inwardly still. Let go and give yourself space to simply be with your experience. Whatever emotion, sensation or thought arises, be still until you feel a natural completion.

MIR Method

The MIR Method was created by Mireille Mettes and is designed to help with emotional and physical pain. Mireille suggests that you do this twice daily, for at least four weeks.

The Steps:

1   Optimise acidity.

2   Detox all toxicity.

3a   Detach father.

3b   Detach mother.

4   Clear Meridians.

5   Supplement all shortages.

6   Balance hormone system.

7   Fulfill basic needs.

8   Optimise chakras and aura.

9   Clarify mission.

Say every step three times out loud, whilst stroking your hands as if you were washing them (see useful resources section for a link to Mireille's instruction video).

Hand Calm

In this exercise, each finger represents a certain emotion – the little finger is self-esteem, the ring finger is sadness, the middle finger is anger, the index finger is fear and the thumb is worry. Massaging these points can instantly assist you to refocus, soothing your system and emotions, rebalancing your inner systems.

Dowsing

Dowsing is another way of receiving answers from your body. I learnt this during my clinical hypnotherapy training. The way it works is by using a pendulum. You interpret the movement of said pendulum to gain answers and perspective. Pendulums are usually made from crystal hung on a single chain. Before using a pendulum, cleanse it so that it only has your energies. You can do this by running it under tap water. Then, let it dry naturally or leave it in sunlight for a short time. To hold the pendulum, I was taught to have the chain in between my forefinger and middle finger, with the top of the chain resting on top of the hand and the remainder hanging underneath. Some people prefer to hold it between their thumb and forefinger – experiment and see what feels right for you. Hold the pendulum completely still and ask your question. Allow the pendulum to move of its own accord. The pendulum moves in different ways in response to questions. All questions need to be formed to receive simple yes or no answers. To find your yes, ask if your name is … (use your correct name). To find your no, ask if your name is … (use an alternative name). For me, when the answer is yes, the pendulum moves backwards and forwards. When it's no, the pendulum swings sideways and for maybe it swings in more of a circular movement. The important thing is to be relaxed and unemotional about the outcome.

This can be used for healing purposes, such as identifying allergies. You can ask if it is willing to increase your metabolic rate, and also use it for finding lost objects and choosing between areas on a map when deciding where to live. I have also used dowsing rods to douse for stuck energies, and I've used it to douse for water too when out in a group exercise.

Past Life Regression

I learned this technique as part of my clinical hypnotherapy training. It was fascinating to see what may have bled through to this lifetime and then heal it. It can often help you understand why certain people are in your life and why you may have some fears about how your unconscious mind works. In part seven I have written a case study, showing how one of my clients couldn't wear anything around her neck until she'd had past life progression, which removed the trauma of being hung.

Emotional Freedom Technique

EFT was especially helpful when I had to go to hospital for a colonoscopy. Prior to the examination, I got very upset, as I'd expected to have some mild analgesic (as when I had an endoscopy down my throat) only to be told the NHS didn't give this anymore. I informed them that I wasn't sure if I could go through with the procedure and got quite tearful. Whilst sitting in the waiting area, in the dressing gown they'd given me to wear, I started doing my EFT tapping to rebalance myself. Another lady came in, who was also upset (having been told the same thing as me) and she joined me in this exercise. When the nurse came back to speak to me, she proclaimed how much brighter I now seemed to be. This is just one example of how tools and processes can help you during everyday, difficult situations. If you're interested in learning tapping, then here's the EFT short form that I was taught:

The first step is to tune in and connect to your feelings. Then rate from 0 to 10, with 10 being the highest possible negative feeling that you're experiencing – i.e. 10 for extreme distress/pain, 5 for upset/frustration, etc.

Acknowledge where the specific emotion is in your body. Now, begin tapping on the side of your hand (little finger side) which is called the "karate chop spot". Whilst doing this, say your statement out loud, 'Even though I am feeling extremely fed up and low, I truly love and accept myself.' If you're unable to love and accept yourself, create a statement that is kind to you such as, 'I like who I am', 'I am learning to like myself' or 'I am choosing to like myself.' The more descriptive you make the set-up statement the better, as it will closely align with your thoughts and feelings.

Then, using shorter statements (adapted from your first one) such as, 'Fed up and low', tap on the crown of your head five to seven times. Move your tapping to the edge of your eyebrow near the top of your nose, repeating the words and still tapping 5-7 times on each following area. Next, move to the outside of your eyebrow, under your eye, under your nose, your chin, your collarbone and then under your arm, again repeating the words. Sometimes it suffices to repeat this process twice. However, something else may arise during the tapping and you can then tap on that instead.

If, for some reason, your feelings have only reduced moderately, then repeat the same activity whilst tapping the karate chop spot, saying, 'Even though I still have some feelings of extreme fed up and low, I love and accept myself.' Then, tap on the other points, saying, 'Still feeling fed up and low.' The setup statement is only said once, but the other points are repeated.

Having carried out this process twice, if there is still some residue, repeat the set-up statement, saying, 'This remaining feeling fed up and low.' Hopefully, this will take you down to 0 on the scale. If it doesn't, then keep repeating the steps until it reduces to 0. There are other variations to this, such as the Choices Method, Movie Method, Positive EFT, Faster EFT, Picture Tapping and more. However, if tapping on your own hasn't eliminated your issues, there may be more that needs exploration. If so, a qualified practitioner can assist you.

When coaching children with EFT, I would sometimes use a teddy as a surrogate if they were too young or didn't want to tap (I sewed buttons onto a teddy on the acupressure points used in the short form). You could also tap on your children directly, if they prefer that option. I made a "feelometer", which you can make together with your children so it is personal to them. This is something first developed by Eddie Brady and is a fantastic and creative tool. Using an A4 card, draw a line horizontally near the bottom of the card. Then draw an arc starting from the beginning of the line right up and over like a rainbow, down to the line on the other side. Create sections and divide into how many emotions you may want to write. You can then get the children to decide on the emotions, such as anger, frustration, sadness, etc. Let them choose relevant colour pencils to represent the feeling (if you want you could also add the relevant word). Then add an arrow made from card and affix in the middle, with a split pin ensuring the arrow is long enough to reach all the segments. This is particularly good if your child isn't able to express their emotion, because they can just point the arrow to the colour.

Retrieval of Your Energies

Think of a traumatic event, relationship or soul memory that you are being called to retrieve your lost energy from. You can say, 'I call back any lost soul fragments, power or light now. Any soul contracts, programmes, hexes, vows from my past, present or future lives in all time and dimensions that are not in my highest good – I relinquish, rescind, release and resolve them all now. All light and power I have willingly or unwillingly/unwittingly given away or had taken from me, I call to be returned now. Any cords or attachments from my past, present and future lives I release now for my highest good, and the highest good of all. And so it is, and so it is, and so it is. Thank you, thank you, thank you.' (The power of three is very potent!)

Alternatively, you can intend all your energy to be returned by visualising it. Imagine that it is returning to a gold and purple ball, situated just above your head. In this ball, it is cleansed and healed, before returning down into your body through your crown. You can also return all energies that aren't yours, seeing it cleansed above the person's head and then back into their body (this energy ball is ENLP based).

Cutting Cords Processes

Energetic cords and attachments are formed between people, places, objects and events. Your energy and energetic space is sacred, so it's important to regularly cut the cords and renew relations to everything and everyone. This is especially important when you no longer want to be connected to someone.

The two processes I will give you here differ, in that the first one involves cutting cords visually with everyone daily, so you can meet each other afresh. The second is a talking process, cutting cords with only those you wish to release from your life.

Visualise a stage, and place everyone in your life on this stage – see, hear, feel or sense the cords between you and them. You can cut the cords with a powerful sword, a laser or any implement of your choice. Ensure all cords are severed and that the hooks have left your body.

Send them back to the owner with love, light and understanding. Fill the void with pink unconditional love, plus anything else you wish to add. There are many sources I learnt this technique from, such as my first psychic development classes, but I know that Doreen Virtue has written something similar in one of her books.

The following cord cutting process is another one I like, which I first came across on my personal Facebook feed. The exercise is scripted by Nicole Vincent. Say out loud or in your mind the following words:

'I release all negative cords I am giving out and send them up to Heaven, so that my needs and desires may be met through divine channels. I ask that all connection points on any living being that I was connected to in a negative way be healed and sealed completely, and return to their perfect pattern through the Light of God.'

'I release all negative cords I am receiving and send them up to Heaven, so that the needs and desires of those that are connecting to me might be met through divine channels. I ask that all connection points on me might be healed and sealed completely and return to their perfect pattern through the Light of God.'

Finally, take a deep cleansing breath. Nicole suggests you repeat this declaration weekly or more often if needed. (See useful resources page for the link to Nicole's website.)

Healing Pyramid

Create a pyramid around yourself, and fill it with healing and love, releasing all your toxins from the apex. In this space you can be centred, as the apex is connected to the cosmos and the base is connected to earth. Being linked in this way enables clarity. Your surrounding pyramid gives you space – a safe haven from the collision of the world's particles and people's thoughts. The pyramid will keep you in alignment, so there's no need for anything on the outside to enter without your permission. Set the intention that only anything that elevates you can enter your pyramid, such as extra energies and possibilities. Find creativity in your thoughts, in your interpretations of the world. Consider things differently than before. Be carefree, entering your journey with trust that every day your needs are being met. All of your baggage can be left outside the pyramid. Whilst in your pyramid, keep your own council, enjoying a beautiful journey with yourself in peace, joy and love. Celebrate you and how far you have come on your bus journey of life. Allow yourself to just be free from expectations – relish just being. This helped me a lot during COVID-19, when our world was awash with fear and judgement. It ensured that I kept myself in good vibrations, keeping in alignment with what felt right for me.

Write With An Open Heart

During the process of writing my book, I took great heart and inspiration from the work of my friend and fellow practitioner Wendy Fry. Her book *Write From Your Heart – Discover Your Author Voice Through Journaling* was particularly great. There are many techniques that Wendy and I have used on journeys that connect us. Wendy has allowed me to share one of her unique and brilliant exercises below:

The Heart Quadrant

Ask yourself this: 'What does my heart need to express right now?' Listen to how it answers. Ask again, even deeper this time: 'What message does my heart want to share?' Being aware of the authentic voice of your heart, with the freedom to speak through journaling, is a huge turning point when it gets down to the business of writing. Consider your unmet needs from childhood. What did your younger self want to say, but couldn't? It's never too late to meet those needs now as an adult, so write from your heart to your younger self with love, encouragement, and support. Our future selves often need a boost too – a champion to say, 'Hey, you can do it. You've got what it takes, go for it, I have your back.' Journaling to and from your future self can be a lot of fun too, especially when you're the cheerleader in your own life.

Sometimes, when we lose connection with our hearts, we go into our heads – looking outside of ourselves for something or someone to fill us up with what we believe is missing. Like a void or a gaping hole, we search for something to complete us. Instead, look within. Express the voice of your heart and discover your authentic voice through journaling.

Copy out the picture of the heart quadrant in your journal or on pieces of paper. Alternatively, you may like to purchase a heart-shaped note pad or make your hearts from different coloured papers and gift wrap or card. Write inside your heart-shaped flower petals, noting what your heart needs to express. You may have never even stopped to think about what your heart needs. If so, this is the best way for you to discover your authentic voice and the voice of your heart.

After completion, write out either on the back of the heart, in your journal, or on some new hearts, all the choices, affirmations, loving statements and acknowledgements which make you feel warm and lovable.

Completing this exercise daily upon waking and sleeping, as well as throughout the day in your journal or on the heart shapes, will have a dramatic effect on your ability to openly express yourself. In turn, this will improve your inner and outer communications.

My Heart Says Yes. My Head Says No

Our head and heart can conflict at different times; two crucial parts of you in disagreement, battling with each other for pole position. Have you found yourself unable to make decisions based on that inner conflict, not knowing which way to go? If so, a question I would like you to become familiar with is:

'Am I in my head, or am I in my heart?'

Often, we are in our heads too much, to the detriment or absence of listening to heart-centred communication. As a result, we fail to discover our authentic inner voice. In fact, many people wouldn't recognise this voice even if it stared them right in the face. Of course, it's natural for us to use our heads to analyse and weigh up the pros and cons of a situation. However, this is also where our voice of doom lives. If we're not careful, we could let our heads rule our hearts and our future, never considering the heart's needs or wants. It's time to start again. It's time to write a new chapter and future into being.

Opening Your Heart

An open and expressive heart is incredibly powerful. Read and understand the following:

- *Your heart is wise.*

- *If you listen to your heart, you will find that it knows all the answers to all your questions.*

- *Your heart provides you with a valuable source of information.*

- *Your heart has a blueprint for happiness, joy and compassion for yourself and others.*

- *Your heart stores that which you seek.*

- *Your heart if you listen to it, will tell you what it wants to say, what it wants to share and why sharing its message will have a profound impact on your ability to fulfil your potential.*

The heart is where our true self resides, that place of inner knowing and intuition, the Higher Self, the source, our oneness. Following your heart in the journaling process supports you in discovering your unique voice and connecting with the writer within. Now is the perfect time to write – when we let go of the past and move forward into the unknown, writing what comes through from our heart's message, we grow magnificently. In doing so, we step fully into our power.

Heart Speak Writing Invitation

- *Listen to your heart's needs.*

- *Be aware of the fears in your head.*

- *Make a note of where these fears come from. Are they fears from the past, current concerns or worries about things you imagine happening in the future?*

- *When you think about your fears, who comes to mind? How do you feel physiologically?*

- *Bring yourself back to your heart each time you find yourself going back into your head.*

- *Go back to the heart. Ask what it wants to say.*

- *What does your heart need to feel?*

- *With the wisdom of your heart, what is the journal piece you must write?*

- *Act and write from your heart in every situation*

In my experience, being a writer is about being fearless; when you write and speak from your heart, you discover freedom.

There are other fantastic processes Wendy has created, such as the spotlight process, which helps you get in touch with your thoughts, the percentage of where they are positive and if they are situated in your past or future. The "I am somebody exercise" is particularly great to do in groups. Wendy's book is full of many brilliant techniques to help you get in harmony and start writing. Go to the Useful Resources page to find details of Wendy's website.

Soul Plan

In my life, I have experienced a multitude of things, all of which have given me insights and explained more about who and what I am. One of these was reading Blue Marsden's book *Soul Plan: Reconnect With Your True Life Purpose*, which lead me to having my own Soul Plan reading. I was so blown away by the insights it gave me that I trained to advanced level with Blue himself (see my useful resources page for the link to Blue's website for training). It was very eye opening and explained many aspects of me that I'd not previously understood. Understanding yourself on a deeper level helps you gain clarity and direction. So, if you're interested in discovering more about your worldly challenges, spiritual challenges, spiritual talents, worldly talents, worldly goals, spiritual goals, and your soul destiny, then book a session with me (www.denisedavis.co.uk). 🖤

The Soul Plan method is a new interpretation of an ancient system of life purpose analysis. This method works on the conscious and unconscious level and promises to bring the recipient greater freedom, connection, satisfaction, healing, life purpose, activation and alignment. Soul Plan reading is based upon the sound vibration and intention of your full birth name as written on your birth certificate (you can also have a reading on the name you use if this is different, as this will create an overlay and bring further insights). If considering a business name, it is useful to see what properties the name brings. Once you've experienced your Soul Plan, you will naturally begin to align with it.

In its present format, Soul Plan reading is a remarkably powerful and accurate system of life purpose, guidance, spiritual counselling and healing. Furthermore, this work has a relevance to all aspects of life and can be used for name optimisation, business readings, relationship compatibility and healing of core limiting beliefs, old patterns and issues. It holds the vibration of your soul purpose. It's based on the fact that our lives are divided into two parts: worldly (from birth to age thirty-five/forty) and spiritual (thirty-five/forty until death). These two "lives" are sectioned into three key aspects: your challenges, your talents and your goals. You use your inherent talents to overcome your challenges, to reach your goals. The talents I'm talking about are yours and yours solely. They are based on your life purpose. It's the same for the goals; you might believe that you need to be like this or that to succeed and be happy, but what is it that **really** makes you happy? All these aspects come together as your Soul Destiny – the essence of why you are here.

After the reading there is an Energy Healing period, allowing you to release blocks which create resistance and suffering. It's an amazingly liberating process! Ask yourself this, dear reader:

- Do you know your life purpose?

- Are you still searching?

- Do you have a sense that there is something more for you in your life?

Theta Healing
Theta Healing is a meditative technique which is conducted while the client and practitioner are

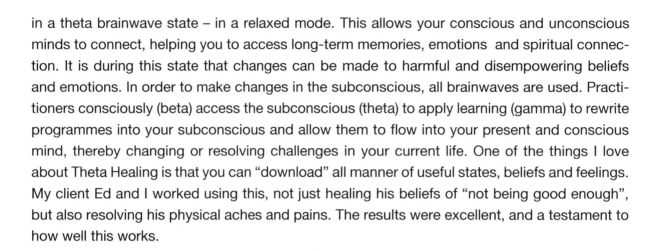

in a theta brainwave state – in a relaxed mode. This allows your conscious and unconscious minds to connect, helping you to access long-term memories, emotions and spiritual connection. It is during this state that changes can be made to harmful and disempowering beliefs and emotions. In order to make changes in the subconscious, all brainwaves are used. Practitioners consciously (beta) access the subconscious (theta) to apply learning (gamma) to rewrite programmes into your subconscious and allow them to flow into your present and conscious mind, thereby changing or resolving challenges in your current life. One of the things I love about Theta Healing is that you can "download" all manner of useful states, beliefs and feelings. My client Ed and I worked using this, not just healing his beliefs of "not being good enough", but also resolving his physical aches and pains. The results were excellent, and a testament to how well this works.

Rewrite Your Story

This is something I've done during various trainings. Particular emphasis was paid to this during "Design Your Destiny" with Christopher Howard and during another training with Andy Harrington. In Christopher's event, we changed our story to our best possible version, by re-writing it from a different perspective. During Andy's event, we wrote the old story and then tore it into tiny pieces, before visualising our best story to the tune of evocative music and perfume, to aid anchoring the new story. So, I invite you to do these exercises today. Today is the first day of the rest of your life. Begin this new day by expressing yourself on paper, creating a fresh "story", noting how the reframe and silver linings that came from your old story have brought you to this wiser and stronger version of you.

Being Present on Earth

For years I felt a longing for "home". I felt as if I didn't fit (home meaning a return to Source, being just energy again, experiencing joy and bliss/no longer being in human form). However, once my grandchildren arrived to ensure I felt happier on the planet and received the most from my experiences, I committed to enjoying the rest of my life to the best of my ability. If you are feeling the same, you can say with full intent, 'I allow myself to be truly home and present here whilst on earth. I release all sadness and grief around my "not belonging", being understood or feeling held.' You can then meditate to call in your perfect home. As mentioned in part one, I recognised my longing to live by the sea and finally brought this to fruition by moving to the coast in Dorset. Meeting kindred souls has also assisted me in feeling at home and finding my authentic self. A root chakra healing, using hematite crystals plus grounding and connecting with spirit also helps me to feel safe and secure.

Smiles – Fake and Real

Smiling releases endorphins. The mind and body affect each other in so many ways, and this is why a "fake it until you make it" smile works well. If you smile, you'll send a message to your brain that you are happy. Your body may also subconsciously alter your posture, making you more upright, appearing confident.

Science has shown that the mere act of smiling can lift your mood, lower stress, boost your immune system and possibly prolong your life. You may think happiness makes you smile, but the reverse can be true too. Dr Isha Gupta, a neurologist from IGEA Brain and Spine, explains that a smile spurs a chemical reaction in the brain, releasing certain hormones including dopamine and serotonin. Dopamine increases your feelings of happiness. Serotonin release is associated with reducing stress. Experts associate low levels of these hormones with depression and sometimes aggression. So, in essence, smiling can trick your brain into believing you're happy, which then activates actual feelings of happiness.

Dr Murray Grossan, an ENT Otolaryngologist specialist, points to the science of psychoneuro-immunology (the study of how the brain is connected to the immune system), asserting that it has been shown repeatedly that depression weakens your immune system, while happiness on the other hand has been shown to boost your body's resistance. "What's crazy is that just the physical act of smiling can make a difference in building your immunity," Dr Grossan is quoted as saying. He continues, "When you smile, the brain sees the muscle (activity) and assumes that humour is happening." Dr Sivan Finkel, a cosmetic dentist at NYC's highly regarded Dental Parlor, corroborates this by stating that, "Even forcing a fake smile can legitimately reduce stress and lower your heart rate." Likewise, a study performed at the University of Cardiff found that people who could not frown because of Botox injections were happier on average than those who could frown.

Energy Healing

Energy Healing is based on the premise that a vital energy flows through the human body. The goal is to balance the energy flow in the client. A healer is a conduit for universal energy, which flows through them to their client's body. Your body knows where the healing energy is needed, which isn't always where your brain thinks it is. For example, you may have a pain in your leg, but you also have unknown sorrow deep in your heart – thus the energy may heal this before releasing your leg pain. I utilised this healing method after my divorce, because I was so hurt and emotionally unstable. The result was that I felt more balanced and calmer after my sessions.

I've used this healing method on multiple clients in the past. One client, Marcus, came in with pain in his tummy. He was a bit skeptical at first, as he'd never had Reiki Healing before. After the session Marcus was absolutely astounded at how much better he felt. Not only had his pain gone, but he felt brighter and uplifted. My other client Kirsten had been experiencing a bout of headaches – she even had one when she arrived. Like Marcus, it was her first time having Reiki, and she was so happy and relieved after her session. Energy Healing is a great way to energise or relax you (according to your body's needs), alongside Reconnective Healing, which my clients have had awesome results with.

Memory Recall

Relive and re-immerse yourself by recalling past fun times, allowing yourself to access feelings, sights, sounds, taste and smells. Let all these good feelings permeate your body right down to a cellular level and out into your auric field. Sit with these until you notice you have had a change of mood, feeling more positive. Visual rehearsal is when you relax into a hypnotic/meditative state and imagine your life how you'd like it to be, using all of your senses. Remember that your mind cannot detect whether your experiences are real or imagined. So, go ahead and use your visions to create your desires.

Prayers and Wishes

I often talk to Archangels, Angels, my Guardian Angel, the Ascended Masters, my Star Family, my Higher Self, God/The Universe, (Creator, Source, Intelligence, Beauty or whatever you like to call it) to give thanks for all that I am and all that I have. I also commune with my spirit guides and channel information from collectives and higher beings. There are many wonderful books detailing the different angels that can assist us. I've read too many to list here. I also love using my various Angel Oracle cards, with my favourite one being "Doreen Virtues" – which I regularly use.

Vision Boards and Mind Movies

A vision board is a tool to help clarify, concentrate and maintain a focus on your life goals. It's a board on which you display images and words that represent whatever you want to be, do or have in your life. It is a fabulous way to keep you motivated, on track and encouraged. Visualisation encourages you to be forward thinking, to expand from your current situation. It's a reminder to you that you don't have to be in the same situation forever. If you're unhappy, it will encourage you to do more. If you're already in your comfort zone, it will encourage you to reach further. Visualisation physically shows your mental goals. When the images in your mind become physical, you create an image of your future self, which you move towards. Imagining can give you a sense of purpose, giving your mind a chance to think about the decisions and actions you make. As Arnold Schwarzenegger said, 'If I can see and believe it, then I can achieve it.'

Creating a vision board is a powerful and tangible way to say 'yes please' to the abundance you'd like to receive and deserve in your life. It works, because it makes you put your attention on your desires, unconsciously scanning the world for items that match them. It's not that your desires weren't there before, it's just that you hadn't noticed them before. For example, if you want a grey Mercedes, then you will regularly see them. When you continue to give your attention to the things you want and you have a visual of them, you can attract those things into your life. The more you surround yourself and your mind with things you want to experience, the more you'll experience those things in your life – energy goes where your attention flows. Once you've clarified your vision and displayed it where you can see it daily, your job is to look at it as often as possible, noting the opportunities in your life, so you can pursue your goals and desires. The symbols and words are a visual for your unconscious to know what your wishes are. On my birthday each year (which I view as my new year) I make a large A1 card vision board, which I display near my bed, so that I see it each morning on awakening. I also make a smaller A3 card with words and symbols drawn in colour, which I place on my wall above it, with two A4 mandalas on my dressing table, one for optimal health and one for abundance (love, happiness and money).

Before attending Dr Joe Dispenza's advanced workshop, we were asked to create a "Mind Movie". The pictures and words serve as a visual message to your unconscious mind and the Universe, showing what your wishes are, helping to bring them to fruition. This works similarly to a vision board, but in some ways is better, as it uses more of your senses – you can add music, positive statements and even subliminal messages, to get empowered to reach your goals. The short videos you create are designed to get your mind in peak "manifesting mode". By watching your Mind Movie daily at least once or more, you are mentally imagining your goals and desires in a way that feels as if you're already living in that reality. The optimum way to manifest is to use both a static vision board and Mind Movies.

Healing Art

Creating art in different formats such as mandalas, future pictures, picture tapping, free flow abstract painting or crafting, gives you a sense of control, relieving stress and tension by taking your mind off your problems. It's a wonderful way to express yourself. By providing a fantastic outlet to process your emotions, it can help you recognise and acknowledge feelings lurking in your subconscious. Art fosters self-awareness and can be done at home on your own. However, I also love creating in groups, so I attend local one-off events or short courses. Art reconciles your emotional conflicts, as the creative act of crafting helps focus your mind. Even gardening or sewing releases dopamine, a natural antidepressant. Art improves memory, resilience and reasoning, and serves as a further way of releasing blocks and manifesting your desires, through doodles, mandalas, symbols or whatever intuitively feels right for you. You can create mandalas for anything. I have created many mandalas of my own for various reasons, including healing and manifesting – I just set the intention before creation. I even created a mandala for my Soul Plan, using the symbols at the centre of my mandala in the Star of Creation. See the photo below for how this looks:

Carl Jung gave his clients ready-made mandalas to colour, as a way of healing. There are many already created available in the shops. At my first spiritual development circle we were given a very basic, almost empty circle and told to create a wonderful mandala, before bringing it with us to our next session. The following week we would place them anonymously in the middle of the room. Later in the evening we would pick one and give the person a reading of how they were feeling when they were creating it.

Another method I mentioned earlier in the book is to fold an A4 piece of paper in half and draw your current issue on the left-hand side and what you want on the right side. Once you have finished, cut the left side off and disperse – you could even tear it up into tiny pieces. My preference is to burn – a releasing ritual which has been used for thousands of years in many diverse communities, particularly by shamans in the indigenous communities. If you still have issues that demand more than creating at home, then you can contact me to book a session (www.denisedavis.co.uk). ♥

Walking the Labyrinth

Labyrinth walking is an ancient practice used by many different faiths for spiritual centering, contemplation, and prayer. You can walk slowly while quieting your mind and focusing on a spiritual question or prayer. You can also walk the labyrinth to contemplate your life, identifying and releasing challenges on the way to its centre. Then meditate and set your intention whilst there, focusing on your desires on your exit from the labyrinth. A friend and I did this together at the Wisdom Retreat and Conference Centre in Romsey, where we reunited as sisters, recognising this as a past life reunion. It is usual to walk the labyrinth alone, which we did until meeting in the center for our reunion, before exiting separately. Chartres Cathedral in Paris has a wonderful labyrinth which is only open on the summer solstice and on Fridays at certain times of the year.

I was fortunate when a friend gifted me a miniature sandbox to create my own mini labyrinth with tiny tools. I had to use something small like a pencil to "walk" the labyrinth, as it was tiny, but it was most enjoyable. Another friend had a labyrinth mowed into her garden, which I was lucky enough to walk round a few times. I have also printed out a labyrinth on A4 paper and used my fingers to walk the labyrinth, before releasing on the way towards the centre and focusing my positive desires on the exit.

Aqua Detox

I often consult an Aqua Detox ™ practitioner, particularly when I have had X-rays, to release all the toxins and to reset my body. I combine this with a homeopathic remedy to repair and heal. The Aqua Detox is an effective way to re-balance, re-energise and detoxify the body. The technology of the Aqua Detox system was based on the original research carried out by Dr Royal Rife in the 1930s. He studied the effect of passing a low voltage electrical current through the water and its association with the body. Dr Rife discovered that this would stimulate the meridians of the body.

The Aqua Detox foot spa comprises a foot bowl filled with warm salt water that is connected to a control panel. This control panel delivers a minor charge through the water via an electrode called an array, which resonates with your individual bio-energetic field. You place your bare feet into a footbath of warm saline water and relax in a chair for thirty minutes. The water changes colour because of the chemical reaction, which happens while the water is being ionised. The colour of the water will change regardless of the presence of feet! While you are relaxing, the water will immediately change colour, as millions of ions enter your body. The body will absorb the electrons and a natural rebalancing of the cells in the body will take place. It's an effective way of cleansing the body from heavy metals and other toxins. There are numerous benefits of this, including aiding detoxification, stimulation and balancing of the body's energy meridians. You may feel great, sleep better, and have more energy and an improved outlook on life. If you're worried about pain, then this is a great treatment for you, as the charge delivered by the array is tiny. Some people will comment on a slight tingling in the feet, but this is normal. Many people feel nothing at all.

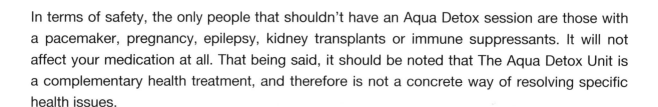

In terms of safety, the only people that shouldn't have an Aqua Detox session are those with a pacemaker, pregnancy, epilepsy, kidney transplants or immune suppressants. It will not affect your medication at all. That being said, it should be noted that The Aqua Detox Unit is a complementary health treatment, and therefore is not a concrete way of resolving specific health issues.

Emotion Code

The Emotion Code is a simple and easy way to release any unwanted trapped emotions that you may not even realise you have hidden. My clients found this an excellent way to feel better swiftly, without having to re-immerse themselves in any distressing memories. I often use this method on myself and have sessions with other practitioners. The Emotion Code was created by Dr Bradley Nelson, to help you find and release any trapped energies that inhabit your body. These energies limit your ability to feel love, joy and to create success. There is also a book of the same name. You can find the chart on the internet to use this to work on yourself, or work with an experienced practitioner if you prefer.

There are various muscle testing processes available. Here, I have written the two I use the most. You can use the sway test – this is when your thoughts and emotions produce a certain response in your immune system, affecting your motor response (movement of your body). To do the sway test, first stand up and find your neutral position. Make sure you are hydrated, as this may affect your response. To find your yes, say the following: ask if your name is … (use your correct name). To find your no, ask if your name is … (use an alternative name). What usually happens is that when you say your real name, your body moves slightly forward, with your feet remaining in the same position. When stating a wrong name, your body usually sways backwards slightly. Having found your yes/no position, you can now ask questions. Remember to phrase them for a yes or no response. I sometimes use the sway to ask whether to buy a certain food.

The test I prefer to use for the emotion code is one I call the finger pull. To do the finger pull, make a circle with your thumb and index finger. Insert the other thumb and index finger through the loop you have already made, to create another circle. Hold light tension in the circles. As you ask your question, gently pull your second loop to see if it disconnects from the first circle. When it remains locked, your answer is yes. When the second loop disconnects, then your answer is no. For images, type into Google "loop fingers kinesiology". Alternatively, if you prefer to release your physical pain or emotions with someone assisting you, then book a session with me (www.denisedavis.co.uk). ♥

Access Consciousness

Gary Douglas was the pioneer of Access Consciousness, and now works collaboratively with Dain Heer. According to the latter, Access Consciousness is about seeing life from a different point of view. It is based on the premise that you are not wrong and that your consciousness can shift anything, giving you access to the possibilities that exist when you no longer believe you are stuck. The aim of Access Consciousness is to create a world of consciousness and oneness, where everything exists and nothing is judged. It enables you to change everything you think you cannot change, and create everything you desire in a different and easier way. Access Consciousness empowers you to know what is true for you. As I mentioned earlier, I use the access sayings, 'How does it get any better than this?', 'All of life comes to me with ease, joy and glory' and 'What else is possible?' No one is allowed to share the access clearing statement, but it is easy to find on the Access Consciousness website.

Copper Wand and Copper Water Bottle

I sometimes sleep with my copper wand (which has a pointed clear quartz crystal tip to amplify its properties) on my bedside table, so I can feel the benefits and sometimes I just hold it for a few minutes. I put my drinking water into a copper bottle, which helps me to get the most out of it, and I bless it before drinking as I do before eating. When buying a copper bottle, make sure you do plenty of research, because if it is of poor quality then it can have detrimental instead of beneficial effects. Copper is an essential trace mineral, necessary for survival. It is found in all body tissues and plays a role in making red blood cells, maintaining nerve cells and the immune system, due to the fact that it has a unique combination of anti-inflammatory, antibacterial and antiviral properties. It is purported that copper helps your body form collagen, absorbs iron and plays a role in energy production. It's said to protect cognitive function, promoting immune function and iron absorption. It also aids in digestion, anti-aging, is an energy boost and assists thyroid function. Wearing a copper bracelet is said to protect against heart disease, bone density and osteoporosis, arthritis relief and joint pain. Additionally, copper helps to support healthy cell renewal and rejuvenation, so that while your body is fighting off infection, it is also working to replace the damaged skin cells, thereby increasing the speed of skin healing.

The Journey

Shortly after James left me, I had a health scare with suspected colon cancer. My grandfather and father died from this – it is said to be hereditary through genetics. But, having read Dawson Church's *A Genie in Your Genes,* Bruce Lipton's *The Biology of Belief* and Candice Pert's *Molecules of Emotions,* I believe we can make changes to our genetic predispositions. Before receiving my results, I decided I would use complementary therapy as my first port of call instead of chemotherapy, should the results be positive. So, I booked a Journey Session before I knew what the outcome was. Of course, if you are suffering from cancer or another illness then your first port of call should always be to see a doctor, as I am not a medical expert.

This session was interesting, because I gained numerous insights, including that I was projecting my challenges and blaming others. It made me very aware of my thoughts and speech patterns. The session intrigued me so much that I trained with Brandon Bays for The Journey, to work with both adults and children. The process comprises nine steps on the physical journey. You guide your client to Source, going on a journey of discovery, uncovering emotions, associated memories or people, guiding your client through the memory process, and then through the campfire process and dialogue, emptying out and forgiving. You see how the area of the body has changed and get advice from it. Finally, returning to the doorway where the journey began, you say farewell to the mentor and guide your client back to consciousness.

My Appreciation Jar

I use heart-shaped sticky notes that are glued together with the letters "TIA" (today I appreciate) at the top. I then write underneath what I appreciate, before placing the notes in a jar.

The key is to feel the emotion of gratitude. As previously mentioned, I express my gratitude and thanks at various times of the day for anything and everything and say why. When feeling low, you can then look at what you've previously written to engage with those happy feelings. This exercise rewires your brain to a more positive viewpoint. If you want to do this with your children, then leave a gratitude pebble by their bed and have them hold it at night, saying thanks for things they have enjoyed that day (or any object they want to have as a symbol of appreciation). An alternative would be to draw a big heart. Inside it, draw a picture and/or write sentences of things they are grateful for that day. Encourage them to think both big and small.

Focusing on the positives in your life lifts your spirit – the act of appreciation will not only create enjoyable feelings but bring more of the things you have gratitude for into your life (see law of attraction part seven). When thinking of those you love, send out your love to them – feeling it deeply in your heart – knowing that on some energetic level they are receiving it.

Spread Your Love

Share your positive feelings, compliments and hugs with those you care for. I've always been a tactile person, hugging and kissing those I care for, linking arms when walking and showing other public displays of affection. I believe it's important to spread joy to others, as it makes me feel good too. Dr David Hamilton states that hugs and kindness increase longevity for both giver and receiver.

Being of Service

When my kids were young, I volunteered in their schools, helping children to read and assisting with art and design lessons. Being helpful or in service to others helps creates a sense of purpose. For example, I go singing each month. Once we know the songs well, we then sing at care homes for the residents. Other ways you can assist are:

- Helping a neighbour with their shopping or walking their dog when they're poorly.

- Keeping lonely people company one evening a week. This can be family, friends, neighbours or strangers.

- Helping at a charity shop or at the hospital.

- Listening to children read in a school or helping with school trips.

- Being a surrogate grandparent to those who don't have any and would love one.

Really it's just about helping those in need, offering them kindness, love and appreciation. There may be many others you can think of, which suit you better.

Oracle Cards and Readings

I regularly use my oracle and tarot cards, but I also have lots of other cards too. I just love having so many choices, although I mainly use just two sets for my professional readings. The rest I use only for me and my friends. I find that these cards are all very helpful, especially when I need reassurance that I'm on the right path. This you can do for yourself, or consult a professional reader. When I trained in the advanced tarot course, I was directed to sense, feel and see what the cards showed me instead of focusing on the general meanings. I believe you can do the same with your own cards, but you have to relax, tune in and have no expected outcome. Look at the colours and what you feel/sense they mean. What words come into your mind when you look at the pictures and numbers on the cards?

Often, a fellow reader and I do spontaneous readings for each other, sometimes when out we will use any objects around us. Occasionally I consult other readers, which usually confirms what I already "know or feel", but I also gain some insights that I was unaware of. Pamela, one of my clients, came to me for a reading. The guidance she received lead to her expansion and making changes to her career. She said she felt fulfilled and satisfied for the first time in ages. A reading is essentially a snapshot in time, of a possibility that may occur if you continue down the path you are currently on. Of course, free will means you may change your course, as there is an abundance of possibilities in this life (part seven explains about the "field of possibilities").

Celebrations

Celebrate your successes, big and small. Even if it's just that you got through another day, treat yourself in whatever way you like best. It may be a pampering soak in the bath, reading, listening to a celebratory song, giving yourself a pat on the back, sharing your win with a friend or having a yummy bar of your favourite chocolate…

Create a success list, so that you can reflect when you're feeling low. Do whatever feels good to you. Recognise how far you have come since you were a young child and the obstacles you have overcome.

Reach Out

When feeling lonely, ring a family member or a friend. If they are all busy and you wish to be near others, you could go to workshops, coffee shops, the library or the gym. I feel less isolated from people and feel a sense of belonging when I do this, which is especially vital as I live and work alone. It's true that I like some time on my own, but not all the time every day and evening. I even took to going out when writing this book, as I was becoming too much of a hermit. In fact, you could go anywhere really where other people are, such as a museum, an art gallery or leisure centre. Join classes, do something uplifting, learn something new or meet up with group of friends to just chat and have a cuppa.

Pamper Treatments

Having a body massage is relaxing, especially if you fully "let go" and allow yourself to sink into the experience. In Dawson Church's book *A Genie in Your Genes,* he suggests that massages may cause a piezoelectric effect, which can release stuck emotions from your body. There are other treatments that I find fabulously relaxing too, such as reflexology, acupuncture, scalp massages and facials. Another uplifting treatment for me is having my hair treated and styled (which may be true for many women). Have treatments with various people until you find the one that gives you the greatest benefits. I found that some massage therapists and reflexologists were either too gentle or too rough – I now have excellent people who place me in a state of calm and rejuvenation.

Read and Watch Films

Reading inspiring books or watching wonderful movies is a good way to transport yourself into another time and place, a world away from your current challenges. This stops you overthinking and feeling sad or low. Comedies are particularly cathartic, as when you laugh you're releasing positive hormones, similar to when you smile.

When grieving the loss of my expected future after my divorce, I found the book *The Afterlife of Billy Fingers* by Annie Kagan. In the book, Billy suggests that we have as many experiences as possible, of all different "flavours". I also found it reassuring that my beliefs of the afterlife, lives between lives, and reincarnation, are real. *Many Lives, Many Master* is another reaffirming book about past lives and reincarnation.

Over the years I have read thousands of fabulous books, so I'm unable to mention them all, otherwise this chapter would be a tome! Listed below are a tiny fraction of the ones I enjoyed:

- *Who Moved My Cheese?* by Spencer Johnson.

- *Jonathan Living Seagull* by Richard Bach.

- *The Celestine Prophecy* and its follow-on books by James Redfield.

- *Synchrodestiny* by Deepak Chopra.

- *Rise Sister Rise* by Rebecca Campbell.

- *A Return to Love* by Marianne Williamson.

- *The Alchemist* by Paulo Coelho.

- *The Four Agreements* by Don Miguel Ruiz.

- *The Gene Keys* by Richard Rudd.

- *The Book of Knowledge: The Keys of Enoch* by JJ Hurtack.

- *Men are from Mars, Women are from Venus* by John Gray.

- *The Five Love Languages* by Gary Chapman.

- *Conversations with God* by Neale Donald Walsh.

- *The Ringing Cedars of Russia* series by Vladimir Megre.

- *F**ck It - The Ultimate Spiritual Way* by John Parkin.

There are so many other authors too, such as Doreen Virtue, Matt Khan, Sonia Choquette and Caroline Myss. I also love reading novels and have found this a wonderful way to pass time, as well as taking my mind off what is happening during COVID-19.

Sunshine

Sunbathe carefully for quick bursts (not in midday sun) to relax and take in vitamin D, which helps counteract depression. We are like plants and need the light to survive (photosynthesis). I have to be proactive in my self-care during January and February, as my mood dips from the lack of sunlight. So I walk outside and take vitamin D3, K2 and magnesium, which helps absorption of the D. It's healthy for you to be out in daylight, as long as you can wrap up well for the weather. Why not go for a walk, followed by a pit stop to take in the beauty around you? You could take your holiday during January or February, visiting a sunnier climate in order to get your sunshine "hit". After James left, I took St. John's Wort capsules for a while, as this helps lift depression (they are a natural plant).

Mental and Dance Breaks

It is important to take mental breaks, especially when thoughts, worries and stress are clouding your over-crowded mind. So give your mind a rest from onerous tasks, walk around the office, go to the bathroom, just breathe and ground yourself or go outside for ten minutes and notice five things around you – using all your senses. When you return to the task, your mind will be rejuvenated with a fresh perspective. Move every thirty minutes to relieve the body of sitting in the same position for hours. This also gives your eyes a rest if you've been focusing on a task for a long time.

If I'm ever unsure of the cause of my negative feelings, I may ask my body questions, sometimes using a pendulum or doing the sway test to get a "yes or no" answer, which as I said earlier is biofeedback from your body. At other times I may just sit quietly and go within for the answer. As mentioned, in my morning practice I may look at photos and scrapbooks to remember happy times and to connect with the love I have for those I care about.

My Abundance Jar

In the abundance corner of my home, which is in my bedroom, I have a money jar. I also have a pile of serviettes on my bedside cabinet, which look like fifty-pound notes. On top of this I have a real fifty-pound note so that it appears as if I have a lot of money. I have cash in each handbag and my car so that everywhere I look, I feel abundant. I use my money stashes as a focus for being grateful for all the money I have had and will receive in the future.

Plants

Studies have shown that having indoor plants can boost your mood, productivity, concentration and creativity. They also reduce stress, fatigue, sore throats and colds. Plants clean indoor air by absorbing toxins, increasing humidity and producing oxygen. They add life to a sterile office, give privacy and reduce noise levels. Plants can help to reduce "sick-building syndrome". In 1989, Dr Bill Wolverton, a leading scientist in NASA's Clean Air study, revealed that "when the building occupants are away for a time, the symptoms usually diminish, only to recur upon re-entry to the building." The cause of sick building syndrome is indoor air pollution, usually from toxic emissions from synthetic building materials, airborne mould, viruses and pollutants, along with energy efficient construction like making spaces as airtight as possible, which reduces the air circulation. These contributors release toxin emissions such as benzene, formaldehyde, trichloroethylene, xylene and toluene.

It isn't just commercial buildings where these appear, as the toxic compounds can be found in many homes too. Many wall paints, rubbers, vinyl, laminates, computer parts, furniture, carpets and plastics all break down over time and release compounds in the air. The brilliant news is these can be improved by adding plants to absorb the harmful toxins, breaking them down and storing them in their soil to use later for food. Snake plat, pothos, rubber plant, ZZ plant, bird's nest fern and philodendron are good plants to use. Finally, plants have phytoncides and other airborne chemicals. These chemicals help to reduce your stress, which boosts your immune system.

Studies in Norway have shown that illnesses drop by 60% through the use of plants in the home. When you have plants in your home, it also increases your compassion as you care for a sentient, living thing. The phytonutrients help to settle your mind, creating a safe space and environment.

Group techniques and activities

Sound Healing

Sound Healing uses unique aspects of sound to improve your emotional and physical wellbeing. By using specific rhythms and frequencies, you can downshift your brain from the beta state of normal consciousness to the theta state of relaxed consciousness, and the delta state where internal healing can occur. Everything in the universe has a vibrational frequency (more information in part seven). In the brain, all your neurons fire at different frequencies based on the data they receive from things around you. Those vibrations interact with every cell in your body. When you have a Sound Healing session, you are immersed in the experience, listening to music, chanting or listening to sounds from instruments like gongs.

In ancient Greece, they used music to aid mental disorders. Music boosts your morale, helping you work faster and more productively. Science has linked sound with boosted immune function and lowered stress levels, even noting that it can improve the health of premature babies. It has other benefits too, such as normalising blood pressure, promoting relaxation, reducing pain, depression, fatigue and anger. Sound waves from gongs, tuning forks, singing bowls and more can alter your brainwave frequency. Humans hear frequencies from 20 hz up to 20,000 hz, but this doesn't mean that you aren't affected by sounds you're unable to hear. When you have two vibrating entities near each other, the stronger vibration will affect the weaker one, with the two entities eventually synchronising – which is entrainment. In your ear there is a vestibulo-cochlear nerve, which connects to your vagus nerve and is the major parasympathetic nerve in the body. This affects your nervous system and is responsible for rest, digestion, stress reduction, muscle relaxation and lowering blood pressure. Your vagus nerve helps control hormone release, digestion, blood glucose levels, inflammation, heart rate and blood pressure. An inactive or blocked vagus nerve is dismal news for health, but stimulating it with sound can bring your body back to harmony and balance.

I am blessed to know a few sound healers who also use gongs, so I regularly have a "gong bath". A gong or sound bath/journey is when a facilitator plays the gong or other instruments, whilst the participants lie down and relax, allowing the sound to wash over and into their body. As a sound healer I love to give and receive gong baths in a group. I have had clients come for bespoke one-to-one sessions where the intent is personal, private and exclusive. Drumming circles are another superb way to "beat the blues" – and there are group meetings throughout the UK for this purpose.

Sound Healing can assist with:

- Anxiety disorders;

- Depression;

- PTSD;

- Dementia;

- Autism and ADHD;

- Learning difficulties;

- Behavioural disorders;

- Cancer;

- Mood swings;

- High cholesterol;

- Coronary artery disease and stroke;

- Insomnia and other sleep disorders.

According to Lynne McTaggart, doing things in groups exponentially increases the benefits of any healing approach. Her latest book *The Power of Eight* argues that eight is a great number to achieve very effective results. However, a group giving healing (whatever the size) is always more effective than just one person doing it alone.

Mantras and Chanting

To follow on from part five, a mantra is a syllable, word or phrase that is repeated through speaking, singing or whispering. It's often used as a mindfulness practice. It can serve as a mental protection from unwanted distractions or emotions, sleeplessness or coping with fears. For others it is part of their spiritual practice. Mantra recitation is used to focus the mind and heart, and to connect with the Divine, which is both within you and around you. One benefit is that it helps keeps your mind focused and receptive to the blessings of the present moment. Explore what you want from your mantra chanting – do you want to maintain/regain your health, do you have thoughts whirling around that distract you, or are you looking to forge a deeper spiritual connection? Many people find this is a wonderful way to relax and soothe their mind, lower blood pressure and reduce their stress and anxiety.

Mantras align your vibration to create awareness. The vibrations from mantras have the power to rearrange your molecular structure. You can chant silently in your mind or out loud, whatever is your preference. You can set an intention if you wish – my client William said that his mantra practice helped him overcome destructive personal habits and brought him closer to the Divine. William also said it helped him be more patient, keeping his vibrations and mood at a good level.

Sit and focus on your breathing to relax before you start. Scan your body to see and feel where you're holding tension so you can let it go. Once relaxed, chant your mantra and repeat until you want to stop. Some people use 'Om Mani Padme Hum' which means 'great compassion' as a mantra. Others use affirmations – you could create your own, starting with 'I am...' For example:

- *'I am content in this moment, my heart guides me. I let go and let God in. Om Shanti Om.'* (Shanti means peace.)

- *'Om Namah Shivaya.'* This means, 'I bow to Shiva'. (Shiva representing your Higher Self and everything in nature it represents.)

- *'I AM that I AM.'* This reaffirms the presence of the Divine that is everything and everywhere.

- *'Aham Prema'* – I am Divine love.

You can find more mantras on the internet, along with the ones previously mentioned in this book, to discover something that fits with what you want to feel that day. Chanting is an excellent way of healing the throat chakra and heart chakra, releasing emotions through self-expression. You can use a word that means something to you or signifies your goal, such as: 'harmony', 'love', 'peace', 'faith', 'I am at peace', 'I am love(d)', 'I am harmonious and balanced', 'I am full of light and love', 'past, present and future are one' and 'love is all around me, love is everywhere'. Repetition is key, so dedicate an amount of time to chanting.

Mother Earth Lodges

A Native American sweat lodge or Mother Earth lodge is a ceremonial sweat bath. It is a purifying ceremony that uses intense heat to stimulate vision and insight. I asked around and went to a lodge that others I knew attended. That way I felt I was working with someone with experience and would be safe and secure. In some places the use of clothing is optional. I used a swimsuit with a sarong, some wore just a towel or underpants. (There are naked lodges, so do your research before you book a session to find one that suits your preference!) In any case, the ritual helps detoxify the body by stimulating blood circulation, causing you to sweat out impurities.

Traditionally, a sweat lodge is held in a dome shaped structure, low to the ground and created with natural wood such as willow. The builders then cover this with tarpaulin and sometimes put blankets on top, which keeps out the rain and light. The rocks are heated outside, then brought inside into the middle of the lodge and placed in a dugout pit. It's usual to have four rounds, with fresh rocks added in each round, thus building up the heat. The person performing the ceremony is the one to add water to create steam. They also add herbs such as sage or sweetgrass. Some like to smudge everyone's aura before entering the lodge, to aid with the purification, although not all do this. The leader usually chants in Native American tongue. One round is a healing round, where you can wish/share what you desire as an outcome i.e. release pain, to give thanks, to heal, to seek wisdom, to purify mind, body and soul.

The lodges are a fabulous way to rebirth and heal. I was lucky enough to attend some that were run by an indigenous Native American Indian (one nation) who flew over regularly from the states to hold the lodges and share his teachings. Many miraculous outcomes have occurred by attending these. I personally know two infertile women who became pregnant after attending our sweat lodge, whilst others healed physical and emotional symptoms.

Prayers and Wishes

Prayers and wishes to God/The Universe, Archangels, Angels and other Celestial beings, especially when shared as a group, are extremely powerful. When this happens, the energy and the intent are extrapolated. We also gift healing to each other and the world at large, in our group ceremonies and workshops. Many spiritual teachers have claimed that if you see a white feather or a penny, hear a song or hear parts of a conversation, it is a sign from the angels that you are on the right path or to listen to what is being said – as it is relevant to you. During my clinical hypnotherapy training, I researched the power of prayer on the outcome of cancer patients' recovery. Those who had said their own personal prayers, and those who'd had group prayers held for them or received good wishes, were shown to have improved their health at a faster rate. I believe this is due to trust and faith in something greater than ourselves, creating feelings of being supported. There are numerous studies validating the benefits of prayer and possible reasons why it works. I requested prayers for my little grandchildren when they were in hospital very poorly, and I believe this helped with a positive outcome. Many people also ask me to pray or send distant healing, which they believe will be helpful, then they let me know the positive results. It could be the placebo effect – who really knows, but the bottom line is that it works! Positivity is powerful!

Meditation Groups

Meditation is a magnificent way to release stress and increase longevity – there are many studies demonstrating its benefits. I fully encourage you to include meditation as a habitual process, training your mind to focus and redirect your thoughts. You can use it to increase awareness of yourself and your surroundings. People also use meditation to develop other beneficial habits and feelings, such as a positive mood and outlook, self-discipline, healthy sleep patterns and even increase pain tolerance. Some benefits of meditation are:

- Stress reduction;

- Anxiety control;

- Emotional health improvement;

- Enhanced self-awareness;

- Lengthened attention span;

- Reduced age-related memory loss;

- Generates kindness;

- Helps to fight addictions;

- Improved sleep;

- Helps control pain;

- Decreased blood pressure.

Spiritual development sessions usually include meditation, reading objects and cards, and doing insightful activities. This increases your self-awareness, enhances your intuition and when meeting regularly in a group creates a greater sense of community. So, find a group near you to help you explore more of who you are.

Summary

In this chapter we have looked at activities that you can do alone or with a practitioner, and group activities. Try some out and see which works best for you.

Invitation

 Pick three activities from the book which you will implement today to harmonise your heart. Write about your expectations of how you will feel. When you have carried out the activities, write how you felt and see if they correlate.

Insightful Questions

When you have finished the invitation above, take a notepad and pen. Sit quietly, free from any distractions, in a relaxed manner. Look at each of the questions below, one at a time. Allow the question to just flow freely in your mind, percolating if you will. Then, capture your answers on paper, giving you an insight into where you are right now. This will help you shift your perspective, so that you become less stuck.

- *What is the greatest challenge you have right now?*

- *What benefits have you got from this issue/s?*

- *What would you like to release?*

- *What is preventing you from moving forward and having the life you desire?*

- *What are your desires? What's behind them? Is it something you want to move away from or something to move forward to?*

- *Have you found a process(es) that you will use when you're feeling out of balance?*

- *Will you research more on the mind and body connection?*

- *What will you now put into your life, to harmonise your heart?*

- *What insights/benefits have you received from your challenges?*

- *Have you discovered what your top ten values are? Are you in alignment with them?*

Having completed all the questions, consider positive ways in which you could make changes. Can you think of any other ways you could make changes, which haven't been mentioned in the book?

Part Seven

Understanding Energy and Vibration

Everything is Energy!

Everything is energy and everything is connected. From the water in the ocean to the clouds in the sky, the trees, the animals and the people around you – everything comes from the same source and ultimately returns to it. According to quantum physics, a particle vibrating because of the sound of your voice can affect a molecule inside a star at the edge of the universe. This phenomenon is known as quantum entanglement. The greatest illusion of this universe is the illusion of separation. Your thoughts and feelings are energy, so they have an influence on everything and everyone on the planet. In this way, you create your own reality, as your mind rules over matter.

Energy is the basis for material reality, with particles conceived as a quantum vibration in a field. For more clarity on this, read Lynne McTaggart's book *The Field* or Marja de Vries's *The Whole Elephant Revealed*. Quantum theory researchers have discovered that not only do particles consist of energy, but so does the space between them. This is called zero-point energy and was discovered by the German physicist Max Planck in 1911. Dr Harold Puthoff first measured this sea of energy, discovering that if you heat something by adding energy, the molecules move faster and faster. For example, heating water causes the water to evaporate. It works in reverse too – if you cool the water down then the molecules move slowly, eventually freezing and solidifying.

Life energy has many names. In China, it is known as Chi. In Greece, it's called Pneuma and in Hawaii it is known as Mana. There are numerous other names across the world for this phenomenon, with differing concepts according to culture. However, what they all have in common is that they speak about the subtle energy that is universal, which includes all and penetrates everything. This energy forms matter. It has healing and magnetic qualities, and it's what us healers tap into when working with our clients. According to Marco Bischof, in his book *Tachyonen, Orgonenergie, Skalarwellen*, "The zero-point energy field is the prime source of the universal life energy that has been described and used by every culture in its own way."

Morphic Fields

We live in a swirling sea of zero-point energy. Our body forms fifty billion new cells a day. Interestingly, biologists have no answer to how a cell knows it's part of a toenail on the foot or to the behavioural sentience of other cells in the body. It is what they call morphogenesis – the origin of form (in Greek, the term morphe = form, genesis = origin). Your arms and legs are genetically identical, however have varying shapes. So, while we know that genes supply the building blocks for the material of the body, the blueprint for organism design has yet to be found.

It's been suggested that this blueprint is held in the morphogenetic field, which is self-organising and holds the matter in a way that is comparable to how the field around a magnet organises iron filings. Rupert Sheldrake, a well-known scientist and biologist, has written extensively about "morphic" fields in many of his books, supporting his ideas with the results of scientific research. In his book *Morphic Resonance*, Sheldrake says that morphic fields contain information, scenarios with step-by-step plans, comparable to the blueprint of a house, as well as instructions which tell you where to begin. An example is the way that termites construct their hills. Two groups build in different places, meeting at exactly the same place high in the air. No one termite is directing or controlling, they are all working together in harmony and know what to do. Morphic fields not only contain old information such as the blueprints for building, but can take in new information too. A well-known example is the "hundred monkey phenomenon".

100ᵗʰ Monkey Phenomenon and Connectivity

Scientists observed the Japanese monkey Macaca fuscata for a period of thirty years. In 1952, on the island of Koshima, they started providing monkeys with sweet potatoes dropped in the sand. The monkeys seemed to like the taste of the potatoes, but disliked the dirt that covered them. An eighteen-month-old monkey named Imo solved this problem by washing them in a nearby stream. She taught her mother this trick and in turn her playmates taught their mothers too. This was gradually picked up too by various other monkeys. Between 1952 and 1958, all the young monkeys had started to wash away the sand from the potatoes, making them more palatable. Only the adults who imitated their children "learned" this improvement. Interestingly, some other adult monkeys kept eating the dirty potatoes. However, a complete change occurred in the autumn of 1958. At the time, several Koshima monkeys were washing their potatoes – no one knows how many exactly, but they have posited that around ninety-nine monkeys on the island had learned to wash their potatoes. Later that morning, a one-hundredth monkey learned to do the same. Totally unexpectedly and surprisingly, by the evening almost the entire tribe was engaged in this endeavour. The added energy of this hundredth monkey somehow created an ideological breakthrough. What was even more surprising was the fact that this habit "jumped" across the sea, where monkey colonies on other islands as well as the mainland troop at Takasakiyama, began washing their sweet potatoes too.

To sum this up, when a certain critical number (mass) achieves awareness, they communicate this new awareness from mind to mind. Although the number may not be exact, it shows us that when only a limited number of people know of another way, it may remain the conscious property of these few people. But there is a point at which, if only one more person tunes in to a new awareness, the field is strengthened, so that everyone can pick up this awareness. This story originated from writing by Rupert Sheldrake and has been used as a metaphor/legend phenomenon by Ken Keyes Jr. to show the power of critical mass on the morphogenetic field.

Every species of animal, plus every system, has a morphic field and therefore a collective memory. It's a bit like a comprehensive book, where all the records are kept of animals', people's, and organisations' experiences. Carl Jung termed this the "collective consciousness". In esoteric terms, this is often referred to as the "akashic record", symbolising the world memory, which contains all events that have occurred since the beginning of time. In a company, it stores everything that has ever happened within the organisation. The sea is the field of the company's culture, a way of doing things that is greater than all the workers that influence them.

The 100th monkey phenomenon is reassuring, because it shows that if enough people in the world are focused on creating peace, with good-intentions, then this will positively impact our collective lives. Social behaviour is an enormous catalyst for change. During the COVID-19 pandemic, I focused on how I wanted our world to be once we were allowed to go back out again and congregate. I know many other like-minded people who did the same. We shared our visions on Facebook as well as doing regular group meditations.

The Connectivity of Everything and Everyone

Even though everything is vibrating at different frequencies, we're all connected through an invisible web of energy. Sometimes a person, animal or thing really resonates with you; you feel a strong sense of connection. Philosopher of the mind, biology and physics Tam Hunt and psychologist Jonathan Schooler explain a theory of consciousness, working on "what physical processes underpin mental experience, linking mind and matter creating the sense of self". Hunt and Schooler suggest that every physical object, including you, is vibrating and oscillating. The more synchronised these vibes are and the more complex your connection with the world around you, the more sophisticated your consciousness. They posit that synchronised vibes are central to all physical reality, including human consciousness.

To reiterate, this means that all things in our universe are constantly vibrating; even objects that appear to be stationary are vibrating, oscillating and resonating at different frequencies. Resonance is a type of motion, characterised by oscillation between two states or two beings. When different oscillating things are close together for a time, they begin to vibrate in sync. For example, neurons in the brain, birds gathering, the moon and earth – spontaneous self-organisation. Being in sync is akin to a communication between entities. When using instruments they can entrain to each other, and the same applies to people if there is a resonance. When my client Penny visited me for a session, she was in a very distressed, upset and anxious state.

However, after a very brief time she informed me she had never felt so relaxed and calm in all her life! And that was before we had even carried out any coaching work. Entrainment occurred because I was in heart coherence, calm, relaxed and focused.

Hunt believes that the billions of neurons firing in your brain together are exceedingly sophisticated, creating a rich and dynamic sense of self, which Hunt calls "perception". This varies widely, but even seemingly inanimate objects like rocks have a rudimentary level of consciousness – receiving information from the world. A rock is an object in relation to the world and therefore can "experience" existence very basically. In a 2001 paper in the *Journal of Consciousness Studies*, Hunt explains that "literally every life form and every speck of dust right down to a subatomic particle is influenced by the world through the various forces that act upon it. An electron is influenced by the charged particles close enough to have an impact and from objects that exert a gravitational pull, thus the electron behaves accordingly. To exist in the universe every particle in the universe feels some pull and push from the various forces around it."

What humans have is a "macro consciousness" (unlike the rock which has a "micro consciousness"), which gives us our rich sense of self, where we experience our existence. All the relatively simple vibes and oscillations that occur individually in various physical aspects of the brain, working together, become extremely complex and provide us with self-awareness. As explained in an article by QZ.com, "This resonance theory of consciousness provides a unified framework for understanding mind and matter that includes neuroscience, the study of human consciousness of subjective experience, neurobiology and biophysics. It explains the differing degrees of consciousness in various physical systems." (https://qz.com/1490276/the-science-of-vibes-shows-how-everything-is-connected/) Or, as Hunt puts it, "It is all about vibrations and shared vibrations."

This all helps to explain why Sound Healing is so important. When my youngest son was teaching in London, I went to his school to give a Sound Healing lesson. The children were so receptive, even though they hadn't seen large gongs or many of my other instruments. After learning about sound and its healing properties, most of the children laid down on the floor for my gong bath. The feedback afterwards was lovely. Two particularly stand out, one for its profundity – the child said that the experience made his soul soar. The second was a little boy's observation: he said that he loved watching my bottom wiggle when I was playing and moving. This probably stuck in my mind as it wasn't very politically correct, but was still amusing!

As I mentioned earlier in the book, I give sound journeys in groups and for individuals on a one-to-one basis. At the beginning of her personal sound bath, my client Karen set her intention, directing this towards work. She said that she was so relaxed during the session that she was transported to another realm, where she received ideas and inspiration. Karen implemented these ideas and her business went from strength to strength. Another client, Leslie, had a pain in his leg when he came for a Sound Healing session. He underwent a remarkable transformation, in that he was pain free for the first time in months. Both their bodies went into entrainment with the sounds. The Universe "knows" what the client needs, which isn't always the same as what the client perceives their need to be.

I was blessed to hear Dr Jude Currivan speak at a conference many years ago, where she discussed the idea of the universe as a cosmic hologram. She also has a book of the same name. The Scientific and Media Network, which is a joint research study by teams from UK, Italian and Canadian universities, revealed the first observational and cosmological scale evidence to support the premise of our universe being a cosmic hologram. They did so by analysing irregularities in an energetic relic of the early universe, known as the cosmic microwave background, whose radiation was emitted 380,000 years after our universe came into being. They published their findings in the *Physical Review Letters Journal*. During their research, they found significant evidence to support the view that our universe is being innately informed and holographically manifested. "Holography" is a huge leap forward in the way we think about structure and creation of the universe. Scientists have been working for decades trying to reconcile Einstein's theory of gravity and quantum theory – and some believe the holographic theory may do this. As per the Scientific and Medical Network: "Lead researcher Johannes Handsteiner of the Institute of Quantum Optics and Quantum Information in Vienna used light from distant astronomical sources entangled with laboratory photos, to experimentally show the reality of nonlocal connectivity of our universe to a distance of at least 600 light years and supporting the view that our universe is fundamentally inter-connected. These discoveries are backed by evidence across many fields and all scales of existence of our universe, existing and evolving as a unified entity; innately informed and holographically manifested. For the first time quantum and relativity theories can be reconciled by considering energy-matter and space-time as complementary expressions of information." (https://explore.scimednet.org/index.php/further-evidence-that-our-universe-may-be-a-cosmic-hologram/)

This increasingly compelling evidence reveals that reality is informational based, that mind and matter are essentially unified and that consciousness isn't something we have – but fundamentally what we and the whole world **are.**

The Law of Vibration

This law is the foundation for the Law of Attraction. To understand it, one must hold the principle that everything is energy. Quantum physics shows us that everything in our universe is energy, on the subatomic level there is no matter – just energy. This is often referred to as the "Unified Field" or "pure potentiality". Dr Rupert Sheldrake calls it the "Morphogenic field" and Lynne Taggart "The Field" – I believe these are all one and the same. I was blessed to have spent time in their company at conferences learning about neuroscience and experiencing practical tools such as their meditations.

As I mentioned previously, everything in the universe moves and vibrates at differing speeds. Your own frequency differs from other things in the universe and that's why it may appear that you are separate from what you see around you. However, there is no separation, as you are in fact living in an ocean of energy. You and I are connected. Everything, from cars to tables, rocks, chairs, beds, trees, flowers, animals and your thoughts and feelings, are all vibrating at their own frequency. Despite items looking solid, they're all pure energy and movement, which is invisible to our eye – hence the illusion of appearing solid. The idea that seeing is believing is inherently flawed. Before the advent of the microscope, no-one would have suspected that you had infinitesimally tiny "creatures" in the form of bacteria living on your skin. The Dept. of Medicine at the NYU School of Medicine in 2007 found evidence of 182 species of bacteria in skin samples.

Believing helps you see, going beyond your five senses with an open mind. The Law of Vibration is real; all day long you are a transmitter, sending out into the universe your thoughts and feelings which impact the world. When you think of electricity, you know it is real even though you're unable to see it – it's what powers your TV, razor, hairdryer, kettle, computer and so much more. Your frame of knowledge is constantly challenged, as science is discovering more all the time. Once upon a time it was accepted that the Milky Way was the only galaxy, whereas now it's only one of billions of galaxies.

Having an open mind allows you to believe that something can be real, even if science is unable at this point in time to "prove it". The invention of the dog whistle showed us that we're unable to hear all sounds available. The same is true with infrared and ultraviolet light, which humans are unable to detect with our bare eyes. Unknown technologies and inventions have helped us "know" these truths. Life, as you currently understand it, is constantly changing. What appears impossible today may be taken as a given in the future. Who knows, maybe the universal Law of Vibration will one day be part of the school curriculum, giving your children a broader perspective of their world. Who would have thought years ago that you could speak to and video-call others around the globe, send emails, receive texts, take and send photos, watch movies, book train and plane tickets, monitor your health and exercise, access the internet for information and more, all without visible wires? Hopefully, in the near future everyone will take it for granted that the Law of Vibration is real and they'll realise the importance of holding positive thoughts and beliefs whenever possible, as this has a huge impact on the world as a whole.

The Law of Attraction

The Law of Attraction is the ability to attract whatever you are focusing on. This has also been named "the Law of Cause and Effect". Thoughts can turn into things. If you focus on negative doom, you will emit negative vibrations, whereas if you focus on positive outcomes and thoughts that you aim to achieve, you will find inspiration and a way to achieve them. However, it is imperative that you feel the outcome has happened already. Take the first step towards your goals and then make a daily choice to take another step, and then another. For me, I felt inspiration to write this book and chose regularly to carry on with this project. Some days I made a different choice, to rest or catch up with a friend, which meant the outcome took longer to achieve. There are some writers who set themselves a daily number of words to write, but my preference is to write for a certain amount of time, whilst giving myself flexibility to end earlier or much later according to how my body and brain feels at the time. When editing my first draft I was working all day and evening because I had a deadline in mind, which motivated me. This law dictates that whatever can be imagined (especially in a meditative relaxed state, feeling, hearing and seeing in your mind's eye) is achievable, provided you take action on a plan to get where you want to be. Sometimes this is to do nothing but just rest and sit with your body, allowing a flow of ideas to enter. Some of you may already be aware of how much impact the Law of Attraction has on your day-to-day life. Whether you are doing it knowingly or unknowingly, every second of every day you are acting as a human magnet, sending out your thoughts and emotions (which are often unconscious), attracting back more of what you have put out. So, awareness is key!

The Law of Attraction can be seen in Buddha's teachings, "Karma – what you give out returns to you manifold", in the Bible via Proverbs 23:7, "As a man thinketh in his heart so is he" and through the works of prominent creators, artists and renowned thinkers, such as Shakespeare, Blake, Emerson, Newton and Beethoven. Modern advocates include Oprah Winfrey, Jim Carrey and Denzel Washington. Some people have difficulty adjusting to this concept – that every decision made in your life, both good and not so good, has been shaped by you. This is especially tough if you have been experiencing some exceptionally difficult circumstances. However, the positive aspect is that once you have awareness, you can take responsibility for your thoughts and feelings.

The work of quantum physics has helped to shine greater light on the incredible impact that our minds have on our lives and the Universe in general. We are co-creators. The universe is always on our side, providing us with what our vibrations emit. The affirmation, 'I love the Universe and the Universe loves me' makes me feel safe and loved. You can omit Universe from this and replace with the Creator, God, Beauty, Grace, Intelligence, Source or whatever is your preference. The important thing is that you have faith and believe it is true, knowing that everything is working for your benefit.

By making these affirmations, you are creating pictures of your intended life, making choices and taking actions that will actualise what you have envisaged. If you don't like the current picture, remember you can change it! As Bob Proctor puts it, "Money is a servant, you are its master. The Law of Attraction focuses on the concept of self-confidence and faith in the Universe. You need to let go of all feelings of doubt in yourself and the Universe bringing you your desires, for it to be effective." Everyone visualises, whether or not you know it. Now, I want you to take a moment and complete the following exercise:

Sit still, relax, and recall your front door. Think about its shape, colour and where the letterbox is situated. Do the same with your fridge. Open it up in your mind's eye and recall where you have placed your milk. According to Rhonda Byrne, author of *The Secret*, visualising is the great secret of success.

When you clear emotional baggage and limiting thoughts, you create a vacuum to bring in the new. So work on clearing these and then make positive affirmations straight afterwards, to fill the void. Instead of thinking about what you don't want, switch to focusing on what you do want. What is the one step you can take towards your final outcome and keep choosing daily? Check within, to ensure that you're not resisting. This is an invitation to be conscious of everything you're doing, being mindful and conscious about how you allow yourself to think of things.

When making affirmations around an issue in your life, you are allowing the energy of it to filter your subconscious. Your feelings are fuel for manifestation, so feeling and action help to activate the energy. Think of a vast ocean. If you sit on your boat moored on the beach, with no fuel and no navigation chart, then you won't be able to move forward into the sea towards your intended destination. Once you've taken your first step, it allows everything else to expand and flow sets the laws of motion in action. When you are static, it's harder to get something to move – but if you are already moving then it's much easier to push. So, will you take your first step today? What do you wish to create? Start with something small first, to give yourself confidence. As Dr Joe Dispenza puts it, "Your life right now is an outward expression of the thoughts, beliefs and actions of your past self."

Another way to enhance the manifestation process is to create a vision board, mind movie, crystal grid and manifesting artworks such as a mandala, as I mentioned earlier in the book. I look at and listen to them all regularly to infuse my body with the feelings of joy from having them in my life (acting as if I already have them). When stating my gratitude, I believe it's more potent to add the reason why i.e. I want a house *so I can* entertain, feel safe and secure. I want my home to be close to the sea and forest, *because* I love being surrounded by nature. I am grateful for having an abundance of money available, *since this serves* as a vehicle to fulfil my purpose for fun, adventures, sociability and assisting others to fulfil their potential, helping them to be the best they can be. When holding my spiritual development and meditation groups we often hold the intent and make affirmations for each other and the world, thus setting in motion the unified energy of us all, which extrapolates from the individual energy. The power of your imagination is phenomenal.

Ensure that being controlled by those around you doesn't hamper your co-creating. I've often found that my clients, who were told how to avoid getting into difficulties when they were young, grew up anxious – as children they never learnt to make their own mistakes and sort their own lives out. Of course there is a difference between this and just not taking any responsibility, but everyone is self-responsible at the end of the day. You may meet people who want to control the entire universe and you may meet others who never want to control anything, even themselves. It is fascinating how we are all different, but also how our actions impact everyone else. As a child, if you had no boundaries then you may have not felt safe in the world. Equally, if you had too much guidance, then you may experience difficulties in managing your own life as an adult.

Your life is a learning journey. There's no right or wrong way, just as long as you follow your own truth, even if that differs from others. But, understanding brings about acceptance. We all have free will to be the driver of our own bus. I once heard of a small company where the boss fired thirty people, leaving them with no staff. What was fascinating was that once he no longer had staff to control, he left too. The new Aquarian age is about unity, not control but empowerment, collaboration, win-win, thinking as a collective, cooperation, authenticity, integrity and transparency, unlike the competitive, service-to-self Piscean age that has just ended. This goes beyond people and relates to the planet and its resources as a whole.

The Earth, which is a world of time and space, is a place to enact out different roles over different time periods, in millions of different ways. Which role did you choose this time? Did you choose a man or a woman? Which country did you pick? What parents and siblings did you choose? What circumstances did you place yourself within, to learn and grow and move through time and space in a manner of your choice? Maybe you thought you were unfortunate, randomly placed where you are, doing what you are doing because of some past life wrong doing, a karmic retribution for dark deeds in former lives? Or maybe you're a random victim of evolution, which placed you in the worst circumstances whilst another person got to win the lottery? Now you know that science says different!

From a higher perspective, life is a flow of living consciousness from which to plant seeds at any point in time and space. Linear time exists as a matrix to measure progress, a layer of historic content to learn and grow within, linear in history but holistic in experience. Each Age provided different experiences, perceptions, concepts and understanding that were added to the ever-growing library of collective conscious awareness. Your individual experience is one that allows growth, not just by the trials and tribulations of personal experience but by the opening of the heart to the callings of your inner soul. You are the result of all your soul has ever manifested, a wealth of knowledge and wisdom beyond your few years in this space-time continuum. Your thoughts are on a certain vibrational frequency and therefore part of the vibrating universe. The Law of Attraction suggests that you attract what you send out. So, if you're in a positive mode, you'll receive positive vibes in return. Your thoughts are cosmic waves of energy that penetrate all time and space. They ripple out into the sea of energy that many call "the universe" or "collective consciousness".

In his book, *The Science of Getting Rich,* Wallace Wattles speaks of a thinking stuff from which all things are made, "a thought in this substance produces the thing that is imaged by thought". When you know that your thoughts and emotions are vibrating and that "like attracts like" you can have a positive impact on your own life, by holding positive thoughts more of the time and releasing your negative emotions, thus allowing you to replace these emotions with positive, higher vibrational feelings. Unfortunately, many of you will have been "programmed" from a young age to worry about fears, scarcity and not being good enough as you are. This is partic-ularly true right now during the COVID-19 pandemic, with many people fearful and distressed. The fear affects your immune system by lowering its functionality, which could mean you're more likely to attract the virus. Fortunately, as I have my "tools", I never went into fear and held the belief that I would be fine – although I had the odd wobble when I couldn't get any food, as all the click and collect slots had been taken for weeks in advance. When I am aware of my negative thoughts and feelings, for example, thinking that I will go hungry as I can't get any food, I counteract my negative thoughts by saying, 'Clear, cancel and delete' whilst wiping away the thought, with my hand in the air like a windscreen wiper, before focusing on what I do want – a plentiful fridge full of yummy food. When others vehemently disagree with my beliefs on Facebook, I allow them to write their comments underneath my post, as I feel freedom of speech is important. I choose to be kind rather than right. Changing your thought patterns and emotions means you have a greater chance of attracting into your life those things you want. Combine this with daily gratitude for the things you love in your life, and you have the blueprint in place for a wonderful, self-nurturing existence.

Michael Dooley, author of *Notes from the Universe*, which I occasionally share on my Facebook page, offers humorous reminders of life's magic and miracles – with your divinity being one of the biggest reminders. He explains that you should think of your dreams as if they have already happened. Esther and Jerry Hicks also expound this theory in *Ask & It is Given*, as does Rhonda Byrne in *The Magic*. When I first encountered the Law of Attraction (after reading *The Secret* by Rhonda Byrne), something felt missing, as I struggled with getting the correct feelings and being in alignment. However, I found another book that took the subject in depth, which I found extremely helpful. This book was Michael Losier's *The Secret Behind The Secret* as it gave me suggestions on how to get the feelings as if I already had my wishes fulfilled. Instead of making a positive statement that was totally untrue, I would say something like, 'I love the thought of having a new partner or more prosperity...' By saying this, I could get the feelings and then make the 'I am' statement, such as, 'I am in a loving and committed relationship' or 'I am abundant and prosperous'.

It is important that your feelings and thoughts are engaged, as both vibrations go out into the universe, and need to be vibrating at the same frequency. My suggestion is that at least once a day you imagine the life you dream of, in full technicolour, with sounds and emotions, as well as smell, taste and sight. Having done this, stop looking for your manifestations, as this implies a lack of them, which isn't the vibration that you want to be sending out!

More Affirmations

A simple aid to your manifesting process is to use affirmations. You can say them inside your head, but speaking out loud is much more potent, as then you are speaking them into existence with feeling. Writing them down ten times every day declares your wishes to the universe. My client Russell really wanted to get the job he was shortly to be interviewed for. So, I told him to do these exercises upon awakening and before he went to sleep. Another aspect I suggested to Russell was to visualise his build up to the interview. He needed to see himself getting out of bed feeling great, enjoying his healthy breakfast and his journey to the interview going smoothly and easily, before arriving at the office feeling confident and focused. I wanted him to imagine the interview going splendidly, with him being able to answer all the questions clearly and concisely, with ease and confidence. Finally, he needed to visualise the sound of his phone ringing and his accepting the job offer. I suggested that Russell repeat this throughout the day whenever possible, every day until the interview. I often tell my clients to make affirmations for the entire planet, such as, 'We are all living in peace, with abundance, prosperity and good health.' To reiterate, your mind and thoughts are much more powerful than you imagine! Again this became even more pertinent during COVID-19, as it helped to raise the world's vibrations, counteracting the fear and distress being felt on a global level.

Gratitude Aids Manifesting

Can you change your mind now – suspend belief and be open to the fact that you can change future events, right now, by thinking positive thoughts, visualising and making affirmations? Even the simplest things can make a difference, such as letting a car in front of you from a side road in heavy traffic, opening the door for someone or paying a compliment. Whilst out walking at the beach or in the New Forest, I state positive affirmations and gratitude out loud. I express my gratitude for all manner of things big and small, even for my eyelashes, which make a wonderful frame for my eyes and also protect them from dust and grit. I express thanks to the Universe, Spirit, my Guardian Angel, friends and family on both sides of the veil, my star family, Mother Earth and my Higher Self. I express love to all, with gratitude for all that I have and all that I am. I say that I will continue to follow guidance with an open mind, ears, eyes and heart. I envision a love bubble that envelops me and everyone in my life. So, as often as you can, remember to send loving, healing energy from your heart, spreading it as far as you can throughout the planet, galaxy, universe and the multiverse. Thank you, I love you.

We are a friendly bunch down here on the south-coast, so I'll smile and say, 'Morning' to people, but inside I'm really saying, 'I love you, I see you' (which you can understand more if you have seen the film "Avatar", as it's like saying 'Namaste'). Each of your thoughts are energy, going out into the ether and exist as a possibility for future events. You will receive extra benefits of absorbing positive electrons and grounding through your feet by walking barefooted when on grass or at the beach. While you're walking on the beach, walk close to the water, so you can get the additional benefit of the negative ions from the crashing waves, which make you feel good.

Why the Law of Attraction May Not Have Worked

The Law of Attraction seems simple in theory. However, you may have carried out these imaginings using all your senses and still not received your desires. This could be because underneath it all you don't believe that you can have what you want. You may feel undeserving, guilty, unworthy or other negative thoughts and emotions. You need to be in complete alignment with your wishes, feeling and believing you have them already. This is easier said than done, especially if you are emotionally invested in the outcome. The art is to be unattached from the outcome, but in love with it at the same time, so that your vibration is a match for what you want. For example, if you want more money and consequently pray, wish and say positive affirmations around money, but subconsciously believe that money doesn't come easily to you, this will prevent you from fulfilling your desire. This can be exacerbated by harmful beliefs, such as thinking that people would be jealous and dislike you if you became rich.

When growing up, my client Jonathan was often told, 'No you can't have that, I'm not made of money' or 'Money doesn't grow on trees' and other similar sayings, which then became part of his negative programming. In the first session we released his beliefs around scarcity, showing him that just because he has plenty of money, it doesn't mean he's taking away anything from others; showing him that he deserves to have money, and can work smart rather than hard to achieve his goals. In the next session Jonathan wrote his goals and we did "Time Line therapy" to place them in his future. Having cleared out his limiting beliefs and negative emotions around money, I taught him the accelerated learning processes, plus an Energetic NLP process called the "Eight Agendas That Run Your Life" that creates alignment with your mind, body and spirit. During his last session, I took Jonathan to his best possible future using Future Life Progression. He was amazed by the advice and insights that his future-self gave him and by the possibilities that he saw. I am pleased to say that the future he saw is coming to pass and he is now "happy as Larry", as the saying goes.

Amazingly I have met two people who haven't experienced scarcity in any form, and they live and breathe as if they are money. They both separately said, 'After all, money is just another form of energy and is like air, it is just there.' It was so refreshing to meet them and hear their experience. Although they had little understanding of how the rest of us sometimes struggle with money issues, they still had empathy and compassion. These people were wonderful and philanthropic, using their wealth in altruistic ways to help others.

Your Unconscious Mind Rules

Your unconscious mind and beliefs are far more powerful than your conscious mind. The latter is the ruler of your life, so it's important to get both to tally. Since birth you have been created, building a blueprint of what you believe in and your truths (these are your truths and not necessarily universal) formed by your relationships, particularly those close to you, through your teachers, peers and by the media. New ideas are not always immediately accepted, particularly if they contradict what you hold to be "true". As discussed many times throughout this book, affirmations are a good starting point, as you will soon notice that you're in alignment when saying them, noting if you feel good. If you don't feel good, then you'll hear the voice in your mind saying, 'Well that's not true because...' These are known as tail-enders.

As I've already said, one of the things I like my clients to begin with is, 'How wonderful it would be if…' This helps them to connect with their feelings and desires, preventing tail-enders from arising. Next, I get them to sandwich an 'I am' affirmation in between, whilst they still have the wonderful feeling of their desire. Doing activities such as this will start to re-programme your subconscious mind. Affirmations need to be repeated often, combined with envisioning yourself enjoying your desires (acting as if you already have them). In order to have the Law of Attraction work for you, it's important to have attention, desire, feeling and intention, allowing and acting as if you already have what you wish for. Then, take an action step towards your goal.

Questions Again

As I said earlier, a variation of affirmations are actually afformations, invented by Noah St John. Here, everything is in a question format, such as: 'Why am I feeling so energised?' or 'Why do I have a wonderful loving relationship with my partner?' Questions expand your consciousness. As adults, you have become more solution focused. Asking a well-thought-out question is one of the most effective cognitive tools. Most historical discoveries occurred because of fearless individuals who were driven and enthused by their questions. The Wright brothers asked, 'What if we could fly?' Copernicus wondered, 'Is Earth really the centre of the Universe?' and Isaac Newton thought, 'I wonder what caused this apple to fall down?' Edison pondered, 'Are there other ways to light up our homes besides candles?' Not only did they ask smart questions, but they also kept on "failing" until they found their solution. Failure is only feedback to try again, but with change and improvement for next time. When you ask purposeful questions, you engage your reticular activating system, expanding your consciousness from where you are now to all future possibilities. An example, using afformations, could be, 'Why am I letting go of my past with ease and gratitude?' Asking questions stimulates your innovative capabilities, because your mind is a natural problem solver. The brain is a versatile and malleable device that loves to brainstorm, conceptualise, analyse, process and soak in new data. This vast potential can be easily tapped into with the right questions.

Questions act as cues that direct your thoughts towards specific directions. Once you ask a question, the part of your brain known as the RAS (reticular activating system) immediately gets to work to find answers. The RAS is a portal that filters all incoming information and impacts what you pay attention to. If you focus on something like a creative project, building your vacation itinerary or solving an issue at work, your mind will create ideas, thought patterns and solutions that you may not have had otherwise. As Albert Einstein said: 'If I only had an hour to solve a problem and my life depended on the solution, I would spend the first 55 minutes determining the proper question to ask. For once I know the proper question, I could solve the problem in less than five minutes.'

Decluttering Revisited

To repeat, decluttering is critical for manifesting, because it disperses the energy in your environment and gives your dreams space to manifest. It is time to let go of any items that carry old energy and no longer serve you. This is truly a magical and miraculous process, helping your home, office space and body feel lighter and clearer. After my husband left I completely changed the entire house, giving all my furniture to a local charity. I even had the fireplace replaced. I lived without furniture for what seemed like eons. I sat in the lounge on a camping chair for more than a year until I could afford to buy a sofa. I gradually bought lighter and brighter furniture, changing from rosewood mahogany to light oak. I even painted the rosewood spindles and handrails in the hall white, as all the doors were white but the handrails were rosewood and didn't match. I converted my children's playroom into a consulting room, removing the fixed train set and Scalextrix from the wall and all other fixtures and fittings. It felt good to have the entire house feel and look totally different.

Three of My Manifestations

When following my soul's calling by moving to Dorset, again I gave away all my furniture but this time included everything else too: even fine bone china sets, silver cutlery and most of my wardrobe. I wanted fresh energy, a new start. I was renting in Tuckton for six months and downsizing to a much smaller house, so releasing some of it was necessary. Again the camping chair came in handy! This particular house was over my budget and didn't fit all my requirements, but I just knew it was mine and that I had to have it. I felt compelled to buy it. The house was quirky, with the bedrooms downstairs and a vast window in the upstairs lounge, which let in lots of light. My main focus for manifesting this house was that I wanted somewhere light, bright and airy with plenty of storage, which was exactly what I got. Despite the estate agent not believing I would get the house at my desired price, I just "knew" I would – it was as if the house called to me.

An example of my almost instant manifestation was when I was in Egypt on a spiritual pilgrimage. A few of us were sitting looking at the Sphynx and wishing to go down, to be close to it and be in its amazing energies. Within a few moments, a "guide" came up to us and asked if we wanted to go down to the Sphinx. We duly paid the money and followed him. How naïve was I to believe that this was like all the other times when our retreat leader gave "baksheesh" to guides, who then allowed us to enter tombs and do meditations. Hindsight is a wonderful thing. I hadn't really given any thought to my desires, which was rather silly, as I should have included safety into the equation.

My fellow companions were closer to the Sphinx than I was when we heard horrendous shouting and yelling. An Egyptian policeman with a gun was running towards us. This was my first experience of "freeze". Unlike the other people in my group, I only had ballet pump shoes and not walking boots, so I couldn't move fast. I gave up running as my fear deepened. The others all ran off and left me! The policeman caught up with me and gripped my arm so hard I thought it would burst. He then screamed in my face that he was taking me to jail! I was powerless and petrified. All the fears from childhood returned with a vengeance – a powerful male scaring me stupid! Plus, I already knew that prisons in the Middle East were dire, as a friend's cousin had been put in prison when I lived in Doha.

I wondered why I had created this awful ending to my wonderful pilgrimage…then one of my male companions back to help me. He pleaded gently but firmly with the policeman and apologised. Two of the burly "guides" who were part of the scam came down to help. Despite being free, I wasn't able to walk – through fear – so my male companion helped me along. Once I was free and back with the others in our group, I burst into uncontrollable sobs. The guides were apologetic, as this hadn't happened before and they were concerned with how distraught I was. The silver lining was that I realised that there are some wonderful older caring men in our world. I had already seen evidence of the younger caring generation of males with both of my son's behaviours and both of my daughter's partners.

Another time I experienced almost instant manifestation was when travelling from Abu Dhabi to Doha. I was boarding the plane at Abu Dhabi to Doha and had to walk through the business class to get to my economy seat. This was an unfamiliar experience for me and I thought *wow this looks comfy I wouldn't mind being in here.* I continued to my seat and didn't give it another thought. However, within ten minutes I was approached and asked if I would like to go to business class, as there weren't enough people up there to balance the plane. It was fabulous – a gorgeous large seat that converted into a bed, a lovely little table with a tablecloth and real china with my meal. As I still had another long journey to the UK (from Australia where I had been to visit my son and family), I wished for the same again. However I was more emotionally invested in the outcome and hadn't let it go, so I failed to manifest it. I had forgotten to feel and know that I already had it. I've found that the smaller things without too much attachment are easier to draw into my life. If I really want something then I find it harder to let go of the outcome and imagine that I already have it. Now, ask yourself the following questions:

- What are you willing to let go of today?

- How will you let go of things that no longer serve you so easily?

- Where are you placing your focus?

- Can you think of times when you have created something you wished for with minimum effort?

Note, you attract the things you **don't** want into your life by giving them focus and attention, so place your focus on what you **do** want in your life.

The Importance of Taking Action Towards Your Desires

Where are you spending your valuable energy? Is it worth it? Is it contributing to your life? Is it helping you move forward? Be honest with yourself. Only you know your inner world, inner peace and mental wellness. If self-development and growth is a priority for you, then you will remember to stay centred and do things to prevent yourself being sucked into the drama of others and of the world stage. You will keep your positive mindset thriving instead of reacting. Initially, you may get pulled in, but that's just the beginning of your learning curve. You'll react less and less as time goes by, provided you keep vigilant and keep practising. Again, this has been so helpful for me in remaining calm and balanced, especially during the COVID-19 pandemic. You truly do have the power to decide how you respond to life's trials and tribulations and to decide which direction your bus takes. Often, it is beneficial to take a step back and be an observer, thus being unaffected by emotions.

Action Required to Co-Create

If you have desires, then it's important not only to be vigilant about your emotions, but also to take steps towards your desires. A client of mine, David, wanted a new Mercedes. The problem was, he couldn't afford it. The first thing I encouraged David to do was to visit the sales garage, where he took one out on a test drive – so he could feel, see, hear and sense what it was like. This helped him to visualise himself driving his car every day and trust that he would have it. David combined this with affirmations such as, 'I am loving driving my wonderful new Mercedes' and afformations such as, 'Why am I loving taking wonderful trips in my Mercedes car?' David's life transformed, he used this technique and made practical positive changes in his life across the board. He called me eighteen months later to say that he was so pleased to be driving his new Mercedes, in reality!

My client Jenny desired a new man in her life, so she wrote a list of his characteristics and how she would feel when in this wonderful relationship. Jenny signed up to dating sites and went to places where her ideal man would hang out. Jenny also worked on issues around her fear of commitment, getting hurt again, being vulnerable and opening her heart. She worked on loving herself, so that she was coming from the right place and not wanting someone to rescue her, unlike her original dreams of a knight in shining armour riding to the rescue. Jenny became a strong, capable, independent and loving person who manifested her ideal man. It was wonderful to be part of her journey, seeing her remove people who had taken advantage of her kind and passive nature, with her once again taking the wheel. She now was fully in charge of her own bus and only allowed other people to board if they had respect, love and supported her dreams.

If you don't take any actions towards your desires then you will appear unwilling to fulfil your part as co-creator. Consequently, the Universe won't take action, as it is waiting for you to start something – even if that's just to write about your wishes, how you will feel or what you will do as a first step. Your desires will remain a wonderful vision, just a dream.

Go inwards and explore. Remember you are the driver of your bus! Will you choose your inner peace every day? Why are you here, what do you want – to be happy, to make a difference? What will you incorporate into your life now, just for you, that will increase your good vibrations?

Endless Number Of Possibilities

Quantum physics discovered that most elementary building blocks of matter are entirely malleable and change behaviour according to the needs of the situation. Upon research, it was established that these building blocks behaved as either particles or waves and sometimes both at the same time. This changeability persisted until they were measured or observed. Once this occurred, the blocks changed into something solid. What this meant, was that the researchers could influence the outcome, just as long as they held expectations. In other words, the essence of a particle or a wave depends on your point of view – nothing is certain, there are an endless amount of possibilities. Everything consists of a turbulent sea of zero-point energy and information.

During my master NLP training, I had to chop an inch-thick wooden board, using only my hand. In order to do this, I had to perceive the board as fluid and "see" my hand going through it, which it did. I had to repeat this at another event, as well as bending a metal rod with my throat – the bending rod video is on my YouTube channel. The first board still sits in my lounge as a reminder that not everything is as it appears and that we need to be fluid with life, as well as a reminder that we are more powerful than we imagine.

We are the ones who make the world static, stationary and solid. It is by your firm convictions that the furniture you use is of solid matter, that you can safely sit on it without falling through. So, in essence, reality differs totally from what we see as real. We live in a sea of possibilities, but you affirm your reality with your strong beliefs. When using affirmations/afformations you **can** have an impact, provided you have a firm, solid conviction and that you've set your intention and expectation of your desires. Therefore, you have a responsibility for what you think, believe and feel. Every thought has an influence on you and your surroundings. A negative thought has a negative impact and a positive thought has a positive effect. Hence it is important to self-monitor thoughts and feelings, as these are how you create your reality and future.

My client Martin was a good example of this. He was a top manager in a large organisation, but was experiencing difficulty in giving his regular presentations. For years he had given presentations with ease, but when he stood up to speak he would now go into freeze mode. He'd come to me to correct this problem. Upon further investigation, I discovered that there was a great deal going on in Martin's life, all of which was causing him anxiety. From divorce to living in two different locations, separation from his children to unhappy staff in his workplace, it's fair to say that he was taking on enormous responsibility, all of which was making him unhappy and stressed. After doing clearing work on his limiting beliefs and negative emotions, we then worked on getting Martin into alignment and regaining his confidence. We looked at being more self-aware, authentic and congruent with his true self. During our last session I used FLP, transporting Martin to a possible future where he gained insight of his next steps – to have full and frank conversations with his ex-wife, new girlfriend, children and co-workers. I helped him to share his vulnerability and honesty, so that other people in his life felt able to do the same. Martin saw himself giving presentations with focus, ease, enthusiasm and confidence. His future-self gave him advice, telling him to take one step at a time, to ensure he had "me" time and to do things for fun, to appease his inner child.

An example of a past life that was still affecting a person in the present, was my client Mandy. She came to me distraught, as she couldn't wear anything around her neck – not even loosely tied scarves or necklaces – because it felt like she was being strangled. Her boyfriend did not know this and had bought her a stunning necklace. Mandy hadn't told her boyfriend why she hadn't worn it because she was ashamed and embarrassed. She wanted to wear it but felt like she was choking every time she tried to put it on.

The first thing we did was a past life regression. This was highly illuminating, as Mandy saw herself being hung, accused of using witchcraft in the 1600s in Devon, England. Her soul still recalled this and was trying to protect her during this lifetime, by preventing her from wearing things around her neck. Before bringing her back to the present, I asked Mandy what she needed to do to heal her body and herself from this trauma – she said to forgive herself and those who had "shopped her" to the authorities. Mandy then hugged her body in the past and

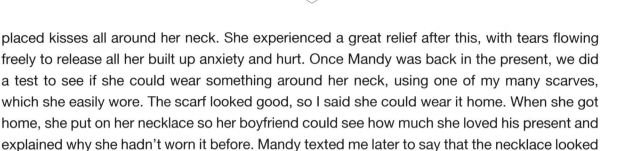

placed kisses all around her neck. She experienced a great relief after this, with tears flowing freely to release all her built up anxiety and hurt. Once Mandy was back in the present, we did a test to see if she could wear something around her neck, using one of my many scarves, which she easily wore. The scarf looked good, so I said she could wear it home. When she got home, she put on her necklace so her boyfriend could see how much she loved his present and explained why she hadn't worn it before. Mandy texted me later to say that the necklace looked lovely on and seemed to make her eyes more sparkly. I wonder if this was a combination of being free from her distress and now feeling blessed…

Resistance to Change

Sometimes, even with the greatest will in the world, you can unconsciously sabotage your efforts through deep-rooted fears and hurts that you may or may not be aware of. The following recount is of my own experience with resistance, procrastination and possible self-sabotage.

Having embarked upon writing this book, working well and writing copiously with enthusiasm and excitement, I awoke one morning in a low mood. I felt sadness and fear, which had arisen seemingly out of the blue. These emotions seemed to be present for no apparent reason, although background circumstances around my finances were of some concern. So, maybe an old pattern of poverty consciousness had crept back in. Had I slipped out of my trust and faith in the Universe that all was well and would be well? After all, I was still here, with a roof over my head, clothes for my body and food to eat. Had I gone into my future, which had led to anxiety and fear? I am human, so I sometimes still need to remind myself of things I "know", such as to stay in the present.

I questioned whether any resistance was surfacing to my writing, as I would be "seen" and open to judgement once the book was out in the public domain. Were there fears around success, failure and maybe others I was yet unaware of? My low mood had me questioning my purpose for being on the planet and if there was any point. My kids all had families and very full busy lives, some friends were no longer part of my life and I felt no raison d'être. Even writing didn't feel fulfilling. At one point I asked the Universe to show me what my purpose was or to "beam me up Scotty". Don't misunderstand me, I was not suicidal, but feeling adrift, lonely and a bit bleak – fed up with striving financially and trying to work out how I was meant to sustain an income (I had experienced a health issue which meant I hadn't had many clients for a while). This had taken me off track for over a week, and I didn't want it to continue any longer. I recognised the signs and didn't want to slip into full-blown depression, so I did more of my feel good practices, enabling my mood to improve day by day. To ensure I remained in good form I had some healing and coaching – some were gifted, others energetic exchanges, and some were paid for.

Despite feeling much brighter during the day and fulfilling my usual practices, I was still waking up feeling yucky, with a bleak sensation in my solar plexus. I didn't understand why. I assumed that sometimes it was what had gone on in my dreams, and other times it was down to whatever was going on in the collective. This meant I spent even more time completing a comprehensive morning practice to uplift myself before rising. This included:

- Self-hypnosis.

- My little cell ditty.

- Positive visualisations.

- Listening to guided meditations, solfeggio frequencies and upbeat songs.

- Saying affirmations/afformations.

- Statements such as 'I am well and happy throughout my day.'

- Using Access Consciousness, the Emotion Code and tapping, to clear negative and trapped emotions.

- Brain-dump: expressing thoughts, feelings and beliefs on how I was feeling in the moment by journaling.

I also listened to channellings during the day or evening when I felt called to, so I could gain more insights on what was happening to the planet and what others were experiencing physically and energetically. I found this reassuring, as it usually confirmed what I had felt/channelled.

Another thing I did when I woke up feeling below par, was to hug myself, which I did before bedtime too. I would begin with my arms crossed across my chest cuddling my shoulders whilst on my side, followed by some hands-on healing (one hand on my heart and the other on my solar plexus). Sometimes I would use my "Harmonise Your Heart" technique. I would say thank you for all I appreciated and why. To reiterate, it is important to me to fall asleep in a pleasant manner, as this impacts not only my quality of sleep but also how I wake in the morning.

To this day, I'm unsure if this incident was another resistance and procrastination, a test of whether I am still walking my talk or just a natural occurrence. Did I unconsciously create challenges to prevent me writing my book? Who really knows? It certainly set me back for a short while, but with determination, discipline and following my own tools, I overcame my difficulties and continued my writing with joy, just as before.

A while later, something inexplicable happened. I'd been out for an enjoyable afternoon of painting in a group, then a coffee with a friend. Once I got home I became uncoordinated, imbalanced and nauseous. I was unsure if I would make it downstairs to my bedroom and was incapable of doing anything other than lying down. I considered that I might be dying – as I had never felt so strange and awful, before I became totally incapacitated. Fortunately, I'd had time to check my blood sugar levels to see if they were low. Although I knew really, it wasn't anything to do with that – I wasn't hypoglycaemic, as it felt distinctly different. I then spoke to God/Universe, saying, 'Although I had requested a while back that you beam me up, you obviously decided against this. Well, I've changed my mind, I definitely don't want to leave now thank you, not at least until after my daughter's wedding. In fact, I am lucky to be alive and wish to continue my life indefinitely, thanks. But if it is my time, then I'm going to meditate and relax now.' I thought I would either die in my sleep or awake in the morning. Was this a case of resistance, or a test? I've no idea, but it was definitely a lesson of sorts. I couldn't text or phone anyone for help. Luckily, I didn't die overnight and the next morning I managed to Google and also text a friend to see if she knew what may be wrong with me. My friend said she would pop round, but I said not to, as I was still recuperating in bed. Fortunately, my friend arrived unexpectedly, having ignored my plea – so I literally dragged myself up the stairs to answer the door. She took me to the doctor who arranged for me to go to hospital for a brain scan, because I could not walk unaided and had terrible coordination. Having to sit upright in the surgery had spiralled my body into feeling extremely poorly again.

In hospital, the nurses discovered that I had a high temperature and that my blood sugars had risen because of an infection. I "knew" my brain was fine and received confirmation of this when the doctors decided against a CT brain scan. They did many blood tests to determine the extent of the infection and check it was lessening, as well as monitoring my blood sugar levels. With all the tests, I resembled a pin-cushion! They gave me two different types of antibiotics intravenously, as well as regular insulin shots and an anticoagulant. In between examinations I did meditations, visualising myself being healthy and well, which helped me to remain calm and relaxed, as it was quite a frenetic process and the acute ward was extremely busy and noisy. Luckily, the body is so clever and knows how to repair itself, so after just one day they discharged me. This is a testament to both allopathic and complementary treatments at their best, working in tandem. How blessed I am that the Universe let me live another day – I'm meant to be here to finish this book, to watch my delightful grandchildren grow and thrive and to see my youngest daughter marry. Weirdly, the source of infection was never found.

After my brief hospital spell, I had to rest. I couldn't do anything much. But by healing and coaching myself (with help from a fellow coach), taking supplements, wearing my VoxxLife neurotech socks (they have a code that transmits messages to the brain to create homeostasis in your body, which sped up my recovery), good hydration, nourishing food (hospital food isn't the greatest) and decent sleep (which had been impossible in hospital) I regained my physical strength and felt fantastic. My appreciation and gratitude was huge and my trust and faith that all was well remained intact. With my good vibrations I was sending out love and light into the world to counteract some of the turmoil, fighting, anger, confusion and other emotions swirling around Brexit in the UK and the world at large. I was able once again to help clients who were going through their "dark night of the soul" and other challenges. I felt that this book was another way I could be of service, encouraging you to be proactive in your healing – a legacy if you like.

Again I wondered, with all these experiences, thoughts and emotions swirling around in my mind and body, whether I was being tested. It felt like perhaps it was a test from the Universe, to see if I was "walking my talk" and practising what I preached. Life was very challenging, but I decided not to "clear" my emotions straight away with processes. I didn't want to risk bypassing these emotions, I wanted to give them the chance to dissipate, for me to receive insight and understanding. When I did this, the tears flowed, without me even knowing the cause. I am okay with this – you don't have to always know why. The most important thing is that you remain vigilant and persevere, whatever your circumstances, as nothing ever remains the same. Life is constantly changing and you can always turn lemons into lemonade to make the best of every situation. Look for your silver linings, even if you have to dig deep to find them.

To regain inspiration to continue writing this book after my spell of ill health, a fellow psychic friend suggested I take myself out of the house to write. I chose a local restaurant that I have a soft spot for – where I am in awe of nature; it has magnificent panoramic views of the sea and the cliffs of the Isle of Wight. I started with a pot of tea, whilst admiring the glorious sight of the sun glinting in a panel on the vast expanse of water, with large fluffy billowing clouds drifting across the sky – I felt such gratitude for our wonderous world. The rest is history! I chose other lovely spaces and could write at home again too (which became very important once we "self-retreated" due to COVID-19, affording me time to finish the book). My spirits had risen and were happy because I was doing what I was meant to (carrying on with my writing, following my destiny).

Resistance often occurs when your ego is fearful that something might not work out well for you, and so wants you to remain where it perceives you to be safe. With this in mind, it can create scenarios to sabotage you. Whilst at my clifftop café, with the sumptuous views of the sea, I noticed a song playing in the background. It was "Lean on Me" by Bill Withers, which was again a reminder of how important it is to have people in your life with whom you can have mutual support and understanding. I regularly say out loud and in my mind, 'Everyone in my life loves, respects, honours and supports me', 'Everything in my life is a source of love, peace and joy'. This allows those that don't have a strong connection with me to leave, as they don't resonate with me anymore. I had a session with a coach who was also a writer, which encouraged me to continue writing, as well as giving me some good tips.

Ancestors and Descendants

Continued from part six – during many of my own trainings and client sessions, ancestral issues featured a lot. Are you being called to heal your family line or free yourself from living a life similar to your ancestors? Science says that our genetic traits and characteristics are passed down at least seven generations – some studies say fourteen generations. Releasing family patterns and ways of being that no longer serve you, frees you up to create a new, updated version of you! When you heal your ancestral lineage, it is said that this healing travels back to your ancestors and forward to your descendants, clearing the epigenetics. This can also inspire others to make change in their lives.

- What old ways of being are you ready to let go of?

- What part of your future do you wish to rewrite?

- What new goal(s) can you aim towards?

Feeling "Off" is Expansion

Matt Kahn says that "feeling off" is not about how misaligned you are. Instead, it reflects how much self-care is needed to support you in making huge leaps of consciousness, on a daily, weekly and monthly basis. Once you're able to make these leaps, you will have outsmarted even the spiritual ego, with the wisdom that only unconditional love may know. For me, this unconditional love has to come from you, to you. It's also important to afford others this unconditional love, as they may be going through transitions and challenges too. So it's not wrong to feel off, it's just a sign of massive expansion. Can you allow yourself to welcome in this healing self-love, even when life doesn't feel the way you desire?

To reaffirm, Dr Joe Dispenza states that you need to do things differently if you want change to happen, otherwise you'll get the same results. According to him, when you continue to do things the same way, you are bringing your past into your present. With this in mind, I vary my routes when attending places such as the gym, sometimes I use my left hand to brush my teeth, I dress in a different order and I even change the side that I get out of bed! Making these changes tells the Universe that you don't want your life to continue exactly as it has been. Dr Joe Dispenza's *Breaking The Habit Of Being You* explains this in more detail. He also has many YouTube videos and workshops if these are your preferred way of learning.

Spirit/Soul

Pierre Teilhard Chardin – a French philosopher – said, 'We are not human beings having a spiritual experience but are spiritual beings having a human experience.' This means you existed in spiritual form before incarnating here on earth. We are eternal souls that live on after our bodies die, as pure energy. Your soul quietly observes what you think, feel and do. It existed before this life and will exist still afterwards. When you take the time to be still and go within, you can reconnect with this part of yourself.

Spirituality is your own individual relationship with the Divine and how that manifests for you. Call it God, the Universe, or whatever name you prefer to label something which is far greater than any of us. Somewhere deep inside me, this resonates as a truth. I believe that I am more than my thoughts, emotions, physical body and life situations I am experiencing at any one moment. I once heard about a five-year-old boy who requested alone time with his new baby sister, so he could feel a closer connection with God. How awesome is that! Such innocence and faith from one so young. The power of love heals all ills, combined with intention, acceptance and faith. The Beatles were right when they sang "All You Need is Love". God is love, the Universe is love – love is within you and all around you. This all-encompassing love has been so important to me during COVID-19, when I've sent out even more love to our wonderful planet and received loving support from people in both the physical world and the etheric realms.

It seems that for many people, we come into this world with an innate wisdom and knowing of our infinite and spiritual nature, but through conditioning of life we forget who we truly are. We forget our magnificence. Your successes and failures, the opinions you hold and your behaviours all override this, until you believe you are your body, that your reality and world is solid and unmalleable. From a young age, we are consumed by our thoughts, many of which tend not to be of the helpful kind, and some are extremely harmful, especially when we start to believe these thoughts to be true. The truth is, you are just a witness to them. Thoughts just happen, you don't have to believe them to be true. Most of your life is spent in a trancelike state. You are very suggestible in this state; hence marketing companies make millions persuading people to buy things that they don't really need. I record TV programmes in advance – whizzing through all the adverts and violent parts so that I'm not affected by them in either a positive or negative way.

As you become more entrenched in your thoughts, you can become neglectful of the senses. Your thoughts are the gateway to your spirit, to your present and to your expansive self-aware-ness. Deep down in your cellular memory there is a spark of remembrance of the stardust whence you came. Tune into the sounds that reach your ears, feel the sensations happening inside you, experience your breath as you inhale and exhale. Feel what it is to really exist in all aspects of you – spiritual, emotional, mental and physical. When in this present awareness, your thoughts can evaporate and your ego can step back. It is as if you are one with life and everything in it.

During quiet moments in our busy lives, it is good to reconnect with the belief that we are eternal Souls or Spirits. Your Soul/Spirit is a piece of the Divine – your God spark within, where unconditional love, forgiveness, compassion, peace, happiness and harmony live. Your Soul is here to experience life and its lessons. Emanuel Swedenborg suggests that the natural and spiritual world co-exist. The natural world comprises all you can see, whereas the spiritual world consists of the unseen, such as Heaven, Hell, people and places in your imagination. Swedenborg believes that a person's inner state is reflected in their surroundings. The physical world is constantly reminding you of its presence, so you have become more concerned about your body and life circumstances than the things you cannot visibly see.

Swedenborg believes that all depression, anxiety, poor body image, unhappiness and disap-pointment stems back to a lack of divine love for yourself and a lack of knowledge about who and what you truly are. By not remembering the magnificent being you are and failing to appre-ciate your uniqueness, you create your own discomfort.

Remember, you are special. Just like snowflakes, no two people are ever created exactly alike – each person has their own part to play in the world. Each snowflake has the same basic structure of six arms that create a hexagon when the tips are connected. Each flake requires a bit of dust or pollen as a nucleus around which to form. Every flake is made of water and formed by atmospheric conditions, including temperature, moisture and air pressure when it falls. Likewise, each human has the same basic structure, two arms, two legs, a neck/head that form a pentagon when the tips are connected. Individuals are also made mainly out of water, with some protein and fat with small amounts of vitamins, minerals and carbohydrates. People are influenced by conditions, genetics, geography, society, culture and collective consciousness.

Like a single snowflake, you occupy a unique place in time and space. All humans are similarly unique in this space-time way. Your minds are predisposed to see either similarities or differences. When considering uniqueness, it may be easier for you to think of snowflakes and humans as being equally unique, whereas others may more easily focus on the differences – we are both similar and different from a snowflake. Humans share similarities on several levels. Similar worldviews bring people together, i.e. passion for justice, a thirst for knowledge, personality, characteristics and a similar history. You may also come across people who you feel close to, which is your interpersonal energy vibrating at a similar frequency. When it comes to finding the meanings in coincidences, your uniqueness is primary. No one can see and experience the meaning from your viewpoint. You bring a unique history, filled with personal symbolism that only you can call up to examine the synchronicities. Although you can consult with others, hearing yourself through the mind of others can help you clarify what you are thinking, just by expressing yourself.

Swedenborg purports that your body separates from your Soul when you pass over. As spiritual beings, it's important that you take the opportunities for your souls to grow through the challenges and experiences that occur (this corresponds with what Billy Fingers says in Annie Kagan's book). Swedenborg says that if you don't learn the lessons from your situations, then they repeat either more in this lifetime or again in another incarnation. The silver linings or blessings from the insights gained during/after these events are what mature you, help you grow strong and have compassion for others who can benefit from your experiences and learning. So, not only do you achieve soul growth, but you also help others on earth too. The more you raise your vibrations, the greater your impact on your world – good vibrations ripple out into the world, building more love, peace and compassion.

With the above in mind, there are so many things you can do to make a positive difference. Try to always see the best in people, knowing that they are a Soul just like you, that they are having a human experience with difficulties that no-one knows about. Make someone's day by smiling at them, as I stipulated before. Smiling is contagious, therefore will fire off happy vibrations. Love your life in its myriad of colours in its full glory, believing that your desires will come true and focusing on what you **do** want instead of what you **don't** want. An affirmation I frequently use as reassurance is, 'Everything is always working out for me.' As you might have guessed, I am a spiritual person. While I was brought up by religious parents and I attended church regularly until the age of twenty-six, I found the church and the congregation to be hypocritical, preaching one thing but not putting the sermons into practice (especially after my mother's death). I do not take everything in the Bible to be gospel, but I appreciate the allegorical messages which teach you to be as impeccable as you can be. Love your neighbour and treat others as you would like to be treated.

Unfortunately, religion has become the basis of enormous conflict in our modern world. Human beings have warped the central message behind religion, creating futile wars, when the entire basis of religion is to be the best person possible and love everyone, as we are one human family. When I was teaching in a school, I discovered that the five major religions all have more-orless the same message, from the Bible to the Quran – it's about acting with love, compassion and integrity, knowing that we are all just human beings, whatever our creed, culture and beliefs. Although I don't attend regular church services (when I do it is often at a spiritualist church or major cathedral with magnificent vibes, weddings or funerals), I have always believed in God/the Universe, even when very young.

In my story, I said that spirits visited me in our very old house in Hemel Hempstead. I was terrified when this happened and didn't understand that they were just trying to let me know they were around. I have lots of experiences of spirits being with me and now I always acknowledge them and say thanks for coming. Sometimes they come with a message and other times just let me know they are present. They also come when I deliberately tune in to gain guidance or reassurance, especially when working with clients.

Your connection to the Divine and other higher beings such as Angels, Spirit guides, Guardian Angels, Ascended Masters and your Star Family is through your crown energy centre, which I mentioned briefly before. Your connection to your "inner God spark" is through your third eye centre in the middle of forehead. It's also where your psychic abilities manifest from:

- **Clairaudience** is when you hear messages similar to thoughts, but these are not your own.

- **Claircognisance** is when you know something, but don't know how you know.

- **Clairvoyance** is when you see spirits and pictures.

- **Clairsentience** is when you feel and sense things about people and places.

If you're currently experiencing challenges in your life, consider what your understanding with your soul/spirit is.

Good Vibrations – Butterfly Effect

The butterfly effect says that small things can have a non-linear impact on a complex system. The concept is imagined by a butterfly flapping its wings somewhere in the world (say Chicago), and causing a typhoon elsewhere (in Tokyo, for example). The idea is based around the sensitive dependence of global conditions. A very small change can make the system behave completely differently. Infinitesimal changes in the starting position of a chaotic system make an enormous difference after a while. This is why even large computers can't tell the weather for more than a few days in the future. Even if weather was perfectly measured, a small change or error would make the prediction completely wrong.

That being said, while some systems (like weather) might appear random, chaos theory says that these kinds of systems or patterns may not be. If people pay close enough attention to what is really going on, they might notice a chaotic pattern. This is true for you on a personal level as well. Each one of us is here to be the best person possible, sending out good vibrations whenever you are able. As I said before, when you re-programme you must update your belief systems and perceptions to the highest frequency possible. This transforms and elevates your vibrations, which go out into the world creating a ripple effect, so every time you're feeling happy, contented, fulfilled, compassionate, loving and experiencing positive emotions, you are being of benefit to those around you and the world at large.

Summary

In this chapter we have looked at:

- ❖ How everything is energy and connected to everything else. From the water in the oceans to the clouds in the sky, the trees, the animals and everyone around you – your thoughts and feelings influence everyone and everything on the planet.

- ❖ The way that critical mass awareness is communicated from mind to mind.

- ❖ The Law of Vibration. All objects are pure energy and movement, which is invisible to your naked eye, hence the illusion of appearing solid.

- ❖ The Law of Attraction, which suggests that you attract what you send out. The Universe can co-create with you to bring your desires to fruition.

- ❖ The endless number of possibilities at the basic subatomic level, where nothing is certain.

- ❖ How your ego tries to keep you safe, by resisting change.

- ❖ Spirituality, your soul and its impact on the world around you.

- ❖ The Butterfly Effect – where a small change can have a big impact over time.

Invitation

Revisit your soul's desire, as outlined in part one of this book. Has this changed in line with your increased self-awareness and the changes you have made whilst reading this book? Are you now dreaming bigger, better, smarter with more confidence, clarity and focus? Have you made changes to your routine, gone to new places, met new people? Look at the parts of your experience in which you can make a difference, here and now. Make notes. The changes you have discovered can now be your starting point to write your current wishes. You can revisit your goals every three to six months.

Insightful Questions

When you have finished the invitation above, take a notepad and pen. Sit quietly, free from any distractions, in a relaxed manner. Look at each of the questions below, one at a time. Allow the question to just flow freely in your mind, percolating if you will. Then, capture your answers on paper, giving you an insight into where you are right now. This will help you shift your perspective, so that you become less stuck.

- *What experiences have you had that felt like destiny? Who have you met that you know on a soul level?*

- *Who has come into your life for a purpose? Have you recognised the reason?*

- *What experiences have you had, where your own positive vibrations have been matched to create your chosen reality?*

- *Are you ready to be who you were destined to be? Are you ready to relax into the truth of what has always been present within?*

- *What changes could you make today that will positively affect your future?*

- *How can you move forward, right now?*

- *What else can you do or invite, in order to inspire and ignite change and kindness in the world – for yourself and for others?*

- *How much fun can you have whilst here on the planet?*

- *What choice can you make today that would make an alternative possibility right away?*

- *What gift are you bringing to the world?*

- *What magic can you be, that no-one else can be?*

- *Are you willing to have a fabulous life? To be more abundant? And if so, more of what? Less of what?*

- *Are you ready to rise above the chaos and discord around you, to be more at peace, in love with life and yourself?*

- *What are your beliefs about being, having and doing everything you want?*

- *What is your body asking for today?*

- *How is your inner child feeling currently?*

Having completed all the questions, form some positive plans to achieve your desired changes. Remember, a vision remains a vision unless action is taken!

Part Eight

To Wrap Up

Thank you for reading my book. I trust it has been helpful in giving you things to consider and ways to improve your life. My hope is that, over the course of these pages, you have found some inspiration – empowering you to drive your bus with more control, calm, focus, fun and fabulousness, creating a harmonious journey through this wonderful and often chaotic and frenetic life. This will not only make you feel good, but also send out wonderful ripples to your environment. Before you go, let me leave you with some final advice:

A life well lived is full of losses, tragedies, adventures and triumphs. Life has encouraged me to plough through utter devastation and despair, reaching liberation and freedom, opening my heart to self-love and continually exploring more of who I am, in my own indomitable, badass way. My journey hasn't always turned out as I expected or planned. People, things and circumstances have fallen away despite my wanting to cling on, knowing that if the time is right for them to leave and explore, they should be free to do so. But I am not unique in this respect – everyone goes through trials and tribulations. I have learned to appreciate the good things, to find the silver lining wherever it exists and to treasure the memories of my best moments. Most importantly, I have learned to let people go when it is right to do so, with love, light and blessings.

Remember that the people with whom you surround yourself will either raise your standards or lower them. Either way, this will encourage you to become the best version of yourself. No one becomes great on their own – we all need people to hold us accountable, reminding us of our essential purpose and challenging us to become greater than we are now. So, seek out your precious people – there are others around, ready for the next step, just like you. You are already exactly where you chose to be, doing exactly what you chose to do at this time. If it doesn't feel good, then this is a sign to make changes and do/be something that feels right and light. Your feelings are the measurement of all you do, giving you awareness, meaning, purpose and destiny, leading you to experience the divine flow of love and life within your heart.

Over the past few years, I have broadened my horizons, gained self-awareness and consciously followed my intuition. I've learned more about connectivity, that everything is energy, that we **choose** before incarnating what lessons to experience for our soul's growth. I've learned to have a greater appreciation for everything that I am and all that I have. I've come to love, respect, support and honour myself – living my life for me! How about you? Are you willing to make these changes? What would it feel like to wake up tomorrow morning, daring to be different and choosing to love yourself just as you are?

Hopefully by this point, you understand that self-love is not an instant thing, it needs to continue throughout your life. So, forgive yourself when you slip – you're human. Just get back on your bus, grab the wheel and veer back onto the right lane. The road can change. Every day is a new beginning and every day can make a difference. Don't die with your song inside you. Remember, the odds of you being you, here and now, are 1 in 400 trillion – if you were not meant to be, then you wouldn't be here. You are blessed with the gift of being present, which many no longer have as an option. So celebrate yourself! Wouldn't it be wonderful if everyone truly loved themselves? When you start the ripple out, setting an example to others, then the 100-monkey effect occurs – resulting in fewer people wanting to read magazines with bitchy articles, ridiculous programmes that humiliate people and the decline of products which we don't really need. There would be more peace throughout the world; wars over resources and religion would die out, because love for ourselves and others would prevail.

Even if you don't feel especially powerful right now, reflect on how far you've come. Revel because you're alive, with greater self-awareness. You are powerful beyond your knowledge. Enjoy your journey to being the most impeccable and happy person you can be, forgetting all of your "should's", "must's" and "have to's".

My wish is that you always remain the driver of your bus. Choose your own path and do it with integrity, awareness and the utmost self-love. If we can take one thing from 2020, it is to love and appreciate one another all the more and to live every day as if it could be our last.

Many blessings and much love,

Denise

p.s. If you have enjoyed this book and found it useful I'd love it if you went to Amazon and wrote an honest review.

Thanks in advance. xxx

Call to Action

Denise appreciates your support.

♡ Leave a review on Amazon.

♡ Pay it forward by gifting a copy of my book to those you love.

♡ Place a copy of the book in a random place, as a participant in the "random acts of kindness".

♡ Share details of Denise's website and services: www.denisedavis.co.uk

♡ **Connect on Social Media**
- Facebook Page – "Harmonise Your Heart", "Dee's Healing Hub" and "Harmonise Your Heart (groups)" plus Facebook "Harmonise Your Health" (VoxxLife info)
- Twitter @Dee_lightful1
- Instagram – denisedavis123
- LinkedIn – Denise Davis – Harmonise Your Heart
- Youtube – Denise Davis – Harmonise Your Heart
- MeWe – Denise Davis – Harmonise Your Heart

♡ To book a session, use my contact form. Should you wish to buy Tropic or VoxxLife items, go to the products tab and click the correct link either "Tropic" or "VoxxLife", which will take you to the appropriate website where you can place your order. To become an associate to sell VoxxLife products, click on the "VoxxLife" link and it will take you to the website where you can sign up.

Thank you for buying my book and being a contributor of love and support to me. When you share this book with others you are assisting them to find harmony with themselves.

Much love & many blessings,

Denise   xxx

Acknowledgements and Thanks

I'd love to acknowledge and thank:

- My deceased parents for their strong work ethic, creativity and intelligence.

- My ex-husband James for the fabulous times we spent together and co-creating our wonderful children.

- My children, who have had infinite patience watching their mum change from a fairly "normal" woman who was acceptable in polite circles (a teacher and corporate wife) to what they perceived as some radical hippy chick with new age tendencies (I was a hippy and biker chick in my teens), whose philosophies don't always match those they were brought up with and live from.

- I love and appreciate spending times of sadness and joy with all my wonderful friends.

- Many thanks to Wendy Fry – author, ghostwriter and writing coach, for her practical writing guidance and wonderful emotional support along the journey of birthing my book. Wendy supports aspiring authors to write and publish their books and fully understands the emotions of writing.

- Thanks to Joshua Brown and Jordan Cooke from Richard McMunn's VIP Author Mentoring Programme for working on the technical side of birthing my book – creating my book cover, proofreading and editing, then printing my book. If you want to self-publish a book, then having the practical guidance from Richard McMunn's VIP mentoring team and emotional support from Wendy Fry is wonderful – because all aspects of publishing are covered. Both parties have worked together for years, making it simpler for aspiring authors to create and publish their books with ease.

- I would like to give thanks to my wonderful photographers Pam Bower-Davis and Jean Dixon who made me feel so at ease in front of the camera and produced gorgeous photos of me including the one on the back cover. Bless you ladies. (P&J Photography)

My Early Readers

I'd also like to say a big thank you to my early readers:

Denise Kennedy for her support and sanctuary when I needed a break from writing, always ready with a cuppa and a chat. Denise's suggestions helped make this book easier for readers to understand, which was greatly appreciated. Lastly for the wonderful smooth tasting water she gifts me – I find it easier to drink two litres of water when it's Kangen rather than tap water.

Alison White for giving me constructive feedback, plus finding my typos and occasional grammatical errors.

Blue Marsden of "Soul Plan Readings" for reading my book and writing an endorsement.

Davina MacKail – Shaman – for reading the book and writing an endorsement.

Anne Jirsch, FLP creator, for reading the book and writing an endorsement.

Sian Goodspeed CEO of "Flying Start Tuition" for reading the book and writing an endorsement.

Pamela Cullinane for reading the book and writing an endorsement.

Maxine Middleton-Budd for reading the book and writing an endorsement.

P.R. for reading the book and writing an endorsement.

Libby Bellhouse for reading the book and writing an endorsement.

Barbie Brinkman for reading the book and writing an endorsement.

Simon Hodges for reading the book and writing an endorsement.

And finally, thank you – dear reader. For giving me the chance to help you in the same way I've helped myself, for reading my story and for sharing this wonderful planet we call home. I am grateful to you, every minute of every day.

About the Author

I have always loved people and been curious about what makes them tick. So, it's understandable that I transitioned from teaching to become a coach for adults and children. I have worked with clients in person and internationally via Skype for seventeen years. I created my "Harmonise Your Heart" process by sequencing together a variety of disparate things I have done for years. Apart from spending time with family and friends, I love spontaneity and travel and welcoming new experiences, as I believe it's important to learn until we depart this realm.

My home is my castle, a sanctuary and a heart space full of love and books. I adore all things heart-shaped (as a symbol of love), so there are ornaments and trinkets in every room, as well as heart-shaped crockery and glassware.

My experience and qualifications

- Degree in Business Studies, plus a Primary School Teaching Qualification;
- An Advanced Floral Designer/Florist;
- NLP & Time Line Therapy Trainer;
- Clinical Hypnotherapy;
- Past Life Regression;
- Future Life Progression,
- Advanced EFT practitioner;
- Energetic NLP (advanced level);
- Soul Plan Reading;
- Sound Healing;
- Access Consciousness;
- The Journey process for adults and children;
- Empowering Learning practitioner (Seeing Spells & Achieving) for Dyslexia and Dyscalculia;
- Reconnective Healing & The Reconnection;
- Reiki Master/Teacher;
- Master Colour Energy Therapy;
- Psychic & Spiritual healing and card readings;
- Mediumship;
- Theta Healing;
- H'oponopono Forgiveness (adv) practitioner;
- Relationship therapy;
- Art Therapy;
- Mindfulness (advanced);
- Emotion Code.

Useful Resources

My details are:-

www.denisedavis.co.uk

To book a session, use my contact form. Should you wish to buy Tropic or VoxxLife items, go to the products tab and click the correct link either "Tropic" or "VoxxLife", which will take you to the appropriate website where you can place your order. To become an associate to sell VoxxLife products, click on the "VoxxLife" link and it will take you to the website where you can sign up.

- Twitter: Dee_lightful1

- Instagram: denisedavis123

- Facebook: "Harmonise Your Heart", "Dee's Healing Hub" and "Harmonise Your Heart" (groups), plus Facebook "Harmonise Your Health" (VoxxLife info)

- LinkedIn: Denise Davis – Harmonise Your Heart

- YouTube: Denise Davis – Harmonise Your Heart

Below are details of people who assisted or contributed to the book:-

Joshua Brown and Jordan Cooke
https://richardmentorme.com
Richard McMunn's VIP author mentoring programme

Wendy Fry
www.wendyfry.com
Transformational speaker, emotional health consultant and writing coach, ghostwriter and best-selling author of *Write from Your Heart, Mothers and Daughters* and *Find YOU Find LOVE.*

Denise Kennedy
www.livinggreener.co.uk
Kangen Water and Ukon

Anne Jirsch
www.annejirsch.com
Future Life Progression training

Blue Marsden
 www.soulplan.co.uk
Soul Plan training

Joel Young
www.joelyoungnpa.com
NPA training

Sian Goodspeed
www.flyingstarttuition.co.uk
Private Tutoring Children

Art Giser
www.energeticnlp.com
Energetic NLP training

Davina MacKail
www.sipapu.com
Pilgrimages in Peru

Mireille Mettes
www.mirmethod.com
MIR method – instruction video

Bach Flower Remedies
www.bachflowerremedies.com
Practitioner trainings

Noah St. John
https://afformations.com

Brain Gym
www.braingym.org.uk
For more info and exercises

Nicole Vincent
www.nicoleRvincent.com
Cutting cords technique

Joe Vitale
www.joevitale.com
Ho'oponopono trainings

Gary Craig
www.emo.com
EFT creator

Brandon Bays
www.thejourney.com
The Journey trainings

Matt Khan
https://mattkhan.org